The Safe Operating Space Treaty

The Safe Operating Space Treaty:

A New Approach to Managing Our Use of the Earth System

Edited by

Paulo Magalhães, Will Steffen,
Klaus Bosselmann, Alexandra Aragão
and Viriato Soromenho-Marques

Cambridge
Scholars
Publishing

The Safe Operating Space Treaty:
A New Approach to Managing Our Use of the Earth System

Edited by Paulo Magalhães, Will Steffen, Klaus Bosselmann,
Alexandra Aragão and Viriato Soromenho-Marques

This book first published 2016

Cambridge Scholars Publishing

Lady Stephenson Library, Newcastle upon Tyne, NE6 2PA, UK

British Library Cataloguing in Publication Data
A catalogue record for this book is available from the British Library

ISBN (10): 1-4438-8903-2
ISBN (13): 978-1-4438-8903-2

TABLE OF CONTENTS

Acknowledgements vii

Preface viii
Nathalie Meusy
*Head of the Coordination Office on Sustainable Development
at the European Space Agency (ESA)*

Chapter One... 1
Global Free Riders
Paulo Magalhães, Francisco Ferreira

Chapter Two 23
The Planetary Boundaries Framework: Defining a Safe Operating Space
for Humanity
Will Steffen

Chapter Three 47
The Spaceship Earth Condo
Clóvis Jacinto de Matos

Chapter Four... 64
Shifting the Legal Paradigm: Earth-centred Law and Governance
Klaus Bosselmann

Chapter Five 83
Legal Tools to Operationalize Anthropocene Environmental Law
Alexandra Aragão

Chapter Six 104
The Common Heritage: Constructive Utopianism
Prue Taylor

Chapter Seven... 131
A New Object of Law: Attempt for a Legal Construction
Paulo Magalhães

Chapter Eight.. 172
Twelve Legal Arguments in Favour of Considering the Earth System
as Natural Intangible Endangered Heritage: In Accordance with
the UNESCO Convention on Natural and Cultural Heritage (1972)
Alexandra Aragão

Chapter Nine.. 180
Earth Condominium: A Legal Model for the Anthropocene
Paulo Magalhães

Chapter Ten 213
The Need for an Integrated Assessment Framework to Account
for Humanity's Pressure on the Earth System
Federico Maria Pulselli, Sara Moreno Pires, Alessandro Galli

Chapter Eleven 246
Structural Conditions to Overcome the Dilemma of Collective Action
Iva Miranda Pires

Chapter Twelve 262
Transforming the United Nations Trusteeship Council for Protection
of the Earth System
Kul Chandra Gautan

Chapter Thirteen.. 274
From Mutual Assured Destruction to Compulsory Cooperation
Viriato Soromenho-Marques

Chapter Fourteen 289
Safe Operating Space of Humankind Treaty [SOS Treaty]: A Proposal
Paulo Magalhães

Contributors.. 303

ACKNOWLEDGEMENTS

The establishment of an interdisciplinary team such as the one formed by the authors of this book, and the detailed development of the main elements of the bold proposal it entails, was only possible as the result of a process stretching along a long time line. Several were the institutions and individuals that, at different stages, contributed to what is now a common achievement, open to the critical judgement of the readers. Without exhausting all the contributions and support, it is our duty and pleasure to refer to those without whom this project wouldn't have been able to attain its final purpose in the shape of the book you are about to read.

In the first place, we wish to thank the Serralves Foundation, in Oporto, Portugal. Within the scope of the 25th anniversary commemoration of Environmental Education in Serralves, an international conference was held, on the 1st and 2nd of November, 2013, on the theme "Educating for the Common Heritage: From the Cultural Intangible to the Natural Intangible". It was within the realm of the conference's preparatory work that the publisher decided to challenge the editors to this endeavour. The conference was also the right venue for the first steps and discussions that brought us to the team and the content that gave life to the problems dealt with and the practical proposals suggested in this book.

Finally, we express also our gratitude to all those who directly or indirectly contributed to the completion of this collective ambition that aims for a better future for humankind and our home planet.

—The Editors

PREFACE

"Les hommes ont oublié cette vérité [...] mais tu ne dois pas l'oublier. Tu deviens responsable pour toujours de ce que tu as apprivoisé."
—Le Petit Prince, Antoine de Saint-Exupéry.

This book opens a new chapter of world history, of our planet's history, and you are lucky to read it, to be part of it. And maybe you will soon live this history not as witnesses but as actors of it in your capacity as simple but nevertheless irreplaceable humans. You and your ancestors have tamed the Earth and you ought to care for it more than ever now. This is the unique last opportunity to do so. This treaty is about this opportunity – it brings to your attention a new concept for protecting the Earth as a system, a whole, from both a scientific and legal perspective, which comes as an obvious and necessary complement of the notion of ecology.

Ecological consciousness was really born when men first went to space and realized how small, how vulnerable our home looked when seen from above; "a pale blue dot" as Carl Sagan called it. When one goes away from the Earth, there are no frontiers – one can only see the oceans, the forests, the deserts, the biodiversity, and, above all, the atmosphere, so thin and so fragile, which nevertheless allows us, human beings, to live in our environment. Catastrophes caused by nature or by people can also be seen from space; in particular, one can see the pollution, the footprint of human activities, which started getting serious with the Industrial Revolution and escalated with what has been called the Great Acceleration some one hundred years later. Space programmes, with their satellite applications and services, help and support the observation of the Earth in all its components: the land (with its forests, deserts, water bodies, its human settlements and cultivated areas), the ocean (with its salinity and currents, winds and waves, and colour variations), the ice (with its glaciers and ice sheets), the atmosphere (with its chemical composition and meteorological variations), and the biosphere, which make the Earth with all its living species unique in the universe. Now with the new Earth observation programmes, such as Copernicus (with the Sentinels satellites), more data, soon available in an open-source mode, will enable us to have a much more comprehensive picture of our planet's elements and their state of health as well as the other consequences of climate change (such as climate refugee flows). This will allow a sound monitoring of the Earth's condition and suggest associated concrete actions in favour of the environment. We must also realize that climate change represents one of the biggest threats for peace and democracy on Earth.

To better live on Earth and, above all, to face the upcoming disruption of resources combined with climatic disturbance, it is very instructive to see how it is possible to survive without atmosphere, in outer space, for instance. In the International Space Station, they have re-created a closed-loop system, a life-support base, and live with an economy of means because resources are limited; in short, it teaches us how to live in a sober manner, which is what we should be doing on Earth.

This is what we should do because the Earth is our home, our spaceship, a closed world with limited resources that will survive us, the only known place in the universe where we can live as humankind, worldwide citizens. We share common goods that we have to care for and protect in order to ensure the future of our planet and allow future generations to live after us.

This is all about sustainability: of human beings, other living species and resources.

When the concept of sustainable development was first officially defined in 1987 by Mrs Gro Harlem Brundtland in the United Nations framework, it was in more of a political context, mainly for the attention of sovereign states with a view of building up a global governance for planet Earth in all aspects of a modern society: environmental, social and economic. Step by step, both private and public sectors committed to sustainable development or the corporate social responsibility principles of accountability, and measured and assessed their performance and evolution under internationally recognized norms and standards. Sustainability has become a strategic tool with which to handle things, do business, create opportunities for innovation, measure data and report on achievements and performance towards share or stakeholders, but also to explain the cost of inaction. And when it comes to climate change, the cost of inaction is tremendous.

It is a good thing that companies and organizations are ensuring the sustainability of their mission but it is now time to endow all citizens with responsibility for their spaceship. We have already seen how powerful and educational the view of the Earth from space is; it has also raised in an intangible way a collective consciousness of how vital it is to act in favour of our home, our condominium, our common goods, our heritage, as this treaty will further explore. We also saw how useful the space applications were as tools for gathering data for a sound monitoring of the Earth System, and there are many more space services available to citizens for monitoring and shaping the society and the planet of tomorrow. Governments can act on a global scale but citizens must act on a more local scale as this can give more tangible and realistic results; the merging of both streams will give an optimal result. A great and encouraging demonstration of this took place on 6 June, 2015 in the framework of the World Wide Views event: 10,000 citizens in 100 countries participated in the widest global citizens consultation organized ever. Their ideas and opinions regarding 30 questions on climate change and energy were collected and all the results have been transmitted to the negotiators of the COP21, the Paris Conference on Climate (30 November–11 December, 2015), where they will be duly taken into account.

The current treaty arrives at the optimal time for action. Within it, you will discover the state of affairs of planet Earth in a multidisciplinary manner and you will find that many theories, political and legal instruments, and tools have already been developed to protect the environment, a holistic approach combining science and law that was deeply needed. This is how the idea of this Treaty of the Safe Operating Space was born.

The environment used to be called "the silent stakeholder" and the Earth System had no *legal status per se*. Since 2014, the Earth has been recognized as a "client" by the European Court of Justice, and with the SOS Treaty, the environment won't be silent any longer. Times are changing…

Nathalie Meusy
Head of the Coordination Office on Sustainable Development
at the European Space Agency (ESA)
30 July, 2015

PS. I would like to thank Paulo Magalhães for the great honour he provided me when he asked me to write this preface. I am confident that the collective efforts of this book will help change the world we are living in.

CHAPTER ONE

GLOBAL FREE RIDERS ...

PAULO MAGALHÃES[1]
FRANCISCO FERREIRA[2]

"A human being is a part of a whole, called by us **universe**, a part limited in time and space. He experiences himself, his thoughts and feelings as something separated from the rest... a kind of optical delusion of his consciousness."

—Albert Einstein

1. Tragedy Without Territory

It is now widely accepted that climate change is a "tragedy of the commons" on a global scale. When a tragedy is occurring simultaneously inside and outside all borders, it does not comply with the principle of territoriality of jurisdictions or of norms. It is a superimposed common reality in all territories, without having a territory. Also, in the dominant view of "territorial obsession", existing is to have territory; being global is not having territory. The underlying principle is the assumption that everything that goes beyond our limits should be considered as external to us – an externality, in the words of economists. Pollution from an aircraft is an externality for the economy and when performed outside the airspace of states, it becomes a legal non-existence for jurists.

Based on this vision, one can define common areas where theoretically all of humanity becomes sovereign over the international commons (*res communis omnium*), in which the "common" is what is left over (open sea,

---

[1] Interdisciplinary Centre of Social Sciences CICS.NOVA - Faculdade de Ciências Sociais e Humanas - Universidade Nova de Lisboa
[2] Center for Environmental and Sustainability Research CENSE.NOVA – Faculdade de Ciências e Tecnologia – Universidade Nova de Lisboa

seabed, Antarctica), the remains of what could not be seized. Pureza (1998) considers that "the *res communis* own regime as a traditional framework for common international spaces is a sequence rather than an antithesis of the national sovereignty principle". The common is not that by which its nature and characteristics are truly common but what remains after appropriation.

In the confrontation between this one-dimensional simplification of the world and the highly complex and deeply interconnected Earth System, we are flooded with more questions than answers: Whose tragedy? Where does the responsibility for acting lie? Who has the instruments to act for the benefit of all? How can we speak about benefiting everyone if humanity, being global, has no territory; a fact that by itself gives rise to its legal non-existence? Yet, are there any organized people in a territorial political community that do not belong to humanity? If humanity exists materially, and is just one single family with a common origin, will it cease to exist just because it doesn't exist in a formally organized political territory? Can the concept of sovereignty exist without the prospect of an unlimited temporal projection into the next generations?

As sophisticated as societies and their technologies can be, the organization of social life leads us invariably to the same primary questions: What is mine? What is yours? What is common or public, or what doesn't belong to anyone? But the reality is always more complex than these simplified operations. To the questions whose simple solutions of separation serve as responses, we can add another: What is simultaneously mine, yours and everyone's in an overlapping and symbiotic way?

As we will see throughout this book, there is no simple answer to this complex question, especially if we look at property not only as a form of ownership over something but also as an organizing tool of social relations. It is at the crossroads of belonging to all, owned by no one, where 'belonging to' does not have any clear legal definition, and whose outcome is often resolved by resorting to *res nullius*. Cappelletti (1975) defines this dilemma as "belonging to all and to no one". Kiss (1982) came very close to the essence of the issue when he asked: "*How can a good that belongs to no one be subject to a legal regime?*" From this paradox, and because legal existence is inextricably linked to some form of "ownership", emerges what was classified as the doctrine of "complex property".

New questions always elicit new answers. However, it is interesting to note that even as we surpass the Earth's borders and launch into the conquest of space, the same classic questions invariably arise. Oosterlinck

(1996), in his article "Tangible and Intangible Property in Outer Space", states: "Property in space is certainly one of the most important issues for the future not only in the context of the more classical form of tangible property such as minerals but also intangible property such as orbital slots on the geostationary orbit, frequencies, etc."

Only with clear and precise legal answers to these primary questions might there surface an element of stability without which the construction of any organization, and therefore the construction of any future, are possible. Transferred from one earthly reality dominated by territorial and tangible dimensions, we are now involved in a spatial reality dominated by apparent emptiness and the intangible. Although within an environment that is strange and cannot be 'comprehended' by our senses, the ability to explore new resources and carry out activities that open new possibilities on Earth created the need to internally organize our relationships concerning the use of these new intangible spaces; therefore the classical questions arise again but with new variations.

Regulating the use of certain goods involves the ability to first describe, measure, locate, and name them, and then to classify them. In other words, in order to regulate the use of a certain good, we have to have defined it.

The legitimacy of a theoretical construction always depends on its explanatory capacity of reality. In space, unlike on Earth, the classification of any legal regime should take as its starting point the reality of the intrinsic characteristics of the goods and not a previous theoretical construction later applied to the goods in question. This process, whose initial impulse is the well-known reality, was similar to the approach carried out by Roman law, which therefore continues to be used in space today. According to Oosterlinck (1996), "Under Roman Law, 'Res', or things, are classified into *res corporals* and *res incorporales*". It was in the Roman legal system where the "emptiness" of space found a concept *(res incorporales)* to explain the new reality of the *areas in outer space or langrangian points, orbits including specific slots of certain orbits, trajectories and to certain extended frequency spectrum*. But even so, "Within *res corporals* a certain number of things are excluded from trade *'res quarum commercium non est'*, normally referred to as *res extra commercium*" (Kaser & Wubbe 1971). That is, there are other features regarding the nature of the good itself that makes its trading impossible, and are essential elements in the definition of the legal regime.

This qualitative approach of Roman law differs immediately from the current approach of monistic simplification, which is merely spatial/geographic, between the things that are within the territory of states and those that are outside the jurisdiction of states.

For Roman law, the *res communis omnium* are available to all and cannot be owned by anyone, not even by a state; for example, the air, rain, flowing river water, the sea, and the shore. Therefore, the origin of the *res communis omnium* was not one territorial division, an abstract criterion where the common is only the part remaining after appropriations; the good's intrinsic qualities led to the classification of its legal status.

It is very interesting to note the distinction between *source* and *resource* in the analysis of the Roman legal system and the constraints that this distinction imposes on the use and exercise of property. In practice, the Romans looked differently upon the issue when considering the sea as a whole and when considering its constituents. In the former case, they qualified it *res communis omnium* and the latter *res nullius*. Or, in more general terms, "*res communis* differs from *res nullius* in that the *source of resources* cannot be appropriated but the resources themselves are amenable to appropriation. (…) *Res nullius* may be subject to appropriation through effective occupation and the will expressed by the (new) owner to exercise ownership (*corpore et animo*)" (Oosterlinck 1996). The intrinsic quality of the good and the possibility of its effective possession, to acquire ownership, were decisive in the classification of the regime applied to it.

The "ocean the whole" was the source, which by its very nature was inappropriable, and the fish in it one appropriable resource. The fact that it is inappropriable and common to all, and therefore global, does not necessarily mean that it doesn't exist or that some of its constituents may be physically appropriable.

That being said, another crucial problem in defining the use and ownership regime was the feature of inexhaustibility.

> These resources were looked at as inexhaustible and their appropriation was physically possible and would moreover only be partial, leaving thus the possibility to others for future exploitation and use of the sea. Hugo Grotius evokes however, though briefly, the possibility that fish could be an exhaustible resource of the sea but in his view this would not alter the legal status of the sea as a whole. (Oosterlinck 1996)

> (…) if it were possible to prohibit any of these things, say for example, fishing, for in a way it can be maintained that fish are exhaustible, still it would not be possible to prohibit navigation, for the sea would not be exhausted by that use. (Grotius 1916)

Therefore, in summary, we can pose some questions that are central in determining property regimes: the possibility to appropriate the good or otherwise; if the good has an in- or exhaustible character, or, better yet, if the use of the good, without a physical appropriation of it, may or may not lead to the exhaustion of it. Throughout the article, the author, using a theoretical analogy between ocean and space, between source and resource, analyses the existing legal regime and the options whose, in his opinion, performance is still required in the organization of the use of this new frontier where natural intangible resources are also limited (as in the spectrum of frequencies or the geostationary orbit). As in all areas in which the law has been called into action, a precise clarification of the various types of ownership is needed in space in order to organize the relationships established around the use of sources and resources, which, by being exhaustible, cannot be used according to a free-access regime.

Synthesizing the previous analysis:

1) Roman law distinguishes between the source that is not appropriable and the resource that can be physically appropriated.
2) Grotius analyses the exhaustible or inexhaustible character, which is decisive in defining the ownership regime, access or use of the good.
3) There are some uses of the good, although not corresponding to a physical appropriation, that can lead to its exhaustion.
4) In the outer space law, intangible property is not only confined to human intellectual property.

Based on this summary, we realize that there are also natural intangible resources in the Earth System that can be exhausted by some uses although they can escape our senses.

With climate change and the discovery that a stable climate is not an inexhaustible factor, that is, the *incorporales* biogeophysical conditions that determine the state of the Earth System have upper and lower limits and therefore are exhaustible, the "appropriation/ownership" of this resource is not realized through a physical occupation but rather through its use, that is, as a change in the qualitative state of its incorporeal characteristics.

One should consider the recent period of relative climate stability, the Holocene (the last 11,700 years after the last ice age), which has been the basis for the development of human civilization (the history of the human species corresponds to a period of about 200,000 years), as a particularly favourable state of the Earth System for our species and for others that share the same ecological conditions. Every time a state, company or an individual contributes to a change in the biogeochemical conditions of this period of stability, which has benefited all humankind, an "externality" in the natural *res incorporales* is generated, affecting all other users of this favourable state as less resource (considering the stable state of the Earth System as a resource) is available to all agents.

The biogeochemical conditions that ensure a stable climate and the favourable conditions of the Holocene are a natural intangible limited resource on Earth. The favourable conditions of the Holocene arose in an evolutionary fashion throughout Earth's history and it is through this evolutionary process, involving the living part of the planet as well as the geophysical, that, for example, the relative concentrations of gases have remained rather constant through time. In essence, it is the integration of the geophysical properties of the planet with the living biosphere that forms the intangible Earth System, a single global system incapable of any legal abstraction of division.

In the source/resource Roman law perspective, the source of this favourable state is the living biosphere and its interactions with the geophysical components. In other words, the sources are the ecological infrastructures, and the resource the biogeochemical conditions of the state of the Earth System.

We have been exploiting a vital resource we did not even know existed; nor did we know if it was exhaustible or inexhaustible. The stable climate was, quite simply, pre-acquired data. The possibility of it being affected by human activity was a hypothesis that did not even arise. The only value we truly recognized was the tangible sources of this unknown global resource. The lack of knowledge was one of the most relevant primary activator of the massive destruction of a huge amount of sources (for example, more than 80% of the original forests).

This is a new situation in regard to its possible classification. First, the natural resource is intangible and as such is not physically appropriated. Second, this good does not recognize land, air or ocean borders. It refers to a specific biochemical structure of the atmosphere and of the oceans, and its integration with the geophysical properties of the planet with the living biosphere that forms the intangible Earth System. In this respect, taking into account their characteristics and the ways in which these *res incorporales* were being perceived over time, we can identify some similar elements in four possible categories:

1) ***Terra Incognita:*** The intangible higher level of integration of the Earth System, because it was unknown, can be considered a true

terra incognita, an "unknown space", traditionally defined as regions never mapped or documented.

2) ***Res Nullius:*** The change in the biochemical structure at the higher level of the Earth System can be considered to have been carried out under the *open-access regime* condition, without rules, and in this sense is a *res nullius.* A good, being a *res incorporales* and an unknown resource, is not suited to traditional effective occupation, that is, a conscious will to ownership (*corpore e animo*). However, its use can lead to its exhaustion.

3) ***Terra Nullius:*** In the Middle Ages, *terra nullius* was used to define unclaimed or unoccupied territories, usually situated between fiefdoms and used as dumps for garbage and deposits. Although intangible and non-territorial, the fact that pollution legally disappears in the legal inexistence of the Earth System allows us to consider it a no-man's land, the place to send waste, and therefore an externality.

4) ***Res Communis Omnium:*** The Earth System is available to all and cannot be appropriated by anyone, not even by a state. When this common property extends to all humankind, the goods come to be considered as *res omnium.* They are the common heritage of humankind so all human beings, both the present and future generations, have the right to access them in a favourable state. However, given its character as an exhaustible resource, it is necessary to create a legal framework for both the use and the benefits realized in the common good.

2. Legal Black Hole

The "global" is, therefore, a new reality that is outside the legal frameworks built to date. Within existing classifications, although we can find some elements that partially adapt to this new reality, there is no legal asset that is simultaneously global and *res incorporales* with the ability to reflect the harmful changes of the biochemical structure of this specific favourable state of the Earth System. In the same manner, there is no way to capture or account for the benefits provided by ecosystems in the maintenance of a favourable state and enjoyed by all on a global scale. This new reality, already accepted and recognized by science and clearly visible from space, still remains invisible to the law.

If we take as a starting point the current prevailing view that the common is not by its nature truly common but what remains after appropriation, and if to this view we join the legal invisibility of the higher level of the Earth System as a whole, what remains is not a *terra incognita* but truly an *incognita sine terra*.

Terra incognita was the term used in the 15th and 16th centuries to mark unknown land – the regions that had never been mapped or documented. After *terra incognita* had disappeared from our maps and the planet had "become spherical", where one could go back to the point of origin without going backwards, a first major step was taken towards realizing the overall unity of the planet at the geographical level of integration. We had, however, to wait until almost the end of the 20th century to realize that the planet and its operating system had more than a well-defined geographical, physical and palpable dimension. A new reality was revealed when we discovered that the gases and substances emitted into the atmosphere not only did not disappear in space but were also interchanged with the land and the oceans, or that what was released into the sea did not disappear into an ocean of infinity. Step by step, science was uncovering the upper level of integration of an Earth System with global and complex interconnections that were difficult to observe and define. However, despite their intangible and systemic nature, these relationships are not an abstract abstraction. Although this higher level of integration requires an abstraction to be considered as such and also explained, it is nonetheless incredibly obvious, based *in res incorporales*, that we are talking about a real world that everyone and everything is part of.

The Earth System is still considered to be *an unidentified legal object* – a ULO (Melot & Pélisse 2008)[3] – resulting in a large *legal black hole* through which vital positive flows (benefits to the state of the Earth System) and negative flows (harm to the state of the Earth System) "disappear" as externalities. The economic externalities are a social disappearance that do not correspond to a ecological disappearance. If the principle of disjunction in natural sciences "hid everything which connects, interacts, and interferes" in law, the paradigm of division "made believe that the arbitrary cut of the real was the real itself" (Morin 1990). The concept of a "system" emphasises the concept of the medium, that is, not only the *physis* as a material basis but also a mediation mechanism of biogeochemical cycles and thermodynamics "in which reciprocal interactions inside the system between the framework and its processes contribute to the regulation of dynamics and the maintenance of their organization, in particular thanks to feedback phenomena" (Lévêque

---

See Chapter 5 of this book, written by Alexandra Aragão

2002). This enables a well-defined characteristic functioning as a single global complex ecosystem, which in reality is a life-support system for the entire biosphere, including humans, on Earth. Of course, the biosphere itself is a critical part of the Earth System, fully integrated with the geophysical components of the system itself.

The legal inexistence of the *favourable state* of the Earth System as an object of law which corresponds to a social invisibility, is a structural problem that hides the most vital factors for human life and prevents the construction of just and equitable solutions.

It is this vision that considers as remaining and *res nullius* everything that does not fit the concept of national sovereignty, which turns us into true *free riders* of the Earth System to which we belong and on which we depend, opening the doors for a collective tragedy.

3. The Greatest Market Failure

While it is true that it is materially or legally impossible to deny any human being free use of the Earth System, the enjoyment of truly common goods without any effective rules means that each individual is compelled to indefinitely increase his/her use of common resources associated with a particular state of the Earth System (e.g., the atmosphere with a particular concentration of constituent gases) because, if one does not do it, another will. All users have an incentive to increase their use without concern for the impact their actions may have on others (and perhaps themselves), and a disincentive in promoting the maintenance and improvement of the common good.

This is the well-known tragedy of the commons model described by Hardin (1968), in which free and unregulated use of a common resource based on the logic of *first-come, first-served* results in a rational actor maximizing individual interest. This places the common resource under such pressure that it becomes degraded and eventually exhausted as a result of overexploitation, thus the "tragedy". "The dilemma is that if a user retracts his/her use and the others do not, the resource will run out in the same way and the user will have lost the short-term benefit that was obtained by others" (Hardin 1968).

The model is now being reproduced on a global scale, with the difference that the good (resource) was until recently unknown and not definable. In this global-scale model, each state, following its own interest, will not be concerned about limiting pollution or maintaining its ecosystems for the purpose of contributing to a well-functioning Earth System in a stable and accommodating state, as the good is freely available to be exploited by all. As there is no legal status for the global good, everyone uses it as *res nullius*, considering it will provide an endless stream of benefits to everyone, where their use does not reduce the potential for use by others (contrary to what is true of the commons).

Incidentally, this legal black hole has also been identified by economists in the *Stern Report*:

> Climate change presents a unique challenge for economics: it is the greatest and widest-ranging market failure ever seen. The economic analysis must therefore be global, deal with long-term horizons, have the economics of risk and uncertainty at centre stage, and examine the possibility of major, non-marginal change. (2006)

The failure to recognize the existence of the Earth System results in the inability of nations to cope with the challenges on a planetary scale. One consequence is that all the benefits from, or damage to, the Earth System are legally non-existent. Without the existence of this common good or the identification of what is the good that presents simultaneously beyond and within all states but needs to be maintained in good condition for the functioning of the Earth System as a whole, we will not be able to turn ourselves into stewards of our common home. An Earth System that does not exist is a matricial failure and theoretical gap, which prevents filling the void that this recently recognized scientific reality requires.

4. Global Free Riders... Get It While You Can

At the heart of this problem are deep theoretical concepts that require some prior conceptual clarification on the characteristics of property, property rights and underlying relations. Since human relations expanded on a global scale through global systemic financial, economic and political interconnections (but ignored the biogeophysical interconnections that underpin the functioning of the Earth System), it is essential to realize how some of these principles of law led to the overexploitation and consequent tragedy of the commons.

The right of private property confers on its owner the power to *exclusively* use a resource, even if such use is rarely done absolutely. This means that, even though an owner has full power over something *plena in re potestas*, meaning the right to use, enjoy and abuse a thing, *ius utendi, fruendi et abutendi res sua* means that he or she is limited by the rules of society.

Rights to common property are held by groups of individuals, excluding access to the resources for all those outside the group but considering rights and duties regarding the use and conservation of the resource.

The *open-access* regime (*res nullius*), the concept of ownerless property, is completely non-exclusive, meaning that the access to goods/resources cannot be denied to any individual. In these cases, one cannot identify a group of users or owners because the available benefits flow to all without any, or almost any, duty regarding the use, preservation or maintenance of the resource.

In economic theory, this inability to exclude any individual's use of a good led to the rise of the *free rider* (Samuelson 1954) issue, in which any individual can benefit from a good without contributing to its production. An individual, following self-interest, will not contribute to the costs of the existence and maintenance of a good but will make use of its existence since it is available to everyone. The individual benefits from the principle of non-exclusion.

The problem of the tragedy of commons is based on the characteristics of free access and the unregulated use of a natural resource, which is limited by nature. Climate change is a tragedy of the commons on a global scale, in which this intrinsically common good, which was overexploited (a specific stable climate of a well-defined state of the Earth System), is not only difficult to define and establish boundaries around but also no human being can be excluded from access to it.

In a situation where either the damage or the benefit is common, without an organization of collective use through a system of accounting benefits and harm, everyone will act as a *global free rider*. Therefore, this is a tragedy not of material resource exhaustion but of the individual occupation of a certain quantity of the biogeophysical space of the Earth System carried out through a change that contributes to destabilising the favourable stable state of the system. In other words, pollution is a contribution to a change this specific state, the *healthiness of the Earth System*. This new form of occupation does not correspond to the traditional concept of territory or a physical appropriation of tangible resources; rather, the new reality must be recognized and conceptualized in order to organize the use of the Earth System. Although a subversive perspective of the dominant view today, the indivisible "whole" makes the issue of management of common goods (i.e., the Earth System) the basic fundamental theoretical question for all discussions on global environmental goods and possible alternative ways of building a sustainable society.

5. A Long Looking-For Period

When we look at the pathway traced by science in perspective, the history of environmental civil society movements and all the high-level negotiations that have been taking place for many decades, we realize that along this route of searching for solutions, the vision that the "common" is just the leftovers after appropriation unfortunately continues to be the starting point from which reality is framed. However, a great effort by the victims of this structural failure is being made and it is imperative to continue this standard negotiations track, even accepting that progress in reaching a solution for our troubled planet has been too slow.

Ten years after Rachel Carson published *Silent Spring,* a book that challenged the idea of the supposed capacity of the environment to absorb toxic pollutants such as agriculture pesticides, the 1972 United Nations Conference on Human Environment, held in Stockholm under the leadership of Maurice Strong, is a decisive mark on the sustainability timeline. While the regional pollution situation in Sweden and the surrounding Nordic and Central European countries achieved a particular focus, it was the first major step at the global level to give environmental issues a high priority. The creation of a sustainable development concept, with the view of integrating different fields of development, which until that time had been fully separated into a cohesive vision solving the environmental versus development dilemma, was a clear breakthrough. *Limits to Growth,* by the Club of Rome, the best-selling environmental book, was published in 1972, one year before the oil crisis. The analysis, interconnections and particularly the results sent a shockwave through both developed and developing countries. The conference led to the establishment of numerous national environmental protection agencies and, most importantly, the creation of the United Nations Environment Programme (UNEP).

During the 1970s, while relevant international agreements such as the Convention on International Trade in Endangered Species of Flora and Fauna (CITES) in 1975 and the adoption of the Convention on Long-Range Transboundary Air Pollution in 1979 came into effect, the world became acquainted with dramatic global environmental problems, including the discovery by Rowland and Molina in 1974 of the role chlorofluorocarbons (CFCs) play in damaging the stratospheric ozone layer, and catastrophes with a symbolic impact that became calls for world action like the 1978 Amoco Cadiz oil spill affecting the coasts of Brittany in France.

The '80s broadened the scope of international action in different areas of the environment. The first World Conservation Strategy was released by the International Union for Conservation of Nature in 1980 with the significant subtitle: "Living Resource Conservation for Sustainable Development". In the document's foreword, it states that "human beings (…) must come to terms with the reality of resource limitation and the carrying capacities of ecosystems, and must take into account the needs of future generations". At the end, the "Towards Sustainable Development" section identifies the main agents of habitat destruction as poverty, population pressure, social inequity, and the terms of trade, and calls for a new international development strategy. While the principles were not disruptive at that time, they started to frame a vision for the next decades concerning the complex relationships between human beings and nature.

The concept of the 'common heritage of mankind', first mentioned in a 1954 convention related with the protection of cultural property under armed conflicts and in the Outer Space Treaty of 1967, achieved a greater maturity in 1982 within the United Nations Law of the Sea Treaty.

In 1987, the publication of *Our Common Future*, or the so-called Brundtland Report, gave a comprehensive vision of the problems affecting the planet and the need for global solutions mostly through the promotion of sustainable development.

The United Nations Conference on Environment and Development held in Rio de Janeiro in 1992 was a real breakthrough. By mobilizing an incredibly larger number of stakeholders and high-level representatives from all over the globe before, during, and after the conference, the Earth Summit or ECO/92 framed the United Nations as the unquestionable international core for further advances in the implementation of solutions for a safer planet with a better quality of life. The publication of Agenda 21, the signature of the Convention on Biological Diversity and the Framework Convention on Climate Change, the Rio Declaration, and a statement of non-binding forest principles probably turned the event into the most important political mark on the sustainable development timeline. The parallel non-governmental organization Forum also added a set of alternative strategies and visions relevant for the framing of a critical view compared to the less ambitious, slow, and sometimes painful negotiation track along the formal venues of the United Nations.

Throughout the 1990s, two major challenges should be highlighted as crucial steps to a better understanding of the international framework concerning sustainable development and the most important global long-term problem for humanity that is climate change – the beginning of the Conferences of the Parties, after the entry into force of the United Nations

Framework Convention on Climate Change (UNFCCC) in 1995 and the further signature of the Kyoto Protocol by 1997, and all the preparatory work for the approval of the United Nations Millennium Development Goals by 2000, where world leaders agreed to a set of time-bound and measurable goals for combating poverty, hunger, disease, illiteracy, environmental degradation, and discrimination against women, to be achieved by 2015.

In 2000, after a decade of global cross-cultural dialogue on common goals and shared values, the Earth Charter was launched. It began as a United Nations' initiative but it was then developed through the involvement of the global civil society, and is currently endorsed by more than 6000 organizations. The Earth Charter proposes an ethical framework for building a just, sustainable and peaceful global society for the 21st century. With 16 principles, the Charter emphasises the need to respect and care for the community of life along the first four principles, with a statement (principle 2a) that frames a relationship between humans and the rest of nature: "Accept that with the right to own, manage, and use natural resources comes the duty to prevent environmental harm and to protect the rights of people."

During the first decade of the 21st century, another paradigm should also be noted – the relationship between the intensive work of more than 3000 experts from the Intergovernmental Panel on Climate Change between science and forecasted policy scenarios, and all the negotiations towards the mitigation and adaptation to climate change, clearly deserving of the Nobel Peace Prize awarded in 2007.

6. The Inevitable Global and Multiple Approach

Even admitting that the negotiations pathway will gradually convey better approximations of a solution, the structural problem still exists, making inevitable a confrontation where "sovereignty defies reality" (Brunnée 1998). This author, in a paper about the conflicts between sovereignty and water management and the difficulties of international law in dealing with shared resources, states:

> My contention is simple: International Water Law, and States, will not meet the "challenges of water" until the reality of interdependence is addressed in its full complexity. This means that international environmental law and international water law must become integrated to treat water for what it is: a component of the environment. From this integration, in turn, must emerge a concept of sovereignty that reflects rather than defies environmental reality.

With the knowledge we have today of the Earth System, a division between the water component and the other system components is not sound but the statement is still valid on the need for sovereignty to reflect the environmental reality.

It has become obvious that solutions are necessary. Within the political framework architecture of existing institutions, we must consider that without a new theoretical approach able to support a new global paradigm for the management of the commons within an international landscape characterised by the multiplication of territorial units, it will be impossible to avoid the effects of a congenital degeneration.

In this context, the preliminary works concerning the ecological footprint, the first quantifiable and integrated analyses on a global scale, date from the beginning of the 1990s. It was more recently, in 2006, that the standardization of this instrument enabled it to evaluate and compare activities, countries and regions worldwide. The ecological footprint enables us to measure human demand on nature and evaluate the availability of resources in a constrained world that is becoming ever-more populated.

The footprint represents both the asset side through biocapacity, the planet's renewable resources such as biologically productive land areas, including our forests, pastures, cropland, and fisheries, and a demand side, with humanity's consumption of natural resources.

Upon reaching 2015, the target date of the Millennium Development Goals, the United Nations took an important broader step, adopting in this same year the 17 sustainable development goals (SDGs). Considered a consequence of the Rio+20 outcome document "The Future We Want", an inclusive and transparent intergovernmental process on SDGs opened to all stakeholders with a view to developing global sustainable development goals: ending poverty and hunger goes hand in hand with the need to ensure sustainable consumption and production patterns; take urgent action to combat climate change and its impacts; conserve and promote sustainable use of the oceans, seas and marine resources; protect, restore and promote the sustainable use of terrestrial ecosystems; sustainably manage forests; combat desertification; and halt and reverse land degradation and biodiversity loss.

Therefore, and with a thorough description of the historical application and usefulness of tracking sustainable development, new guiding principles for assessment system indicators are suggested throughout this book.

However, the ecological footprint does not account for certain key thresholds within our biophysical system, the so-called planetary boundaries (Steffen et al. 2015a; Rockström et al. 2009) that correspond to biogeophysical features of the geological period in the Holocene. This intangible structure that defines the *favourable state* of the Earth System is referred to by the scientific community as the "safe operating space for humanity", a space without territory, a true natural *res incorporales* that is simultaneously inside and outside all sovereignties, which through the cumulative pressure of humanity may drive the Earth System to an undesirable state.

This new known reality, this true environmental *grundnorm*, therefore, should be the basis for any positive law of general acceptance and reasonableness (Rakhyun & Bosselmann 2013). The ULO (Melot & Pélisse 2008) could now have a set of parameters and guidelines that define its stability and existence.

While science is key for evaluating the progress towards a more sustainable planet, the daily reality embraces long worldwide negotiations, with thousands of negotiators talking about (more than defining) a set of policies on multiple dimensions, including the economy, society, the environment, and other aspects such as governance.

Departing from the "current system of nation-state based governance is inadequate for tackling such issues as climate change-induced global warming, pandemic diseases and other threats to human security and prosperity",[4] this book conveys the idea of an Earth Condominium model, and a new global trusteeship as a paradigm shift necessary for overcoming the difficulties the United Nations has had in the last decades to achieve a better planetary outcome concerning different environmental-related matters. Indeed, the perception of informed citizens worldwide is that the UN has not been able to deliver the necessary commitments, measures and actions to tackle many of the issues agreed on within the sustainable development area. However, it is completely unrealistic to rapidly change the modus operandi of this planetary institution. Even though we are far from the desired goals, one has to recognize that the negotiations have been progressing with some relevant achievements. The alternative to bilateral or group country agreements would increase the dictatorship of the will of a few countries, extending the already existing unnecessary divisions.

In fact, the high complexity of the climate change issue makes the science and technical expertise conveyed through the Intergovernmental Panel on Climate Change almost as determinant as political will.

---

[4] See Chapter 12 of this book, written by, Kul Gautam.

The extensive accumulation of negotiation, knowledge and consensus, including the signature of the Kyoto Protocol in 1997, with all the accessory mechanisms such as the clean development mechanism, joint implementation and emission trading between countries, involved a huge process of approval, tracking and monitoring not common to other UN conventions.

The pathway where long-frozen concepts, such as the so-called "firewall" that has been dividing countries into two major groups – developed and the developing, which have been questioned since greenhouse gas emission targets have had to be applied to a much larger number of countries in the post-2020 era, is a paradigm of crucial importance that the negotiations are trying to finally overcome. . The Paris Agreement tries to overcome some of the previously identified difficulties, creating an ongoing bottom-up process based on national contributions with increased ambition to pursue efforts to limit the temperature increase to 1.5 °C above pre-industrial levels. While in some areas, such as financing, the differences between developed and developing countries are still marked, there is optimism that this new push will contribute for some positive steps towards avoiding catastrophic climate change consequences.

The future has to incorporate a combination of strategies where champion countries have to lead the way and engage other countries, and where multilateral negotiations have to unfold and at least partially meet the objectives considered necessary for the minimization of impacts on humanity and ecosystems. Simultaneously, a new legal paradigm where the "commons" are the basis of a new configuration of the relationships between the countries is vital, and should be implemented within a medium or long-term perspective in a parallel but active process that should start as soon as possible. A pragmatic perspective would be the one that takes into account the current *real politic* but at the same time acknowledges the huge theoretical challenge to law to convey a favourable state of *"healthiness"* of the Earth System "which it is not restricted to the global commons but also spans across areas subject to national jurisdiction" (Borg 2007).

A complementary strategy that does not stop or close the ongoing negotiation processes but shifts and integrates them within a new conceptual framework is the challenge embraced by this book. Only a truly accepted agreement can be both binding and implemented and, therefore, successful.

7. The Double Tragedy and Double Challenge

The work of Hardin generated pessimism around the "commons", turning common property management into a failure. The failure deepens when even those who genuinely care about future sustainability and the common good come to the conclusion that the restriction of exploitation of the resource will lead to a comparative economic loss. This is an altruistic feeling that will lead to the self-elimination of the agents resulting from a natural selection process. This logic is valid not only for the exploitation of the resource but also applies to the benefits that can be realized in maintaining/improving the common good.

In the context of the Earth System, one can designate the current situation as a dual tragedy: On one hand, the classical tragedy of exploitation embodied in the destabilisation of the relatively stable Holocene state of the Earth System by unregulated resource exploitation and pollution; on the other hand, and using the Roman source/resource analysis, as no country will enjoy just for itself all the benefits provided from its own sources of the resource (ecological/geophysical infrastructure) in the state of Earth System (common resource), there are no advantages in promoting actions to maintain the Earth System in a stable state. As there is no incentive for individual initiatives to maintain or improve the sources of common good, in the context of competition and legal and economic shortcomings in managing a common resource, it is normal to allow the degradation of the sources to sell raw materials or to obtain other economic gains. The vital benefits provided by the sources of the common resource are worth zero as they are still shared by all on a global scale.

The logic of the tragedy of the commons is doubly valid for the exhaustion of the *resource* and for the destruction of the *sources of the resource*, "the ecological infrastructure" that can deliver benefits to all societies. The short-term logic will prevail unless structural measures that have the ability to change these initial conditions and generate new systemic collaborative effects are implemented. The logic of the tragedy of the commons undoubtedly depends on a set of assumptions related to the motivation of people operating under rules governing the use of the common and defining the very nature of the resource.

A pragmatic approach to this dual challenge has to be innovative. This implies a structural intervention in the framework basics of the sovereign international system that allows the benefits achieved in the state of the Earth System, which currently economically disappear into a black legal hole, to have economic visibility through an accounting system and compensation for the "stewardship of the Earth System". For this structural change to become possible, the global benefits made in the "common resource", which is the Earth System in a favourable state, must be caught in a global legal instrument (Figure 1).

With the work of Elinor Ostrom and the recognition of the Nobel Prize awarded to her, the commons are no longer an impossibility. For Ostrom (2010), "the crucial factor will be a combination of structural features that lead many involved to trust each other, and are willing to take joint action that adds value to their own short-term costs because both see a long-term benefit for themselves and others, believing that most others will comply". This building of trust and reciprocity, as she claims, requires structural features. We argue that the first structural feature in organizing the collective use of a common resource is to define the resource to be managed, and to recognize that it has to exist. Once identified, the natural *res incorporales* state of the Earth System, although physically inappropriable, can be managed. Hugo Grotius (1916), however, defends an exception: "If any part of these things is by nature susceptible of occupation, it may become the property of the one who occupies it but only in so far as such occupation does not affect its common use".

Ostrom (2010) also acknowledged that "it is obviously much easier to build solutions for collective action problems related to small-scale resources than for those related to a global common good". Despite the magnitude of the challenge, there is no other feasible alternative. This is the approach that we will explore throughout this book.

We would like to thank Will Steffen, Clóvis de Matos, Nathalie Meusy, René Oosterlinck, and Pedro Magalhães for the revisions, comments, discussions and suggestions that led to the achievement of this chapter.

EARTH SYSTEM

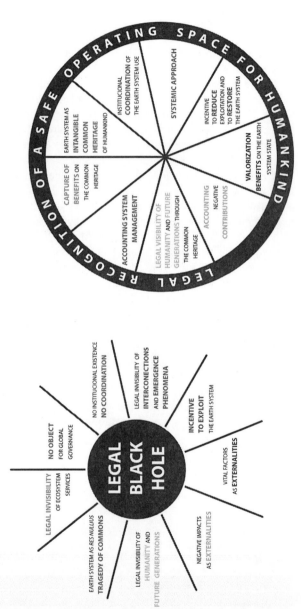

Figure 1. A comparison of the existing and proposed Earth System management regimes

References

Borg, S. (2007). *Climate Change as a Common Concern of Humankind, Twenty Years Later... From UNGA to UNSC.* IUCN Academy of Environmental Law "Towards an Integrated Climate Change and Energy Policy in the European Union". University of Malta. Retrieved from: http://www.iucnael.org

Brunnée, J. (1998). The Challenge to International Law: Water Defying Sovereignty or Sovereignty Defying Reality? In Nação e Defesa (Ed.). *O Desafio das Águas: Segurança Internacional e Desenvolvimento Duradouro*, 86(2), 51– 66. Lisboa: Instituto de Defesa Nacional. Retrieved from http://comum.rcaap.pt/handle/123456789/1501

Grotius, H. (1916). *The Freedom of the Sea.* (The bilingual edition). New York: Oxford University Press.

Hardin, G. (1968). The Tragedy of the Commons. *Science*, 162(3859), 1243-1248. *doi:* 10.1126/science.162.3859.1243

Kaser, M. & Wubbe, F.B.J. (1971). *Romeins Privaatrecht,* trans. F.B.J. Wubbe. 2nd revised and updated edn. (pp. 93–155). Zwolle: Tjeenk Willink.

Lévêque, G. (2002). *Ecologia: do Ecossistema à Biosfera.* Lisboa: Instituto Piaget.

Melot, R. & Pélisse, P. (2008). Prendre la Mesure du Droit: Enjeux de l'Observation Statistique pour la Sociologie Juridique. *Revue Droit et Societé*, 60/70, 331–346. Retrieved from http://www.cairn.info/revue-droit-et-societe-2008-2-page-331.htm

Morin, E. (1990). *Introduction à la Pensée Complexe.* Paris: ESF Éditeur.

Oosterlinck, R. (1996). Tangible and Intangible Property in Outer Space. In *International Institute of Space Law, Proceedings of the 39th Colloquium of the Law of Outer Space,* (pp.271–284). Reston: American Institute of Aeronautics and Astronautics.

Ostrom, E. (2010). A Multi-Scale Approach to Coping with Climate Change and Other Collective Action Problems. *Solutions,* 1(2), 27-36. Retrieved from http://www.thesolutionsjournal.com/node/565

Pureza, J. M. (1998*). O Património Comum da Humanidade: Rumo a um Direito Internacional da Solidariedade?* Oporto: Afrontamento Editions.

Rakhyun, E. K. & Bosselmann, K. (2013). International Environmental Law in the Anthropocene: Towards a Purposive System of Multilateral Environmental Agreements. *Transnational Environmental Law*, 2, 285–309. doi:10.1017/S2047102513000149

Rockström, J., et al. (2009b). Planetary Boundaries: Exploring the Safe
    Operating Space for Humanity. *Ecology and Society* 14(2): 32.
    Retrieved from
    http://www.ecologyandsociety.org/vol14/iss2/art32/
Samuelson, P. A. (1954). The Pure Theory of Public Expenditure. *Review
    of Economics and Statistics, 36,* 387–389. Reprinted in J.E. Stiglitz
    (Ed.) (1966). *The Collected Scientific Papers of P.A. Samuelson,* II,
    1223–1225. Cambridge: M.I.T. Press.
Steffen, W., et al. (2015a). Planetary Boundaries: Guiding Human
    Development on a Changing Planet. *Science Magazine,* 347(6223).
    doi: 10.1126/science.1259855
Stern, N. H. (2006). Executive Summary. In *Stern Review: The Economics
    of Climate Change* (p.1). Retrieved from :
    http://www.wwf.se/source.php/1169157/Stern%20Report_Exec%20Su
    mmary.pdf

CHAPTER TWO

THE PLANETARY BOUNDARIES FRAMEWORK: DEFINING A SAFE OPERATING SPACE FOR HUMANITY

WILL STEFFEN[1]

Dealing with environmental problems is nothing new for humanity. For most of our history, the environmental consequences of our activities have been expressed primarily at the local level and have had little or no impact at regional or global levels. With the advent of the Industrial Revolution, our environmental impacts escalated, affecting waterways and airsheds at greater levels. As we began to recognize that air and water pollution had deleterious impacts on our own well-being, we took action to limit pollution to levels that scientific evidence indicated were safe.

The basic problem in the 21st century is the same, but the scale is vastly different. The human population is now so large and our economic activities so vast that the environmental consequences are being felt at the global level. In essence, we are destabilising the Earth System (ES) and, in effect, beginning to undermine our own life support system (Steffen et al. 2004). The planetary boundaries (PB) framework aims to define a planetary safe operating space within which humanity can survive and thrive (Rockström et al. 2009; Steffen et al. 2015a). The framework is based on a scientific understanding of the structure and functioning of the ES, and of the risks that destabilisation of the system creates for human well-being.

---

[1] Stockholm Resilience Centre, Stockholm University, SE-10691 Stockholm, Sweden; Fenner School of Environment and Society, The Australian National University, Canberra ACT 2601, Australia

1. The Earth System, the Anthropocene and Planetary Boundaries

The ES is defined as the interacting physical, chemical and biological processes that cycle materials and energy throughout the system at the planetary level. Importantly, humans and our activities are an integral part of the ES (Oldfield and Steffen 2004). It is critical for the planetary boundaries framework to recognize that the ES is a *single complex system* that exists in well-defined states. Like all complex systems, the ES exhibits threshold/abrupt change behaviour in aspects of atmospheric and oceanic circulation, which, if triggered, would create serious risks for human well-being.

Over the time period that fully modern humans evolved on the planet, about 200,000 – 250,000 years ago to the present, the ES has oscillated between ice ages and warm periods with approximately 100,000-year periodicity (Petit et al. 1999). For nearly all of our existence on Earth (encompassing two of the ice age – warm period cycles), we have operated in small groups of hunter-gatherers with some impact on the biosphere through, for example, the extinction of megafauna (Martin and Klein 1984) but without significant influence on the structure and functioning of the ES.

About 11,700 years ago, the ES completed its transition into the Holocene, the current unusually long warm period that is expected to last for several thousands of years more (Berger and Loutre 2002). The Holocene is significant for humanity because it is only during this relatively stable long warm period that humans developed agriculture, and then villages and cities, eventually leading to the complex globalised contemporary society that has developed around the world during the last century (Figure 1).

The environmental stability of the Holocene, especially the relative stability of the climate sub-system, has probably played a key role in fostering the development of human societies, beginning with the advent of agriculture.

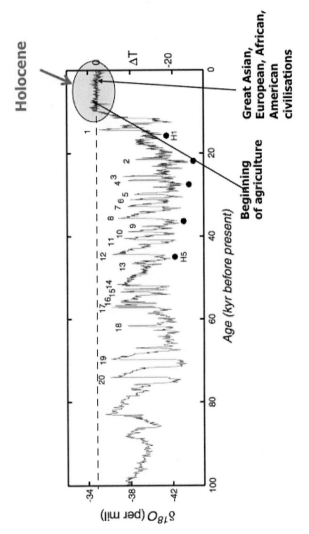

Figure 1. Record of $\delta^{18}O$ per mil (scale on left) from the Greenland Ice Sheet Project (GRIP) ice core, a proxy for atmospheric temperature over Greenland (approximate temperature range on °C relative to Holocene average is given on the right), showing the relatively stable Holocene climate during the past ca. 11,700 years and Dansgaard-Oeschger events (numbered) during the preceding colder glacial climate (Ganopolski and Rahmstorf 2001). Note the relative stability of temperature for the last 11,700 years (the Holocene) compared to the earlier ice age period.

Earth system trends

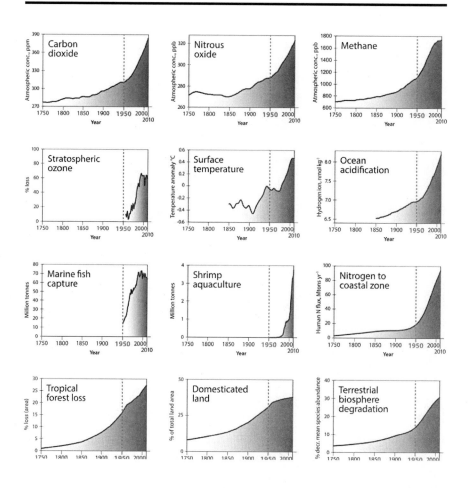

Socio-economic trends

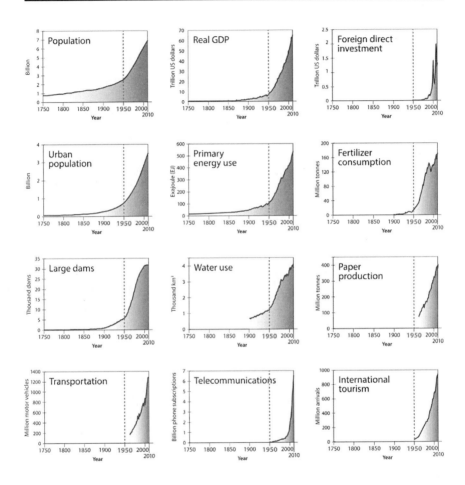

Figure 2. (A) Trends from 1750 to 2010 in globally aggregated indicators for socioeconomic development. (B) Trends from 1750 to 2010 in indicators for the structure and functioning of the Earth System. Details on each of the individual panels and the sources for the data are given in Steffen et al. (2015b).

The Holocene has also proven to be a very resilient state of the ES, a feature important for human development. For example, about 8,700 years ago, not long after the beginning of the Holocene, the Earth suffered an abrupt cold excursion; however, it bounced back very quickly to the much more stable warm conditions of the Holocene (Von Grafenstein et al. 1998).[2] Today, the ES is further demonstrating its resilience via the carbon cycle. Humans are exerting exceptionally strong pressure on the carbon cycle through the rising emissions of carbon dioxide from the combustion of fossil fuels, but the marine and terrestrial carbon sinks are together absorbing over half of them (Le Quéré et al. 2009; Raupach and Canadell 2010), slowing the rate of temperature increase.

Despite this resilience, it is now becoming clear that the ES is on its way out of the Holocene due to an escalating set of pressures arising from human activities (Steffen et al. 2015b).[3] The scale and rate of contemporary human-driven changes to the ES are astounding. The composition of greenhouse gases in the atmosphere, the concentration of stratospheric ozone in the southern high latitudes, and the structure and functioning of terrestrial and marine ecosystems are all now well outside the envelope of Holocene variability (IPCC 2013; MA 2005). Even more remarkable is the post-1950 rate at which human activities are destabilising the ES, a period sometimes called the Great Acceleration (Steffen et al. 2007; Figure 2). This rapid change in the structure and functioning of the ES has prompted the proposal that the Earth has now entered a new geological epoch, the Anthropocene (Crutzen 2002).

The advent of the Anthropocene has serious implications for humanity. The Holocene is the only state of the ES that we know for certain can support complex contemporary human societies. While some may argue that the societies of today now have the technological capability to survive in very different states of the ES, that view is based on beliefs rather than sound scientific analysis. There is much evidence that a large, rapid excursion from the Holocene presents major risks for humans and our societies (IPCC 2014; MA 2005; Steffen et al. 2011). The aim of the planetary boundaries approach is to define a Holocene-like state of the ES based on a scientific understanding of the structure and functioning of the ES as a single complex system. This scientific analysis then proposes boundaries on human perturbations of the Earth System to define a safe operating space for humanity.

---

[2] See also Figure 1.
[3] See also Figure 2.

2. The Conceptual Framework of the Planetary Boundaries

The conceptual framework for the planetary boundaries (PBs) is presented in Figure 3 (Steffen et al. 2015a). The boundaries are organized around a small set of processes that together describe the functioning of the ES. Processes incorporated in the framework include well-known planetary features such as the climate system, the water cycle and the role of life itself in the functioning of the planet. They also include somewhat lesser known processes such as the global cycling of elements like nitrogen and phosphorus and the loading of the atmosphere with small particles called aerosols.

For each process we define a control variable that plays a strong role in the process itself as well as (i) acts as an indicator for the state of the process and (ii) provides a point of intervention for humans to manage our perturbation of the process. For example, we use atmospheric carbon dioxide concentration as a control variable for climate change (although radiative forcing is the more scientifically correct and fundamental control variable) and the amount of deforestation in the world's major forest biomes as a control variable for land-system change.

Figure 3 shows the relationship between the process itself and the control variable. For some processes, there is likely to be a threshold somewhere along the control variable. That is, the process may not be very responsive to changes in the control variable until the threshold is crossed, beyond which, with only a small change in the control variable, there is an abrupt, sometimes rapid shift to another state of the process (left panel of Figure 3). For other processes, there is no known threshold so a change in the control variable leads to a more gradual change in the process (right panel of Figure 3). The latter processes are nevertheless important as they may contribute to the resilience of the ES as a whole, so changes in these processes, even without threshold/abrupt change behaviour, can erode the resilience of the ES.

Even if there is a threshold, the boundary itself is placed well upstream of the threshold (that is, the boundary does not equal the threshold). There are two reasons for this. First, it allows for the scientific uncertainty that may surround the exact position of the threshold along the control variable and, using the precautionary principle, we place the boundary well away from the estimated position of the threshold. Second, placing the boundary well upstream of the threshold may allow society enough time to steer away from the threshold based on early-warning signs of an impending threshold (Scheffer et al. 2009; Carpenter and Brock 2006; Scheffer et al. 2012; Biggs et al. 2009).

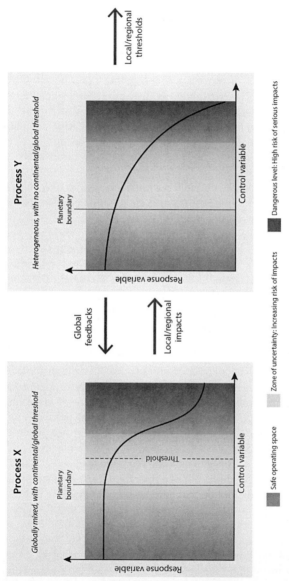

Figure 3. The conceptual framework for the planetary boundaries approach, showing the safe operating space, the zone of uncertainty, the position of the threshold (where one is likely to exist) and the area of high risk. Source: Steffen et al. (2015a).

Each boundary has a zone of uncertainty, the yellow zone in Figure 3, which extends from the boundary along the control variable. This zone encompasses uncertainty in our knowledge about where along the control variable significant change in the process might occur, with deleterious consequences for human well-being as well as intrinsic uncertainties in the functioning of the ES.

In essence, the colour-coding shown in Figure 3 represents a risk framework. Below the boundary in the green zone, scientific evidence shows that there is very little risk of any significant change in the process. This is the safe operating space. The yellow zone is an area of increasing risk. This means that transgressing a boundary may not lead immediately to a negative outcome but that humanity is traversing an increasingly risky zone. Our best scientific evidence suggests that the red zone, beyond the "danger end" of the zone of uncertainty, is an area of high risk for humanity. If the control variable is pushed into that zone, there is a high probability of a change in the functioning of the Earth System that could be deleterious or even catastrophic for humanity.

Two of the boundaries – climate change and biosphere integrity – have been recognized as "core planetary boundaries" given their importance in the functioning of the ES (Steffen et al. 2015a). Climate change represents a change in the energy balance at the Earth's surface. The amount and distribution of energy at the planetary surface are key features of any planet in the solar system, including our own. The Earth, of course, is distinguished from other planets by its abundant life, and the biosphere (the totality of all ecosystems) represents the fundamentally important role that life plays in determining the state of the ES, regulating its energy and material flows and providing the resilience to respond to abrupt and gradual change. Of the nine planetary boundaries, climate change and biosphere integrity, if transgressed, are the only two with the individual potential to push the ES into a new state.

The planetary boundaries, as the name indicates, are designed to operate at the global level but all boundary processes operate across scales, from local to global. Focusing on the global level works well for those boundaries that have globally "well-mixed" control variables, such as atmospheric carbon dioxide concentration, for climate change. However, for several other boundary processes, such as biosphere integrity and land-system change amongst others, the control variables are highly heterogeneous at the global level and so need to be analysed at sub-global levels (Steffen et al. 2015a). Nevertheless, these analyses are restricted to the next lower level from the ES as a whole – ocean basins, large terrestrial biomes and the world's major agricultural zones. This approach is described in more detail in section 1.3 on the individual boundaries and also in Table 1. It is important to emphasise that the planetary boundaries are not designed to address local and regional environmental problems in their own right but rather to complement them by focusing strongly on the global level.

While the boundaries are treated independently of one another, we recognize that there are interactions among them, some of them quite strong. This is particularly true for the two core boundaries, climate change and biosphere integrity, which are connected to all of the other planetary boundaries. However, our current capacity to quantify these interactions is low so they are simply noted in a qualitative sense and flagged as an urgent research priority as our capability in ES modelling strengthens. In general, interactions are likely to constrict further the position of the boundaries along their respective control variables.

3. Identification and Quantification of Boundaries

Table 1: The updated control variables and their current values, along with the proposed boundaries and zones of uncertainty, for all nine planetary boundaries.

Earth System Process	Control Variable(s)	Planetary Boundary (zone of uncertainty)	Current Value of Control Variable
Climate change (R2009: same)	Atmospheric CO_2 concentration, ppm	350 ppm CO_2 (350-450 ppm)	396.5 ppm CO_2
	Energy imbalance at top-of-atmosphere, W m^{-2}	Energy imbalance: +1.0 W m^{-2} (+1.0-1.5 W m^{-2})	2.3 W m^{-2} (1.1-3.3 W m^{-2})
Change in biosphere integrity (R2009: Rate of biodiversity loss)	*Genetic diversity:* Extinction rate	*Genetic:* < 10 E/MSY (10-100 E/MSY) but with an aspirational goal of ca. 1 M/ESY* (the background rate of extinction loss).* E/MSY = extinctions per million species-years	100-1000 E/MSY
	Functional: diversity: Biodiversity Intactness Index (BII)	*Functional:* Maintain BII at 90% (90-30%) or above, assessed geographically by biomes/large regional areas (e.g. southern Africa), major marine	84%, applied to southern Africa only

	Note: These are interim control variables until more appropriate ones are developed	ecosystems (e.g., coral reefs) or by large functional groups	
Stratospheric ozone depletion (R2009: same)	Stratospheric O3 concentration, DU	<5% reduction from pre-industrial level of 290 DU (5%–10%), assessed by latitude	Only transgressed over Antarctica in Austral spring (~200 DU)
Ocean acidification (R2009: same)	Carbonate ion concentration, average global surface ocean saturation state with respect to aragonite (Ωarag)	≥80% of the pre-industrial aragonite saturation state of mean surface ocean, including natural diel and seasonal variability (≥80%– ≥70%)	~84% of the pre-industrial aragonite saturation state
Biogeochemical flows: (P and N cycles) (R2009: Biogeochemical flows: (interference with P and N cycles))	*P cycle*: *Global:* P flow from freshwater systems into the ocean	*P cycle*: *Global:* 11 Tg P yr^{-1} (11-100 Tg P yr^{-1})	~22 Tg P yr^{-1}
	Regional: P flow from fertilizers to erodible soils	*Regional:* 6.2 Tg yr^{-1} mined and applied to erodible (agricultural) soils (6.2-11.2 Tg yr^{-1}). Boundary is a global average but regional distribution is critical for impacts.	~14 Tg P yr^{-1}
	N cycle: *Global:* Industrial and intentional biological fixation of N	62 Tg N yr^{-1} (62-82 Tg N yr^{-1}). Boundary acts as a global 'valve' limiting introduction of new reactive N to Earth System, but regional distribution of fertilizer N is critical for impacts.	~150 Tg N yr^{-1}
Land-system change (R2009: same)	*Global:* area of forested land as % of original forest cover	*Global:* 75% (75-54%) Values are a weighted average of the three individual biome boundaries and their uncertainty zones	62%

	Biome: area of forested land as % of potential forest	*Biome:* Tropical: 85% (85-60%) Temperate: 50% (50-30%) Boreal: 85% (85-60%)	
Freshwater use (R2009: Global freshwater use)	*Global:* Maximum amount of consumptive blue water use (km^3yr^{-1})	*Global:* 4000 km^3 yr^{-1} (4000-6000 km^3 yr^{-1})	~2600 km^3 yr^{-1}
	Basin: Blue water withdrawal as % of mean monthly river flow	*Basin:* Maximum monthly withdrawal as a percentage of mean monthly river flow. For low-flow months: 25% (25-55%); for intermediate-flow months: 30% (30-60%); for high-flow months: 55% (55-85%)	
Atmospheric aerosol loading (R2009: same)	*Global:* Aerosol Optical Depth (AOD), but much regional variation		
	Regional: AOD as a seasonal average over a region. South Asian Monsoon used as a case study	*Regional:* (South Asian Monsoon as a case study): anthropogenic total (absorbing and scattering) AOD over Indian subcontinent of 0.25 (0.25-0.50); absorbing (warming) AOD less than 10% of total AOD	0.30 AOD, over South Asian region
Introduction of novel entities (R2009: Chemical pollution)	*No control variable currently defined*	***No boundary currently identified, but see boundary for stratospheric ozone for an example of a boundary related to a novel entity (CFCs)***	

Table 1 summarizes the updated definitions and quantification of the nine boundaries. Substantial changes have been made to the conceptual frameworks of three of the boundaries (Rockström et al. 2009). The original 2009 "biodiversity loss" boundary has now been changed to a boundary on biosphere integrity, reflecting a more fundamental approach to the role of life in the long-term functioning and evolution of the ES. Land-system change was, in 2009, based on the area of cropland; this has now been changed to the amount of forested land remaining in the Earth's three major forest biomes, with a focus on the role these biomes play in feedbacks to the climate system. This boundary has thus been refocused to highlight the most important roles that land systems (primarily forests) play in the climate system rather than on a highly modified human land system (croplands). The boundary on chemical pollution has been broadened to a wide range of novel entities introduced into the ES by humans, although the focus on further developing this boundary remains on chemical pollution.

As noted above, a sub-global component has been added to several of the boundaries to account for the large-scale heterogeneity in the nature of the relevant ES process as well as in the distribution of the control variable. For example, for biogeochemical flows, the control variable operates at the level of large agricultural zones; for freshwater use, at the level of large river basins; and for atmospheric aerosol loading, at the level of large regional monsoon systems.

Below we provide a brief summary of the status of each of the nine PBs.

Climate change. The control variables here are (i) atmospheric carbon dioxide (CO_2) concentration, and (ii) the more fundamental top-of-the-atmosphere radiative forcing. The boundary (and zone of uncertainty) has been set at 350 ppm CO_2 (350-450 ppm CO_2) and +1.0 W m^{-2} (+1.0-1.5 W m^{-2}). Based on the CO_2 control variable, the climate system is now about halfway through the zone of uncertainty, suggesting that there should be evidence of an increasing risk of deleterious outcomes from the changes already apparent in the climate. This is borne out by the most recent assessment of the IPCC (2013), which shows an increase in the frequency of heavy rainfall events, increasing drought in some parts of the world, increased mass loss from the polar ice sheets, and an increase in the intensity, frequency and duration of heatwaves.

Change in biosphere integrity. Here we adopt a two-component approach, with one component capturing the diversity of genetic material that determines the long-term capability of the biosphere to continue to co-evolve with the geophysical components of the ES, and the second capturing the shorter-term functional role of the biosphere in the ES that ultimately provides a wide range of essential ecosystem services for the well-being of humanity (Mace et al. 2014; MA 2005).

For the first role, phylogenetic species variability would be the ideal control variable but not enough is known yet in a quantitative sense to allow its immediate adoption. For an interim control variable, we use estimated rates of extinction of well-studied organisms and compare current rates to background levels. We place an initial boundary of extinction rate at ten times the background level, while currently observed rates are already 100–1,000 times the background level and likely to go higher (MA 2005), thus placing this component of biosphere integrity in the danger zone. We emphasise, though, that this initial boundary is an initial estimate as we don't yet have enough knowledge of what level of biodiversity loss (e.g., loss of what types of organisms) the ES can tolerate before its resilience and evolutionary capacity are significantly damaged.

For the second role, a biome-level estimate of the integrity of that biome based on an appropriate control variable (e.g., calcification rate for coral reef systems) would be an appropriate approach (Mace et al. 2014). However, we currently lack sufficient knowledge to implement such an approach globally so the Biodiversity Intactness Index (BII, Scholes and Biggs 2005) has been adopted as an interim control variable. The index, which ranges from 100% for biomes and ecosystems where the population abundance of a wide range of taxa are at pre-industrial levels to lower values for disturbed systems, has so far been applied to southern African countries only. We propose setting the boundary at 90% BII, but with a large uncertainty zone of 90% to 30% to reflect large gaps in knowledge about the relationship between change in BII and the functioning of ecosystems and biomes.

Stratospheric ozone depletion. The control variable is stratospheric ozone concentration as measured in Dobson Units (DU), and the boundary is set at a concentration of 275 DU. This process is within the safe operating space around the globe, except for the well-known ozone hole over Antarctica in the southern hemisphere spring when ozone concentration can drop to about 200 DU. This minimum regional ozone concentration has stabilised over the past 15 years but is expected to rise in the future as ozone-depleting substances are phased out.

Ocean acidification. Although this process is closely linked to the control variable for climate change (atmospheric CO_2 concentration), it is important that it has a boundary too as some proposed geoengineering fixes for climate change (e.g., solar radiation management) may cap global temperature rise but would not prevent the increasing acidification of the ocean. The control variable for ocean acidification is the saturation state of aragonite (Ω_{arag}), a form of calcium carbonate formed by many marine organisms. The boundary is set at $\geq$ 80% of the pre-industrial average annual global Ω_{arag}. The current value is approximately 84% of Ω_{arag} so ocean acidification, as a global average, is still within the safe operating space. However, as CO_2 is more soluble in cold water, some areas of the polar seas may already be in the zone of increasing risk (Hoegh-Guldberg et al. 2007).

Biogeochemical flows. In principle, this boundary applies to a wide range of element flows through the ES but for now we focus on phosphorus (P) and nitrogen (N), which are essential for the functioning of life on Earth and have been significantly modified by human activities. However, in future, other important elements, such as silicon and iron, may also be included within this PB. The carbon cycle is included as an integral component of the climate change PB so is not duplicated here.

The P boundary has a two-component approach. One component is based on the prevention of a large-scale ocean anoxic event, with the boundary set at a sustained flow rate of 11 Tg P y^{-1} from freshwater systems into the ocean. The other component of the boundary is based on the prevention of widespread eutrophication of freshwaters and is set at a flow rate of 6.2 Tg P y^{-1} from mined P (fertilisers) to erodible soil, where we assume that intensively tilled agricultural soils are erodible (Carpenter and Bennett 2011).

The N boundary is likewise based on the prevention of widespread eutrophication of freshwaters and coastal seas (de Vries et al. 2013). Based on this approach, we set the N boundary at 62 Tg N y^{-1} from industrial and intentional biological N fixation. That is, the boundary is based on the total addition by human activities of new reactive N into the ES.

The P and N boundaries are related, as the ultimate source of additional P and N to the ES is almost entirely from the application of fertilisers in intensively managed agricultural zones. The current global application rates are about 14 Tg y^{-1} for P (MacDonald et al. 2011; Bouwman et al. 2013) and about 150 Tg y^{-1} for N (Fowler et al. 2013). Both of these values transgress their respective boundaries and are also outside the zone of uncertainty, thus placing them in the high-risk area (Figure 4).

Land-system change. Based on their role in the biogeophysical regulation of the climate system, the three major forest biomes – tropical, temperate and boreal – have been identified as the key biomes in terms of a land-system change PB (Snyder et al. 2004; West et al. 2010). It is important to note that all terrestrial biomes – forests, woodlands, grasslands, shrublands, tundra, etc. – are considered in the biosphere integrity PB and so are included in the PB framework. The major forest biomes are emphasised here because of their significant role in the climate system in addition to their role in the global carbon cycle (part of the climate change PB).

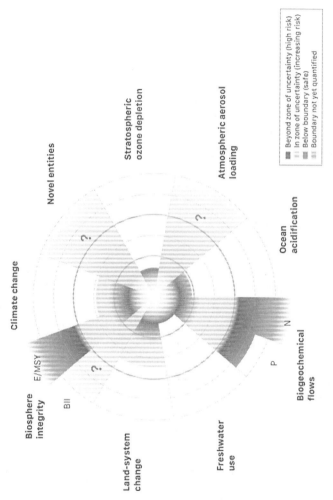

Figure 4. The current status of the control variables for seven of the nine planetary boundaries. Green zone is the safe operating space (below the boundary), yellow represents the zone of uncertainty (increasing risk), and red is the high-risk zone. The planetary boundary itself lies at the inner heavy circle. The control variables have been normalized for the zone of uncertainty (between the two heavy circles); the center of the figure therefore does not represent values of 0 for the control variables. The control variable shown for climate change is atmospheric CO_2 concentration. Processes for which global-level boundaries cannot yet be quantified are represented by gray wedges; these are atmospheric aerosol loading, novel entities and the functional role of biosphere integrity. Source: Steffen et al. (2015a).

The PB for the tropical forest biomes is proposed at a maintenance rate of 85% of intact forest cover, based on research that suggests there is a threshold of clearing for the Amazon basin beyond which the entire forest is more prone to conversion to a woodland or savanna (Nobre et al. 2009; Lewis et al. 2011). Although there is no equivalent research for boreal forests, we have suggested a boundary of 85% of boreal forests be retained, given the important role they play in regulating the albedo of the northern high latitudes. We proposed a boundary of 50% for temperate forests based on their weaker biogeophysical coupling to the climate system (Snyder et al. 2004; West et al. 2010).

Freshwater use. We have retained consumptive use of water from rivers, lakes, reservoirs, and renewable groundwater stores as the control variable for this PB, and propose a globally aggregated boundary of 4000 km^3/yr. However, the hydrological cycle, and human modifications of it, is highly heterogeneous around the planet so we have also developed a component of the boundary based on withdrawals of water for human use at the level of river basins.

The rationale for a river-basin-level PB is the need to avoid major changes to flow-dependent freshwater changes in a large number of river basins. Here we rely on the environmental water flow concept, which defines the level of river flow required to maintain well-functioning freshwater ecosystems. Environmental water flow is dependent on the flow regime (high, intermediate, low) and so the variable monthly flow method (Pastor et al. 2014) was used to calculate the basin-scale boundaries. These vary considerably from basin to basin, and are shown in detail as a global map in Steffen et al. (2015a).

Atmosphere aerosol loading. Aerosols – small particles suspended in the atmosphere – are well known as a local pollution problem but they also play several important roles in the functioning of the ES. For the definition of a PB for atmospheric aerosols, we focus on their role in modulating regional ocean-atmosphere circulation and, more particularly, influencing large regional monsoon systems. We take the South Asian monsoon system as a case study and adopt Aerosol Optical Depth (AOD) as the control variable. The background AOD in the South Asian region is about 0.15, but much larger values have been observed due to human activities such as the combustion of fossil fuels and biomass (Chin et al. 2014). A value of around 0.50 would likely lead to a decrease in monsoon activity, and hence rainfall, over the very populous South Asian region (Ramanathan et al. 2005). Using a precautionary approach, we propose a boundary at an AOD of 0.25, with an uncertainty zone of 0.25-0.50. The mean annual AOD over the region is currently about 0.3 (Chin et al. 2014).

Introduction of novel entities. This PB is fundamentally different from the other eight, all of which are concerned with the human perturbation of natural processes in the ES. This PB is focused on the introduction into the ES of entirely new entities created by humans; these include new substances, new forms of existing substances and modified life forms that have potential unwanted geophysical or biological effects. The characteristics of the types of novel entities of concern are (i) persistence, (ii) mobility across scales with consequent widespread distributions, and (iii) potential impacts on vital ES processes or subsystems. At present, most is known about chemicals, given the rapidly increasing worldwide production and distribution of chemicals, and so they are the initial focus of the novel entities PB (MacLeod et al. 2014; Persson et al. 2013). For now, an initial quantification of this PB is not possible as we don't yet have the screening processes in place for chemicals with properties that may predispose them towards becoming global problems.

Figure 4 shows the current status of the nine PBs. The focus of the figure is on the zone of uncertainty, that is, the area of increasing risk, and so the scales for the PBs have been normalised on that zone. This means that the PBs do not share a common origin in the figure and, in fact, the origins would be in vastly different places. Also, because the width of the zones of uncertainties for the various PBs differs significantly, the distance beyond the outer edge of the zone can be misleading. The focus, then, of the figure is (i) whether or not a process (represented by the control variable) is in the safe operating space (green zone) or in the high-risk (danger) zone (red zone), and (ii) if it is in the zone of increasing risk, how far into that zone it currently lies.

Based on this framework, four of the nine control variables have transgressed the boundary, and two of these – biosphere integrity (the long-term genetic component) and biogeochemical flows – are already in the danger zone. The other two that have transgressed the boundary – climate change and land-system change – are both within the area of increasing risk and have not yet reached the high danger zone.

4. Implications of the Planetary Boundaries Framework for Governance

While humans have developed governance approaches, legal frameworks and institutions to manage environmental challenges at local and regional levels, dealing with environmental threats at the global level presents a fundamentally different and more complex set of challenges. These challenges have sparked a rapidly increasing international research effort on governance issues in the Anthropocene, an effort that is already generating a range of interesting approaches to deal with these challenges (Galaz 2014; Beirmann 2014). Here we highlight several features of the planetary boundaries framework that must be considered when implementation of the framework is attempted.

Scale. The most critical scientific principle that underpins the PB framework is that the Earth System functions as a single integrated system at the planetary level. In effect, it provides a life-support system for humanity. As noted earlier, the Earth has existed in various well-defined states throughout its history but it is only the most recent, relatively stable state that has allowed human civilizations to develop. The PB framework is oriented strongly towards maintaining a relatively stable state of the Earth System, one that is very similar to that of the past 11,700 years. The focus on the global level means that well-known human institutions that operate at the sub-global level – for example, nation-states or large corporations – are not designed to deal with a single entity like the Earth System that is shared by all of humanity regardless of nationality or culture. Furthermore, nations or corporations are not designed to deal with large subsystems of the planet that are critical for the functioning of the Earth System, for example, the climate system, the water cycle and element cycles, either. Dealing effectively with these challenges may require both innovative interactions among existing institutions across scales and the creation of new institutions at the global level (Galaz 2014; Biermann 2014).

Complex systems. Several features of complex system behaviour pose severe challenges to governance approaches for managing humanity's relationship with the Earth System.

(i) Many large-scale features of the Earth System can exhibit threshold behaviour; this means that once a threshold is crossed, a change in the state of the subsystem is inevitable and can occur abruptly. Examples include the Greenland ice sheet, the South Asian monsoon system and eutrophication of large freshwater bodies and coastal waters. As noted earlier, in such cases the subsystem may appear unresponsive to the driving variable until very near the threshold, by which time it is often too late to avoid the crossing of the threshold. This argues strongly for the application of the precautionary principle, based on best available scientific understanding, in managing subsystems prone to this behaviour.

(ii) A feature of complex systems closely related to threshold/abrupt change behaviour is the importance of so-called "slow variables" in the behaviour of the system. These variables may go unnoticed in the observed behaviour of the system but they can slowly erode the resilience of the system so that it becomes more prone to destabilisation by other drivers that operate on much faster time frames. Examples include the very slow fragmentation and contraction of large forest areas by land cover change or the slow erosion of the resilience of coral reefs as the ocean gradually becomes more acidic. At the global level, the same type of process might operate on the biosphere as a whole when a set of human pressures increases the fraction of human-dominated landscapes around the planet; the ultimate outcome might be the rapid transition of the Earth's biosphere into a very different state as a threshold is crossed (Barnosky et al. 2012).

(iii) Some changes in the state of critical subsystems of the Earth System are essentially irreversible in any time frame of relevance for human societies. An example is the loss of a large polar ice sheet like that on Greenland. Although the loss of such an ice sheet may appear slow on human timeframes, its loss is essentially irreversible. Loss of ice sheets is one factor driving the rise in global sea levels, another process that is essentially irreversible on timescales of relevance for humans. This irreversibility provides another strong argument for application of the precautionary principle when implementing the PB framework.

Equity. Inequalities between and within nations are attracting a lot of attention as constraints on the functioning of human societies, especially in terms of the social problems that inequalities can trigger (e.g., Wilkinson and Pickett 2009; Piketty 2014). The PB framework also intersects with human equity issues in a couple of important ways. First, the human drivers destabilising the Earth System and pushing it out of the Holocene are distributed in highly unequal ways around the world; the 18% of the human population that live in the OECD (wealthy) countries account for nearly three-quarters of global economic activity, and with it the consumption patterns that drive the impacts on the global environment (Steffen et al. 2015b). Second, the intrinsic nature of the Earth System itself is unequal when it intersects with the human sphere. For example, the world's tropical forests are more important for the functioning of the Earth System than temperate forests. Tropical forests are located almost entirely in developing countries whereas two of the three largest temperate forest regions, those of North America and Western Europe, are occupied by wealthy countries. Dealing with the complexities of inequality in human societies and simultaneously with the intrinsic inequalities (or "heterogeneity" as scientists call it) in the biophysical world present enormous challenges to the creation of effective governance systems for the PB framework.

In summary, the most critical feature of the Earth's safe operating space for humanity, as proposed by the PB framework, is that it is based firmly on the concept of the Earth System as a single integrated system at the planetary level. The most critical challenge for humanity is to create institutions and governance systems that respect this biophysical reality and manage our behaviour towards the Earth System accordingly.

References

Barnosky, A.D., Hadly, E.A. Bascompte, J. et al. (2012). Approaching a State Shift in Earth's Biosphere. *Nature* 486, 52–58.

Berger, A. & Loutre, M.F. (2002) An Exceptionally Long Interglacial Ahead? *Science*, 297, 1287–1288.

Biggs, R., Carpenter, S.R. & Brock, W.A. (2009). Turning Back from the Brink: Detecting an Impending Regime Shift in Time to Avert It. *Proc. Natl. Acad. Sci. (USA)*, 106, 826–831. doi: 10.1073/pnas.0811729106

Biermann, F. (2014). *Earth System Governance: World Politics in the Anthropocene* (pp.267). Cambridge MA USA and London UK: MIT Press.

Bouwman, A.F., Klein Goldwijk, K., van der Hoek, K.W. et al. (2013). Exploring Global Changes in Nitrogen and Phosphorus Cycles in Agriculture Induced by Livestock Production over the 1900–2050 Period. *Proc. Natl. Acad. Sci. (USA)*, 110, 20882–20887. (first published May 16, 2011; 10.1073/pnas.1012878108).

Carpenter, S.R. & Bennett, E.M. (2011). Reconsideration of the Planetary Boundary for Phosphorus. *Environmental Research Letters*, 6. doi: 10.1088/1748-9326/6/1/014009

Carpenter, S.R. & Brock, W.A. (2006) Rising Variance: A Leading Indicator of Ecological Transition. *Ecol. Lett.*, 9, 311–318. doi: 10.1111/j.1461-0248.2005.00877.x

Chin, M., Diehl, T., Tan, Q. et al. (2014). Multi-Decadal Aerosol Variations from 1980 to 2009: A Perspective from Observations and a Global Model. *Atmos. Chem. and Phys.*, 14, 3657-3690. doi: 10.5194/acp-14-3657-2014

Crutzen, P.J. (2002) Geology of Mankind – the Anthropocene. *Nature*, 415, 23.

de Vries, W., Kros, J., Kroeze, C. & Seitzinger, S.P. (2013). Assessing Planetary and Regional Nitrogen Boundaries Related to Food Security and Adverse Environmental Impacts. *Current Opinion in Environmental Sustainability,* 5, 392–402.

Fowler, D., Coyle, M., Skiba, U. et al. (2013). The Global Nitrogen Cycle in the 21st Century. *Phil. Trans. Roy. Soc. Lond. Ser. B,* 368(20130164). doi: 10.1098/rstb.2013.0164
368(20130164). doi: 10.1098/rstb.2013.0164

Galaz, V. (2014). *Global Environmental Governance, Technology and Politics: The Anthropocene Gap* (pp.189). Cheltenham UK and Northampton MA USA: Edward Elgar.

Ganopolski, A. & Rahmstorf, S. (2001). Rapid Changes of Glacial Climate Simulated in a Coupled Climate Model. *Nature, 409,* 153–158. doi: 10.1038/35051500

Hoegh-Guldberg, O., Mumby, P.J., Hooten, A.J. et al. (2007). Coral Reefs under Rapid Climate Change and Ocean Acidification. *Science,* 318, 1737–1742.

IPCC (Intergovernmental Panel on Climate Change) (2013). *Climate Change 2013: The Physical Science Basis.* Summary for Policymakers. Alexander, L., Allen, S., Bindoff, N.L., Breon, F.-M., Church, J. et al. (Eds.). Geneva, Switzerland: IPCC Secretariat.

IPCC (Intergovernmental Panel on Climate Change) (2014). *Climate Change 2014: Impacts, Adaptation, and Vulnerability.* Summary for Policymakers. Field, C.B., Barros, V.R., Mastrandrea, M.D., Mach, K.J. Abdrabo, M.A.-K., et al. (Eds.). Geneva, Switzerland: IPCC Secretariat.

Le Quéré, C., Raupach, M.R., Canadell, J.G. et al. (2009). Trends in the Sources and Sinks of Carbon Dioxide. *Nature Geoscience,* 2, 831–836.

Lewis, S.L., Brando, P.M., Phillips, O.L. et al. (2011). The 2010 Amazon Drought. *Science,* 331, 554. doi: 10.1126/science.1200807

MA (Millennium Ecosystem Assessment) (2005). *Ecosystems and Human Well-Being: Synthesis.* Washington DC: Island Press.

MacDonald, G. K., Bennett, E. M., Ramankutty, N. & Potter, P. (2011). Too Much or Not Enough: Agronomic Phosphorus Balances Across the World's Croplands. *Proceedings of the National Academy of Sciences (USA),* 108, 3086–3091.

Mace, G.M., Reyers, B., Alkemade, R. et al. (2014). Approaches to Defining a Planetary Boundary for Biodiversity. *Global Environmental Change,* 28, 289–297. doi: 10.1016/j.gloenvcha.2014.07.009

MacLeod, M., Breitholtz, M., Cousins et al. (2014). Identifying Chemicals that are Planetary Boundary Threats. *Environmental Science & Technology,* 48, 11057–11063. doi: 10.1021/es501893

Martin, P.S. & Klein, R.G. (1984) *Quaternary Extinctions: A Prehistoric Revolution* (pp.892). Tucson AZ USA: University of Arizona Press.

Nobre, P., Malagutti, M., Urbano, D.F. et al. (2009) Amazon Deforestation and Climate Change in a Coupled Model Simulation. *J. Clim.*, 22, 5686–5697. doi: 10.1175/2009JCLI2757.1

Oldfield, F. & Steffen, W. (2004). The Earth System. In: Steffen, W., Sanderson, A., Tyson, P.D. et al. (Eds.), *Global Change and the Earth System: A Planet under Pressure*. The IGBP Book Series, (p.7). Berlin, Heidelberg, New York: Springer-Verlag.

Pastor, A.F., Ludwig, F., Biemans, H. et al. (2014). Accounting for Environmental Flow Requirements in Global Water Assessments. *Hydrol. Earth Sys. Sci.*, 18, 5041–5059. doi: 10.5194/hess-18-5041-2014

Persson, L.M., Breitholtz, M., Cousins, I.T. et al. (2013). Confronting Unknown Planetary Boundary Threats from Chemical Pollution. *Environ. Sci. Technol.*, 47, 12619–12622. doi: 10.1021/es402501c

Petit, J.R., Jouzel, J., Raynaud, D. et al. (1999). Climate and Atmospheric History of the Past 420,000 Years from the Vostok Ice Core, Antarctica. *Nature*, 399, 429–436.

Piketty, T. (2014). *Capital in the Twenty-First Century*, (pp. 685). Cambridge MA USA and London UK: The Belknap Press of Harvard University Press.

Ramanathan, V., Chung, C, Kim, D. et al. (2005). Atmospheric Brown Clouds: Impacts on South Asian Climate and Hydrological Cycle. *Proc. Natl. Acad. Sci. (USA)*, 102, 5326–5333. doi: 10.1073/pnas.0500656102

Raupach, M.R. & Canadell, J.G. (2010). Carbon and the Anthropocene. *Current Opinion in Environmental Sustainability*, 2, 210–218.

Rockström, J., Steffen, W., Noone, K. et al. (2009). Planetary Boundaries: Exploring the Safe Operating Space for Humanity. *Ecology and Society*, 14(2), 32. Retrieved form http://www.ecologyandsociety.org/vol14/iss2/art32/

Scheffer, M., Bascompte, J., Brock, W.A. et al. (2009). Early-Warning Signals for Critical Transitions. *Nature*, 461, 53–59.

Scheffer, M., Carpenter, S.R., Lenton, T.M. et al. (2012). Anticipating Critical Transitions. *Science*, 338, 344–348. doi: 10.1126/science.1225244

Scholes, R.J. & Biggs, R. (2005). A Biodiversity Intactness Index. *Nature*, 434, 45–49.

Snyder, P.K., Delire, C. & Foley, J.A. (2004). Evaluating the Influence of Different Vegetation Biomes on the Global Climate. *Clim. Dynam,* 23, 279–302. doi: 10.1007/s00382-004-0430-0

Steffen, W., Sanderson, A., Tyson, P.D. et al. (2004). *Global Change and the Earth System: A Planet under Pressure.* The IGBP Book Series, (pp.336). Berlin, Heidelberg, New York: Springer-Verlag.

Steffen, W., Crutzen, P.J. & McNeill, J.R. (2007). The Anthropocene: Are Humans Now Overwhelming the Great Forces of Nature? *Ambio,* 36, 614–621.

Steffen, W., Persson Å., Deutsch, L. et al. (2011). The Anthropocene: From Global Change to Planetary Stewardship. *Ambio,* 40, 739–761.

Steffen, W., Richardson, K., Rockström, J. et al (2015a). Planetary Boundaries: Guiding Human Development on a Changing Planet. *Science,* 347. doi: 10.1126/science.1259855

Steffen, W., Broadgate, W., Deutsch, L., et al. (2015b). The Trajectory of the Anthropocene: The Great Acceleration. *The Anthropocene Review.* doi: 10.1177/2053019614564785

Von Grafenstein, U., Erlenkeuser, H., Müller et al. (1998). The Cold Event 8200 Years Ago Documented in Oxygen Isotope Records of Precipitation in Europe and Greenland. *Climate Dynamics,* 14, 73–81.

West, P.C., Narisma, G.T., Barford, C.C. et al. (2010). An Alternative Approach for Quantifying Climate Regulation by Ecosystems. *Frontiers Ecol. Environ.,* 9, 126. doi: 10.1890/090015

Wilkinson, R.G. and Pickett, K.E. (2009). Income Inequality and Social Dysfunction. *Annu. Rev. Sociol,* 35, 493–511.

CHAPTER THREE

SPACESHIP EARTH CONDO

CLÓVIS JACINTO DE MATOS[1]

1. Introduction

The oceans, the atmosphere and solar energy can be seen as universal goods common to all living species on Earth. Preserving these common global resources can only be achieved collectively. This will require mutual respect and solidarity among the independent nations that share our common planet. When seen from space, our planet clearly appears as our communal home, it is humankind's home, and thus it should be managed and maintained on the basis of an Earth Condominium. Going a step further, one could even think of our planet as a spaceship taking humankind on a journey around the sun, through our galaxy (as our sun circles the galactic centre) and ultimately through intergalactic space (as our galaxy moves with respect to other galaxies in the universe). Astronauts designate this cognitive experience as the overview effect. The photo of the Earth in Figure 1 on the following page, captured from the NASA *Cassini* spacecraft, perfectly illustrates this argument.

---

[1] Global Navigation Satellite Systems Evolution Programme and Strategy Division at the European Space Agency (ESA) Headquarters. The information and views set out in this chapter are those of the author and do not necessarily reflect the official opinion of ESA. Contact information: Clovis.de.Matos@esa.int

Figure 1: Photo of the Earth (pinpointed by a white arrow) taken from the Cassini spacecraft currently orbiting Saturn. On the top left corner one can see Saturn's bulk eclipsing the Sun, and on the top right corner one sees the fine details of Saturn's rings.

Our planet orbits around the Sun at a distance of 149 million kilometres (1 Astronomical Unit). This orbit belongs to the so-called habitable zone,[2] which affords the adequate energy conditions to permit the existence of water in a liquid state. Therefore, the possibility for our planet to host life sustainably depends strongly on this fortunate orbital situation (any closer to the Sun and liquid water would be entirely vaporized; any farther and the Earth would be a ball of ice). In this respect, life on Earth is already a consequence of the natural space environment of our planet. Presently it is not known if life emerged on our planet through its own organic chemical activity, in-utero, or if it was brought to Earth by an extraterrestrial astronomical object rich in organic compounds (like comets, for example); this is the so-called ex-utero theory, also designated as the panspermia hypothesis. The ESA Rosetta mission, which culminated with the landing of *Philae* on the comet Churyumov Gerasimenko, is a perfect example of the type of scientific research that needs to be carried out to discover new scientific facts about the question of the origin of life on our planet.

---

[2] The "habitable zone" is the orbital region around a star in which an Earth-like planet can possess liquid water on its surface and possibly support life.

Independently of this initial unknown, one can say that since life appeared on Earth, it has always interacted with its natural physico-chemical environment. The different forms of life in our biosphere have so far contributed to the overall equilibrium of the Earth's ecosystem (Holocene geological period) but humankind is now modifying its environment at a faster pace and can no longer adapt to it (Anthropocene geological epoch). This will ultimately lead to the collapse of the global economy, followed by the advent of a new structuration of human societies. Here we propose that as the overview effect experienced by astronauts is progressively absorbed by humans on Earth, humankind will evolve towards the formation of a single unified planetary organism constituted by independent but solidary regions. Although this process will come up against cultural, political, religious, and philosophical obstacles, humankind will progressively become aware of the necessity to collectively control its natural environment. A more resilient and efficient economy will then progressively tend towards a stationary state in the long-term unless a breakthrough in the field of controlled nuclear fusion[3] allows for the expansion of humankind in the solar system, thus allowing the maintenance of the current economic growth paradigm.

The present chapter starts by investigating how the laws of thermodynamics actually account for and anticipate the evolution of the current environmental crisis. In this context the global character of the problems to be solved appears clearly, thus making crucial the role of space assets[4] in managing the Earth as they monitor the Earth environment at global and regional scales simultaneously. Following this review, some reflections about the advent of a new kind of global consciousness for humankind and its possible role in the context of an Earth Condominium are discussed. Conclusions about the future are proposed, showing that believing in humanity itself requires a different mindset.

---

[3] Nuclear fusion should not be confused with nuclear fission, one of the major differences being that some nuclear fusion reactions do not release radioactive elements in the natural environment. In this sense, controlled nuclear fusion is a clean form of nuclear energy; unfortunately, it is much more difficult to control than fission, which is presently used in nuclear power plants.

[4] "Space assets" exist in, for example, space missions, like the Hubble Space Telescope, but also large infrastructures like GPS satellite constellations, launch systems like Ariane and systems of systems like the Copernicus Programme.

2. The Earth System and its Thermodynamics

The Earth can be assimilated to a thermodynamic engine powered by a source of heat located in space: the Sun, with a surface temperature of 5773° C. Part of the solar energy sent to the Earth under the form of light (with maximum power emitted in the green wavelength) is used to produce mechanical work, powering the oceans and the atmosphere and sustaining life on our planet. Another part is converted into entropy, which must be restituted to a cold source under the form of infrared radiation (heat). This cold source is also provided by space; it is the cosmological background, which is at a temperature of -270° C.

The Earth is thus an open system, exchanging matter and energy with its space environment. The membrane regulating these exchanges between the Earth System and space is a thin atmospheric layer, with a thickness equal to 1/1000 of the Earth's radius, 90% of its mass being concentrated below an altitude of 16 km. We all live in it, under a pressure of one bar of oxygen and nitrogen. More than any other part of the Earth System, the atmosphere is shared by all inhabitants, independent of any territory division; it forms the central air conditioning system of the Earth. The air is definitely a common good. The oxygen we breathe represents 21 per cent of its total volume. It also contains a few other constituents, among which there is carbon dioxide, in a proportion of just a few hundred parts per million, which helps to maintain the sea and the Earth surface at an average of 15°C through what is commonly referred to as the greenhouse effect.

The atmosphere is structured in different layers: the troposphere, the stratosphere, the ionosphere, and the magnetosphere. These different components are in a permanent state of evolution and interaction with the other components of the Earth System, which are: the Earth's interior (where the Earth's magnetic field is generated), the hydrosphere (which includes the oceans and inland water areas), the cryosphere (polar caps, lakes, glaciers, and snow) and the biosphere. Approximately 51 per cent of the energy received from the Sun is absorbed by the land, the oceans and the atmosphere, and 49 per cent is re-emitted into space through direct reflection and re-emission by these three components (Joergensen). The timescales that characterise the evolution of these components scale down from millions of years to tens of thousands, as well as shorter seasonal or diurnal variations.

The oceans are the central heating system of the Earth, through the thermohaline circulation mechanism. This convective mechanism depends on water salinity and temperature gradients. The ESA's Soil Moisture and

Ocean Salinity (SMOS) mission is currently measuring the global ocean salinity. Carbon is recycled through the oceans, the atmosphere and the biosphere while its concentration in the various parts of the Earth's system varies with time. Only about half of the anthropogenic emissions sent into the atmosphere remain there. The other half is probably absorbed into the oceans and into the land, with about 14 per cent of worldwide carbon stored in permafrost soils and sediments. Tundra wetlands are considered to be major contributors to the global carbon balance and are anticipated to be highly sensitive to climate change: if they were to suddenly outgas, the resulting global warming effects would be much more dramatic than at present. This is why it is crucial to follow the complete carbon cycle and observe the exchanges between land, ocean and the atmosphere. Because organic components of life are strong absorbers of lethal UV radiation, the atmospheric ozone layer, which stalwartly absorbs this type of radiation, plays a unique role in the preservation of life on our planet. Permanent monitoring of ozone concentration is therefore also essential. Although recent measurements indicate that the Earth's ozone layer is slowly recovering, measurements performed nearly continuously since 1960 have clearly indicated a degradation of the ozone layer being caused by both human activities as well as volcanism. This clearly shows that over two generations, humanity has become a real geological force on our planet (some informally refer to this aspect as the beginning of the Anthropocene geological epoch).

In summary, the atmosphere not only provides the adequate chemical conditions for life but it also protects life from the harmful electromagnetic radiations of the solar light. In this respect, the magnetospheric layer formed by the interaction of the solar wind with the Earth's natural magnetic field plays a vital role in scattering high-energy electrically-charged particles capable of harming living cells if they could reach the Earth's surface.

The biosphere ranges from about 10 km above the ground into the atmosphere down to the deepest ocean floor, including most of the lower atmosphere, the hydrosphere and the upper lithosphere. The mass of the biosphere cannot be estimated very accurately thus scientists modelling the dynamics of environmental systems, agricultural processes, health-related issues (pandemics), and biodiversity base their predictive models on incomplete data. Vegetation is the key component of the biosphere. Phytoplankton, in particular, accounts for the majority of the biomass in the oceans and has a greater effect on our planet's climate through the recycling of carbon than any other living species. Vegetation represents our ultimate source of subsistence – it constitutes the world's pantry. It is the source of the oxygen we breathe and the amino acids from which all animals build up their proteins. Monitoring the evolution of biomass and, more specifically, the global vegetation and phytoplankton reserves also appears to be essential to ensure our survival from now on.

As is the case for any open thermodynamic system, the total rate of entropy production on Earth is permanently maximized such as to ensure that the maximum total flux of energy crosses the system at all stages of its evolution (Roddier 2012; Kleidon 2012). Even natural evolution seems driven by this principle, as illustrated by the plot in Figure 2 where the power dissipated by different natural structures with respect to the cosmological time arrow is displayed.

This has profound consequences for the relationship between human socioeconomic processes and their influence on the natural environment.

Like any dissipative structure, we are mainly adapted to our sources of energy. The dependence of human societies on fossil energy sources for about two centuries is the weakness of present societies. The world population energy consumption currently amounts to a total of 10.5 tons of oil equivalent (TOE[5]) per year, meaning an average power dissipation of 2.2 KW per person. Of this dissipated power, 85% results from non-renewable fossil energies (oil, coal). The other 15% is shared between nuclear and hydraulic energy (dams). Although we have perfectly adapted to this energy environment, we have become less and less adaptable to a different energy context. Oil-based transportation systems (aviation, maritime, road) are key to sustaining the current growth of global economy. This forces humankind to modify its natural environment faster than it can adapt to it. While under time pressure, long-term sustainable solutions are not adopted and instead we do our best to preserve the current infrastructures by opting for short-term solutions, which leads us into a vicious circle and contributes to the present global economic and environmental crisis.

---

[5] 1 TOE = 42 gigajoules

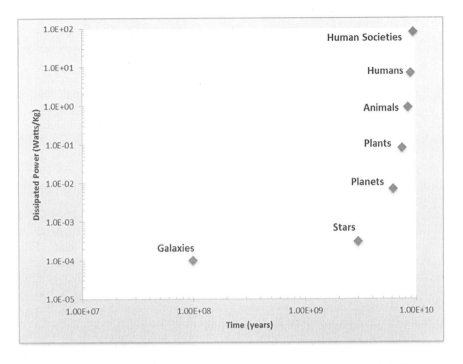

Figure 2: Logarithmic plot of the power dissipated per unit of mass of different natural structures in function of the approximate time at which they have been formed in the universe with respect to the Big Bang.

Economists still have to fully understand that the economy follows the laws of thermodynamics (Roegen 1979). Competition for natural resources will make it difficult to maintain the current complex structures of our society and will be a constant source of conflict. The present situation will tend to increase the gap between rich and poor countries and destroy democratic nations in favour of totalitarian governments. Two economic models are competing: one is driven by the globalisation of the economy, with the creation of a single world currency as the ultimate outcome; the other is formed by independent regional economies with their respective local currencies and promotion of renewable energy solutions (green economy) and /or optimization of the exploitation of oceanic natural resources (blue economy). According to thermodynamic laws, between these two economic models (global versus local) the one that is the most efficient in dissipating (under the form of entropy) the flux of energy flowing through the system will be favoured by nature and will survive.

The main concerns of our societies are thus energy supply and the evacuation of the entropy it generates through its industrial processes (waste management, water and air quality, etc.). Entropy can only be evacuated if all operations in a thermodynamic cycle are reversible. This physical law also applies to humankind. During the 19th and 20th centuries, humankind produced mechanical work and consequently increased the entropy of the natural environment. Now we have understood that to do this in a sustainable manner (over long periods of time), we must come back to the initial state through a reversible operation. This is what we call recycling. It is worth noting that recycling is also the processing model on which the biosphere is based to produce free energy.

Economists, together with civil society actors and the scientific community at large, must understand that an isolated system tends to evolve towards thermodynamic equilibrium. Thus, if humankind wants to survive, there is no other solution than using a source of energy external to the Earth, i.e., the Sun. The use of nuclear energy on Earth, even controlled fusion-based, is also excluded. As using nuclear energy would rely on a much higher power density with respect to fossil energies, this option would increase the Earth's entropy in an irreversible manner at a much faster rate than at present, quickly leading humanity to its end. It is worth stressing here that this complete nuclear collapse can be avoided if controlled fusion energy, when achieved, is not only used on Earth but is also applied for space propulsion, enabling space transportation and settlements to spread across the solar system! If this could be achieved from a technological point of view, the volume of the biosphere would be dramatically increased from the size of our thin atmospheric shell layer to the cumulated size of all solar system objects that could be colonized by humankind. By enlarging the Earth ecosystem to the entire solar system, one would therefore lower the density of produced entropy on Earth while maximizing the total dissipation of entropy at the scale of the solar system (as required by the laws of thermodynamics). Therefore, as anticipated above, control of nuclear fusion alone is useless if it cannot also be applied to space travel in order to increase the physical size of the system by reshaping its boundaries, since its single use to power Earth-based societies would very quickly destroy the Earth's natural environment together with humankind. In summary, either we rely only on solar energy and switch to a stationary economy or we succeed in mastering nuclear fusion and are forced to expand in the solar system to avoid the total collapse of our planet.

3. Space Pivotal Role to Manage Earth's Future

In this section, we invite the reader on a pedestrian tour of the different space missions and techniques that permit the monitoring of the Earth's environment at different scales (global versus regional).

Space-based data are often combined with high-resolution in-situ data in order to identify the dynamics leading from local phenomena to the global pattern behaviour of the Earth System's main components. Altogether they enable the monitoring of the Earth's surface, be it solid or liquid, its shape and motions, and its temperature and vegetation cover. They must also make it possible to measure the composition of gases in the atmosphere, the concentration and circulation of aerosols, and their temperatures. In-situ measurements are required for the cross-checking and calibration of the data as well as reaching parts of the system that cannot be observed from orbit, such as the ocean's subsurface layers. That implies that space systems must be operated by and integrated into a global space system.

Gravimetry satellites, altimetry satellites and global navigation satellite systems are crucial for understanding the internal structure of the Earth, the dynamics of the Earth's systems and the climate. These satellites perform their measurements through the precise knowledge of their positions and their motions relative to the geoid. The geoid is a reference surface whose precise shape allows the determination of the irregularities and time variations in the distribution of mass that induce variations in the gravity field.

Gravimetry satellites use the alteration of their orbits to measure the distribution of mass concentration as they pass over. Gravimetry missions can thus measure variations in the water content as they cycle between the atmosphere, oceans, continents, glaciers, and polar ice caps. The deviation of the local sea level from the geoid can therefore be closely linked to ocean circulation, the changes of which are a consequence of changes in atmospheric forcing, primarily caused by surface wind stress and heat and freshwater flux. Measuring these variations with a great degree of precision is crucial for understanding the internal structure of the Earth, the dynamics of the Earth System and the climate. The ESA GOCE mission has taken advantage of its low-altitude orbit at 250 km, which is more sensitive to the gravity signal, to establish global and regional models of the Earth's gravity field, with 1–2 mGal precision and a geoid with 1 cm accuracy over about 100 km of spatial resolution.

Altimetry satellites directly measure the altitude of their orbits relative to the Earth's surface features (active technic). This is achieved by measuring the time it takes for radar or laser pulses (in the case of Lidars) to travel from the satellite and back. This technique is important for the monitoring of the ocean surfaces and the polar ice caps. The ESA cryostat mission used this powerful technique to monitor the thickness of the Earth's continental ice sheets.

GPS stations provide essential support to all geodesy and altimetry satellites. GPS radio waves are particularly well suited for measuring the concentration of water in the atmosphere and for determining the vertical column density, the profiles of pressure and temperature, and the structure of the troposphere through limb sounding. At altitudes of above 100 km, the ionosphere can also be studied by using the GPS signals as the speed of radio waves is affected by the total electronic content of the ionosphere differently, depending on their respective wavelengths.

Synthetic Aperture Radar (SAR) imagery is capable of indicating changes with time in soil and ocean situations and can easily differentiate between waterlogged and dry land, and is a powerful means for the study of polar and ice-covered areas in general. ESA's Cryosat mission is also equipped with this type of imagery capability. SAR allows the tracking of small changes in the Earth's moving surface that would otherwise be undetectable.

Optical imaging provides high-resolution pictures and observations in many different colours, which helps characterise the nature of soil surfaces and agricultural exploitations. Imaging instruments provide information on the oceans, the land, the cryosphere, the clouds, and the atmosphere. In combination, this allows the monitoring of global climatologic and environmental dynamics as well as biological and physical variables of phytoplankton and land cover. In conjunction with ground-based information, optical imaging is also used in the prevention and forecasting of environmental crises. The use of meteorological satellite images to follow and forecast the spread of diseases transported by animals and mosquitos as they sense climatic changes is very promising. Space remote-sensing optical imaging also allows for the monitoring of volcanoes and earthquakes as well as anthropogenic hazards.

Remote-sensing spectroscopy of planetary atmosphere and surfaces represents one of the most powerful tools for analysing the chemical state of a planet and its evolution. For the Earth, it is one of the main methods used for the monitoring of global warming and atmospheric pollution resulting from biomass burning (forest fires) and industrial activities.

The daily weather and climate depend on the balance between the amount of sunlight received by the Earth's surface and the atmosphere, and the amount of energy emitted by the Earth back into space. This budget of incoming and outgoing energy is called the radiation budget. Radiometers are satellite payloads that can measure the various energetic components of this budget, which is a function of different electromagnetic wavelengths.

All these space assets and techniques complete with each other in terms of information provided, and with ground-based measurements are keys to modelling and understanding the physico-chemical and biological evolution of the Earth. But unfortunately the critical infrastructure needed to consolidate these diverse sources of information in a coherent manner and make space-based data available for the proper management of the planet and the security of its inhabitants is not yet completed. For example, the lack of global data is the major constraint on the development of water resources and improvement of water management at regional scales today. In this case as well, the combination of space-based data and in-situ data is mandatory. When completed, the ESA-EC Sentinel infrastructure (Copernicus Programme) will be a major step in the development of a coherent concatenation of the information delivered by a diversity of space and ground systems. A substantial number of scientific and international organizations already develop or coordinate some of the necessary space and ground-based tools but which organization is globally responsible for ensuring that these tools are available when required and maintained to ensure their indispensable continuity to properly assess the evolution of the Earth on the medium and the long-term scales is not yet clearly defined. There are signs that even the incomplete current capability is in jeopardy.

4. The Awakening of Humankind

As already mentioned, the principle of maximum energy dissipation (maximum entropy production rate) also regulates the process of natural selection. Natural selection has always favoured the systems that maximize the dissipation of energy (see Figure 2); it has thus privileged the development of societies that dissipate more energy. When high-energy fluxes are available, competition becomes more efficient than cooperation in the dissipation of the energy, and short-term comfort is more important than the quality of life of future generations (in the long term).

Once fossil energy resources are exhausted, and if the control of nuclear fusion is impossible, then we will be left with solar energy to maintain a certain standard of living. In these circumstances, the law of evolution indicates that cooperation is more efficient than competition to dissipate the available energy. In contrast, in the scenario where humanity achieves control of nuclear fusion, it is exactly the opposite situation, meaning that competition between individuals and governments takes over from collaborative initiatives. The application of controlled fusion power to the space conquest would thus translate into a competitive harvesting of the solar system, which is imperative, as we discussed previously, to prevent the Earth from being buried by an entropic avalanche.

If we continue moving towards a single unified society, competition between different nations will be tempered and a global planetary awareness will progressively emerge (Roddier 2012). This new type of consciousness (materializing as a kind of planetary exo-brain connected to humanity) will understand that its role and duty are to maintain and preserve an adequate natural environment to sustain life and human culture over long periods of time. This will also be required for its own survival. Original solutions found at regional scales will start benefiting the entire world, leading to a reorganization of all of humankind and towards the emergence of a common planetary culture based on universal solidarity.

What are the entities and intellectual tools that could lead to the emergence of humankind's consciousness (de Chardin 1957)? One cannot give a complete answer to this question but some examples can be introduced at the current stage: in a global context of solidarity, the main task of the World Bank should not be to maintain economic growth but to preserve the natural environment on a global scale. This could only be achieved by preserving the natural environment at local regional levels, and therefore favouring the poorest countries in terms of allocation of investments. This investment strategy would progressively transform into a win-win relationship between the local and the global scale for the different challenges faced by humankind. To open the way to global culture, maybe the elaboration of a "Universal Declaration of People's Rights" by an "Earth Peoples' Assembly", which could take the form of an "Earth Condominium" (Nottale 1998), would be an important initial step.

5. Free Energy: A Key Parameter of Climate Modelling

We are almost in a position to drive our natural environment but we do not have an organizational architecture that meets the functional characteristics of the Spaceship Earth system, which mainly exists in a global state of disequilibrium caused by the dynamics of free energy generation, transfer and dissipation (Kleidon 2012). Free energy is a thermodynamic variable that consists of the total amount of useful work generated, transferred and dissipated in a thermodynamic system. In this sense, free energy is available and useful to produce work; it thus powers the Earth's oceans, atmosphere and biomass. It is also the type of energy human societies desperately need to harness. Presently, the main source of free energy for the Earth System is the sun. Tides and internal heat generation are also sources but much more modest than the sun (oil stores free energy that initially came from the sun).

The rate of humankind's consumption of free energy in industrial activities is of the order of 50 terawatts [TW], which corresponds to one-quarter of the total production rate of free energy by photosynthetic life, i.e., 200 TW[6] (Kleidon). This clearly shows that our activities are an integral part of the Earth System from an energy point of view, thus actively contributing to the consumption and production of free energy.

The free energy budget not only includes consumption rates but also the generation rates of free energy; it thus provides a baseline budget for the availability of different forms of renewable energy. Quantifying the role of the biota in the generation of free energy by the Earth System would allow for a better quantification of how much biotic activity contributes to the planetary disequilibrium of the Earth.

One should therefore develop climate models able to estimate the ability of the Earth System to generate free energy together with the modelisation of free energy transfer through the entire biosphere. This is not properly included in present climate modelling, the main output of which is determining strategies for future free energy appropriation by humans with either a minimum impact on free energy generation by Earth System processes or, at best, an enhancement of the ability of the planet (i.e., Spaceship Earth and its crew) to generate free energy.

The Spaceship Earth Condo should either preserve the Holocene-like state of the Earth System in the case of a deficit in the overall balance of free energy or it should sustainably facilitate the advent of a new geological state, which would be an improvement with respect to the Holocene because it would result from an excess of free energy produced by human technologies (providing they become available without disrupting effects). In other words, if the total balance of free energy indicates

- a deficit, then we are living in a closed world;
- an excess, then we are living in an open world.

---

[6] For comparison, a fission nuclear reactor produces, on average, a power of about 1.5 GW.

In both cases, humankind needs a condo to keep a proper accounting of the free energy on the Earth scale!

6. Conclusion: We Are All Astronauts of Spaceship Earth!

In the past, the finiteness of the area of the Earth was not a problem for the Europeans. When there was no longer space at home, huge areas could be colonized elsewhere: North and South America, Australia, Africa. That time is over, unless space conquest provides humankind with new geographical territories in the solar system. This could only become possible if humankind achieves the promethean dream of mastering nuclear fusion energy and succeeds in applying it to space transportation. If this appears to be technologically impossible, then the only alternative is to adjust to a more stationary society powered exclusively by solar energy. In both cases we are all astronauts of Spaceship Earth (Buckminster Fuller 1969); and the spaceship crew (humankind) at the planetary level needs to understand that it will need for its survival an Earth Condominium that efficiently regulates the interactions of its various regional scale components and solutions for the benefit of the entire crew. As explained previously, this can only be achieved by complying with the laws of thermodynamics and hence by maximizing the total rate of entropy production on Earth in order to maximize the total flux of energy crossing the system at all stages of its development. Ultimately, this means two different possible roles for the Earth Condominium in the future:

- in the case of a stationary society, to optimize the use of solar energy on Earth (green and blue societies)
- in the case of a breakthrough in the control of nuclear fusion, to ensure that this technology will also be applied to the space conquest for the expansion of humankind in the solar system, otherwise the use of this technology will have to be forbidden on Earth

In this context, it is tempting to think about the Earth Condominium as the "Condominium of Spaceship Earth". Indeed, like any spaceship, Spaceship Earth also needs a central computer to make sure that the vital functions of its life-support system are managed properly in order to keep the crew alive. This would be the role of the Spaceship Earth Condominium. The ESA astronaut Wubbo Ockels left a message to humanity that points to this concept (Ockels 2009, 2014). With the same objective in mind, he initiated the Happy Energy Movement,[7] the ten commandments that could inspire the SOS Treaty:

1. Humanity is inseparable
2. Humanity's goal is to survive
3. Humanity needs the Earth and Nature
4. Our goal is to support Humanity and thus the Earth and Nature
5. We need to respect anyone who exercises that goal
6. Everybody is connected with anybody via Humanity
7. Everyone is connected with Nature and the Earth
8. We are all Astronauts of Space Ship Earth
9. Those who disrespect others, will disrespect Humanity
10. Humanity, Nature and the Earth are inseparable

Let us conclude with some considerations on the potential role of scientific research and space exploration to help humankind find its way towards a sustainable future. To start with, one might wonder if the discoveries made today have the same impact on our image of the world as those made earlier. Some of us might have doubts. After 50 years of space exploration, life appears to be firmly restricted to Earth. At the same time, we realize that the Earth is becoming too small for us. We have reached the limits of our growth and are going beyond. Here I would like to adopt a more optimistic view. Although we are stuck on Earth and the Earth is becoming too small to sustain us, wouldn't it be nice to suddenly discover an escape route? To suddenly realize that there is a whole new world we could explore and which would allow us to expand again? I cannot be sure, of course, but somehow such a course of events seems natural to me. "Human" life is too smart to allow itself to be compromised so easily. The problem of the physical nature of time and consciousness raised by bio-sciences, in physics through quantum mechanics (with the measurement problem) and relativity (with the quadri-dimensional nature of the physical world at a fundamental level and the problem of free will) will most probably revolutionize not only the understanding of the universe but also the understanding of the human condition itself. Thus our view of the place of humanity in the scheme of nature and the very concept of what should be the "Condominium of Spaceship Earth" will continue to be an endless frontier.

---

[7] More information available at http://www.happyenergy.nl.

7. Acknowledgement

I dedicate this work to the memory of Prof. Dr. Wubbo Ockels, with gratitude for the inspiration and the happy energy he insufflated in my professional life. I would also like to acknowledge Nathalie Meusy and Paulo Magalhães for inviting me to contribute to the *SOS Treaty* and for their continuous support and encouragement. My profound gratitude goes also to Alice Bernard Gairard for significantly improving the discursive clarity of the original manuscript.

"We all are astronauts of spaceship Earth."
Prof Dr Wubbo Ockels 1946 – 2014

References

Bonnet, R.M., Woltjer, L. (2008). *Surviving 1000 Centuries – Can We Do It?* Berlin: Springer.

Buckminster Fuller, R. (1969). *Operating Manual for Spaceship Earth.* Carbondale, IL: Southern Illinois University Press.

de Chardin, P. T. (1957). *La Vision du Passé* (pp.318–326). Paris: Edition Seuil.

Joergensen, S. E., Svirezhev, Y. M. (2004). *Towards a Thermodynamic Theory for Ecological Systems.* Amsterdam: Elsevier.

Kleidon, A. (2012). *How Does the Earth System Generate and Maintain Thermodynamic Disequilibrium and What Does It Imply for the Future of the Planet?* Phil. Trans. Roy. Soc. A, 370, pp. 1012–1040. doi:10.1098/rsta.2011.0316

Nottale, L. (1998). *Pour une Democratie des Peuples.* Retrieved from http://luth2.obspm.fr/~luthier/nottale/frdalai.htm

Ockels, W. (2009). *We All Are Astronauts of Spaceship Earth – A Farewell to Wubbo Ockels* [TEDxAmsterdam Talk]. Retrieved from http://www.tedxamsterdam.com/2014/05/astronauts-spaceship-earth-farewell-wubbo-ockels/

—. (2014), *Happy Energy. The Movement for a Sustainable Earth and Us; Humanity.* Retrieved from http://delta.tudelft.nl/uploads/delta.tudelft.nl/delta_articles/28268/pdf_f ile/happy_energy_religion_5281.pdf

Roddier, F. (2012). *Thermodynamique de l'Evolution - Un Essai de Thermo-Bio-Sociologie.* Aix-en-Provence: Parole Editions.

Roegen, N. G. (1979). *La Decroissance.* 2.ª Ed. 1995. Paris: Éditions Sang de la terre. Retrieved from http://classiques.uqac.ca/contemporains/georgescu_roegen_nicolas/dec roissance/la_decroissance.pdf

CHAPTER FOUR

SHIFTING THE LEGAL PARADIGM: EARTH-CENTRED LAW AND GOVERNANCE

KLAUS BOSSELMANN[1]

1. Introduction

For several years now, representatives of virtually all states have been hearing, on an annual basis, what kind of law and governance may be required to enable humankind to live within planetary boundaries. Since 2011, the UN General Assembly's "Interactive Dialogue on Harmony with Nature" (http://www.harmonywithnatureun.org/) has been exploring ways of how to shift from a state-centred to an Earth-centred paradigm.

Here are some excerpts from the Secretary-General's 2012 report:

45. Numerous scientists, economists, and legal experts have decried the escalating destruction of the Earth's natural systems (…) They are insisting that, rather than people and planet serving the infinite growth of the economy, the economy must recognize its place as servant to the larger well-being of humans and the Earth itself.

46. In this new system, the rule of law, science, and economics will be grounded in the Earth. (…)

47. A key challenge in developing a global governance system built on the rule of ecological law is reinvigorating a transformed sense of democracy, in which individuals and communities embrace their ecological citizenship in the world and act on their responsibility to respect the complex workings of the Earth's life systems.

---

[1] University of Auckland.

The UN Secretary-General's 2014 report lists a number of recent resolutions and initiatives for adopting the rights of nature and respect for Mother Earth and then concludes that concepts such as Earth System governance and Earth-based law (UN Report of Secretary-General, 2014, para.12) should be further debated in the context of the post-2015 development agenda (UN Report of Secretary-General, 2014, "Recommendations", para. 92).[21]

The terminology used in these UN reports hints of transformed law and governance: law, science and economics grounded in the Earth, the rule of ecological law, a transformed sense of democracy, ecological citizenship, rights of nature, Earth System governance, and Earth-based law. All these terms are useful when describing the concept of law based on responsibility for Earth's ecological systems.

How would such a law differ from international environmental law, and can it be built around or underneath existing treaties and national laws? This chapter seeks to answer this question by showing the continuity and, at the same time, novelty of what could be called Earth Systems law (Bosselmann 1995; Taylor 1998).[32]

New concepts such as Earth Systems law, Earth jurisprudence (Burdon 2011, 2014), Earth justice (Cullinan 2003), Earth governance (Bosselmann 2015) and Earth democracy (Bosselmann 2011a) fundamentally consider the Earth as a central reference point. This puts them potentially at odds with state-centred international environmental law and international environmental governance.

The Earth is more than the sum of its parts; that is, a unifying entity in her own right and very different from the world (of nations). The Earth is one and borderless; the world is divided and diverse. In legal terms, the world has international law resembling division and diversity while the Earth has – nothing. There is as yet nothing in the law responding to the Earth's wholeness and complexity. The standard explanation for this void

---

[2] For further UN documents as well as the national laws of Ecuador, Bolivia, India, Mexico and New Zealand, state and local laws in the United States and policy documents of UNEP and IUCN, see the "Harmony with Nature" website.

[3] There is as yet no coherent terminology around Earth-centred law. Terms similar to Earth System law include Earth-based law, Earth jurisprudence, rights of nature, Mother Earth rights and others. They all share the common belief that law ought to be reflective of ecological interconnectedness and human dependence on ecological systems. For an ecological approach to law generally, see Bosselmann, K. (1995); Taylor, P. (1998) and Bosselmann, K. & Taylor, P. (Eds.) (forthcoming 2016).

is that the Earth is not a legal category. The world is made up of people and countries represented through states hence we have international law, but not global law or Earth law in a true sense.

Seen through the lenses of states, the wholeness of the Earth remains unnoticed, and planetary systems (climate, biodiversity, oceans, etc.) appear discrete entities at the periphery of what states are really concerned with; that is, economic needs. By contrast, ecological realities make the Earth appear whole and undivided. There is a mismatch between international law and ecological realities. As long as we assume an exclusivity of states to define international and national laws, Earth Systems are likely to be captured in a very limited way, usually in terms of their usefulness for human development, which is typically expressed in the concept of sustainable development.

The alternative is not a law without states but a law informed by ecological realities. Earth Systems are not there to serve humans needs; they are simply there. For human needs to be met, laws have to recognize Earth Systems as ecological realities that cannot be overlooked by any living being, including humans. It is this recognition of reality that is currently missing in our international and national laws so our predicament is straightforward: unless law recognizes and internalizes ecological realities, it is doomed to fail. Humans are utterly dependent on the integrity of Earth's ecological systems so they should behave and govern themselves accordingly. No amount of rhetoric (green economy, sustainable development, sustainable development goals) can gloss over this simple truth. The rhetoric of the "Harmony with Nature" reports mentioned above is significantly different yet futile unless put into action. The challenge ahead is to internalize ecological realities into human law and governance (Bosselmann 1995, 120–128; Illge & Schwarze 2006).[4]

The project of internalizing ecological realities is of course not new. It is as old as the history of environmental law. The very purpose and subject of environmental law, that is, protection of the natural environment, should have led to a fundamental 'greening' of law and governance. Instead, the opposite happened. Since their early beginnings in the 1960s, environmental laws have aimed for less, trying to balance environmental, social and economic interests (Tarlock 1994). As if there was a middle ground between life and death, environmental laws and policies have assumed a position of looking after ecological systems while leaving the

---

[4] Conceptually, this is no different from economics internalizing ecological realities; both ecological law and ecological economics are based on strong sustainability.

growth paradigm untouched. However, there cannot be a compromise between sustaining life and life-threatening cancerous growth. Under the growth paradigm, environmental protection was bound to remain at the political periphery, rendering environmental laws to temper around the edges (Bosselmann 1995, 2010; Tarlock 1994; Gaines 2014).[5]

Perhaps surprisingly, such obvious design flaws have never occupied the discipline of environmental law in any major way. Looking over mainstream scholarship of 40 or so years, one can see there has been a relative dearth of critical literature. Most environmental lawyers tend to see themselves foremost as lawyers rather than as ecologists. However, viewing ecological realities from the traditional legal perspective is likely to result in anthropocentrism and reductionism. Viewing political and legal realities from an ecological perspective, on the other hand, is likely to result in ecocentrism and holism (Bosselmann 1995, 101–119). From its beginnings, environmental law scholarship has been divided along these conflicting paradigms.

Yet we have good reason to believe that the paradigm clash will eventually be resolved in favour of ecocentrism as we have one great ally on our side – Mother Earth. There is now overwhelming evidence that Earth Systems are no longer functioning as they must to sustain human life. We are seeing the signs of planetary decline all around us: the oceans, the atmosphere, the biosphere are systems in crisis, and so are human systems: countries and communities are becoming increasingly impoverished socially, economically and environmentally. With the exception of 1 per cent (or less) of humanity, the entire world population of human and non-human beings is suffering. It is as if humanity has given up on itself. Like Dennis Meadows, co-author of the *Limits of Growth* (Meadows & Meadows, Randers & III 1972; Turner 2014),[6] once said: "I have tried long enough to be a global evangelist and have learned that in doing so that I cannot change the world. Apart from that, humankind behaves like someone committing suicide, and there is no point in arguing with a suicidal person once they have already jumped out of the window" (Bosselmann 1995, 63; Meadows 2012).

While we cannot be certain about suicidal behaviour or a life-saving turnaround, we can describe a rescue strategy. At the very least, such knowledge will be useful for attempts to rebuild civilization following

---

[5] For fundamental critiques of environmental law, see, for example, Bosselmann 1995,1–100; Bosselmann 2010; Tarlock 1994; and Gaines 2014.

[6] Meadows, Meadows, Randers, & III (1972). Recent research at the University of Melbourne confirmed that the book was largely correct.

eventual collapse. Central to any rescue strategy must be the objective to protect the integrity of ecological systems and not overstep planetary boundaries. In legal terms, this objective can be expressed as a fundamental principle or *grundnorm* (Kim & Bosselmann 2013, 2015) underpinning the law in general (not just environmental law) and, in a similar way, as respect of human dignity or equality, fairness and justice. To get there, two steps are necessary.

The first step is recognizing the reality of planetary boundaries. Of the nine boundaries identified thus far (Rockström et al. 2009), three have already been exceeded (atmospheric greenhouse gas concentrations, rate of biodiversity loss, and nitrogen cycle) (Steffen et al. 2015). The recognition of planetary boundaries sets a non-negotiable bottom line for all human activities. More particularly, and in the context of the well-trodden concept of sustainable development, it suggests a hierarchical order of its three constituent elements: the natural environment is fundamental and comes first, human social organization exists within it and comes second, and economic modelling only exists within both, not parallel or above them. Only such a hierarchical understanding of sustainable development ('strong sustainability') reflects the reality of planetary boundaries and marks the first step towards a refined rule of law.

The second step is taking the strong sustainability approach to the design and interpretation of laws. One of the most basic legal concepts in this regard is the rule of law. It is the prime tool with which to ensure the control and accountability of governments, and implies that all citizens are subject to the law. But no law can rely on the rule of law in order to be respected. Rather, the rule of law has a moral dimension. It could not be any other way. Historically, the rule of law developed alongside individual autonomy, equality and social justice. This makes it inconceivable, for example, to consider a law justifying the killing of all blue-eyed blond people as in any way consistent with the rule of law. Such a law would be invalid not because of its immorality but because it was not enacted in accordance with the procedures authorized by the rule of law. Even for the rule of law morality matters and is never strictly separated from legality. This poses the question of what sort of morality may be constitutional to the rule of law.

This chapter argues that any law, no matter how aspirational for human purposes, must obey the fundamental rule to not undermine human survival (making all human aspirations possible in the first place). Positively speaking, respect for planetary boundaries and the integrity of the Earth's ecological systems are non-negotiable preconditions for the rule of law. I have called this a rule of law grounded in the Earth

(Bosselmann 2013a, 2013b). Effectively, human law must not violate recognizable physical laws that guide human existence.

The physical reality of planetary boundaries sets certain moral boundaries on human enterprises but they may not be acceptable to everybody. In fact, so far humanity has ignored any moral boundaries on the growth of populations and economies. 'More is better' is still widely accepted and sometimes not even perceived as a moral statement. If we are to accept a morality of 'enough', then we also need to think of its possible legality. So should the law control human development in order to respect planetary boundaries? At this juncture, it must be made clear that any such law could only ever be conceived on moral grounds[7] – there is no objective justification for it – but a case can be made that the moral grounds for respecting planetary boundaries are strong and compelling. They can be perceived as the rules or principles of nature that are discoverable by human beings and relevant to their relationship with the Earth. We would ignore such "natural law" at our peril. In this sense, it is superior to any (human) positive law (Berry 1999).[8]

2. The Rule of Law in an Ecological Context

The rule of law guides all people at all levels (global, national and local). Its purpose is to restrict the arbitrary exercise of power – of people or governments – by subordinating it to well-defined law. If it is therefore law that rules, then the rule of law invites us to further investigate what qualities laws must possess to justify command over people's lives and conduct. As we will see, any law must meet certain minimum standards to qualify as law in this sense.

The historical roots of the rule of law are in England's Glory Revolution of 1688 when *Rex Lex* ('The King is Law') was converted to *Lex Rex* ('The Law is King'). This event had of course ramifications far beyond the English monarchy. It marked the beginning of modern parliamentary democracy. Preventing the exercise of arbitrary power by governments and safeguarding individual rights are core to the rule of law and represent a consensus shared around the world today. Beyond that, however, the consensus is more fragile.

A report for the European Commission (Ehm 2010) acknowledges a variety of meanings of the rule of law but specifically identifies some core

---

[7] Morality is of course behind all forms of legal protection, including, for example, human rights.
[8] Described as the 'Great Law' by Berry (1999).

elements expressed in numerous international documents across legal cultures: (1) independence and impartiality of the judiciary, (2) legal certainty, (3) non-discrimination and equality before the law, (4) respect for human rights, (5) separation of powers, (6) the principle that the state is bound by law, and (7) the substantive coherence of the legal framework (Ehm 2010, 7). The report concludes that it can be deduced that there exists a rule in customary international law that demands the rule of law operates in the states as a precondition for membership in international organizations (Ehm 2010, 16).

International recognition is perhaps the most significant feature of the rule of law principle. If the rule of law can be seen as a defining characteristic of the modern state, then any linking with universally accepted principles – in whatever shape or form – would have ramifications for the contents of domestic **and** international law. This is already the case with respect to universally accepted principles such as respect for human rights, the principle of legality and the idea of a constitutional state based on fundamental rights and obligations. Along these lines, however, what could be more fundamental than protecting the physical conditions that human life depends on and make the enjoyment of human rights possible in the first place? Surely respecting planetary boundaries and the integrity of ecological systems are pre-conditional to human rights and consequently relevant to the rule of law.

So what would it take to **legally** recognize such a principle in the context of the rule of law?

For several years now, the World Justice Project of the American Bar Association has been measuring the strength of the rule of law principle around the world and ranks countries according to their governments' accountability, the absence of corruption, clarity and stability of laws, fundamental rights, open government, regulatory enforcement, and access to justice. The latest Rule of Law Index 2012–13 has the four Scandinavian countries topping the list of the world's most respected countries. They are followed by the Netherlands and New Zealand (with Germany ranked 9th, the United Kingdom 13th and the United States 19th) (The WJP 2014, 36–57).

The interesting thing here is that, with the exception of New Zealand, the top ten countries do not even refer to the 'rule of law' in their respective jurisdictions. Instead they speak of *rätt staat* (Danish/Swedish/ Norwegian) and *Rechtsstaat* (German/Dutch) or *Rechtsstaatsprinzip* and *Rechtsstaatlichkeit* (German). The literal translation of 'rule of law' (e.g., *Herrschaft des Rechts)* would be far too limiting to capture the system of principles and values associated with the **concept** of the rule of law. One obvious difference is that virtually all continental European countries relate the idea of law (*Recht, Rätt, droit, derecho, diritto*) to the idea of the state (*staat, etat, estado, stato*). Both ideas are intertwined and describe the expectation that a government gains legitimacy and legality only through adherence to predefined standards and principles.

It is typical for the Romano-Germanic legal tradition to derive the content of the rule of law from an entire system of mutually reinforcing and limiting principles. Depending on what principles are invoked and how they are defined, it is possible to give the *Rechtsstaat* certain content. In Germany, we speak of *sozialer Rechtsstaat* ('social constitutional state'), *Umweltstaat* (Kloepfer 1994; Callies 2001) ('environment state') or *ökologischer Rechtsstaat* (Bosselmann 1992, 1995; Steinberg 1998) ('eco-constitutional state'). Such contextualized understanding allows for a fruitful discourse on the importance of ecological responsibilities and the rule of law. In Germany, this discourse started in the mid-1980s and prompted a very promising investigation of the Joint Constitutional Commission of Bundestag and Bundesrat. The 1989 final report of the Joint Commission concluded that the question of an ecological rule of law is of such importance that only a wider public debate among the relevant sectors of society could advance this matter. German unification and full-blown neoclassic economics have silenced this debate but it never really stopped. Recently, Michael Kloepfer, a pioneer of German environmental law but not known as an eco-lawyer, observed a process of "ecologicalization of the legal system" and an increasing "ecologicalization of society" (Kloepfer 2013). As the crisis continues to evolve, it is likely that we will see more of this fundamental debate in the years to come.

As in Germany, the past two decades have seen moves towards an ecological rule of law in many other civil law jurisdictions such as Switzerland, Austria, France, Spain, Portugal, South Africa, and Latin American countries including Brazil, Venezuela, and particularly Bolivia and Ecuador. What we could learn here is that, conceptually, the rule of law can be expanded to include recognition of ecological realities. Arguably, the same is true for the rule of law outside civil law jurisdictions, including international law and the Anglo-Saxon common law system (Bosselmann 2013a, 7).

3. Constitutionalising Environmental Rights

Global trends towards an ecologicalization (or greening) of legal systems are best visible at the constitutional level. Constitutions are value-laden concepts, typically encapsulating the idea of democracy, the separation of powers, the protection of human rights, and certain guarantees of social security (Peters 2006). Human rights, in particular, define the core of how a political community aims to function. For the prospects of an expanded rule of law, human rights and their relationship to the environment are, therefore, of great importance.

Many international environmental agreements highlight the links between human rights and the environment. They are visible, for example, in the Stockholm Declaration, World Conservation Strategy, UN World Charter for Nature, Caring for the Earth, United Nations Framework Convention on Climate Change (UNFCCC), 1992 Rio Declaration, Agenda 21, UN Millennium Declaration, Johannesburg Declaration and the Rio+20 outcome document "The Future We Want".

At the time of the 1972 Stockholm Declaration, only a handful of national constitutions addressed environmental issues (Boyd 2012, 47). Today, some 125 constitutions incorporate environmental norms – 107 are in developing countries compared to 18 in developed countries (Jeffords 2011). About 92 constitutions explicitly recognize the right to a healthy or decent environment (Boyd 2012, 72). No other human right has achieved such a broad level of constitutional recognition in such a short period of time (Law & Versteeg 2011).

A human right to a healthy environment is only one form towards constitutionalizing the environment. Some 97 constitutions contain obligations for the national government to prevent harm to the environment and 56 constitutions recognize the responsibility of citizens or residents to protect the environment (Bosselmann 2008, 126).

Clearly, there is a worldwide trend towards constitutionalizing environmental rights and duties with respect to the environment. But will it make a real difference? This is not easy to answer. In general terms, the omnipresence of free market ideology has certainly undermined the efficiency and enforceability of environmental rights but there are also genuine law enforcement issues. For example, the legal cultures in Latin America are markedly different from the continental European legal culture with its emphasis on actual enforceability of constitutional rights. Therefore, the Rights of Mother Earth (as in Bolivia and Ecuador) are not *per se* superior to human rights and state obligations (as in Germany) if they lack enforceability. Fundamentally, we need to consider how constitutional rights – as a socio-legal construct – reflect ecological realities. There are anthropocentric and ecocentric variations.

Environmental rights often refer to access to, and use of, the environment but can also be understood to imply ecocentrism. Alan Boyle rightly observes that "environmental rights do not fit neatly into any category of human rights" (2007, 471) and then asks: "Has the time come to talk directly about environmental rights – in other words, a right to have the environment itself protected? Should we transcend the anthropocentric in favour of the ecocentric?" (2007, 473). Like most commentators, Boyle uses the term environmental rights generically to capture the environmental dimension of human rights (2012).

Anthropocentric reductionism has been one of the main reasons for the ongoing failure of environmental law and governance as mentioned (Bosselmann 1995, 2010, 2011b; Bruckerhoff 2008; Gaines 2014; Jakobson 2012, 196; Tarlock 1994; Taylor 1998, 31). The anthropocentricity of Western concepts of human rights and constitutions is not yet broken but while ecocentrism, the rights of nature, and Earth law are still largely confined to jurisprudential theory, there is a growing perception, even among governments, that the law needs to be grounded in non-anthropocentric environmental ethics. Promoting this shift and working towards a "constitutional moment" (Ackerman 1991; Slaughter & Burke-White 2002)[9] should be the key objective of the emerging field of global environmental constitutionalism (Bosselmann 2015b).

4. Ecological Integrity as a Grundnorm to Guide the Shift of the Legal Paradigm

The never-ending discourse around sustainable development – including sustainable development goals – has yet to discover the fundamental importance and core meaning of sustainability, a concept as old as humanity and well-practised in most societies until the arrival of the industrial age (Bosselmann 2015c). This is also true for Europe. In fact, the origins of the modern concept of ecological sustainability can be found in the forest management theory of the 17th century.

During this era, the notion of sustainability was created to describe the need of ongoing, future-oriented care for forests, the main energy source of the time. The term itself was coined by German engineer and forest economist Hans Carl von Carlowitz, who analysed the European resource crisis while crossing the continent between 1665 and 1669 (Spindler 2012). Inspired by his studies of British and French literature as well as by the experience he gained in his administrative function, Carlowitz eventually wrote his opus magnum *Sylvicultura oeconomica oder*

---

[9] A constitutional moment can occur when there are unusually high levels of sustained popular attention to questions of constitutional significance.

Naturmaessige Anweisung zur Wilden Baum-Zucht (*Forest Economy or Guide to Tree Cultivation Conforming with Nature*) (Bosselmann 2008, 17–19; Grober 2013). The book, published in 1713, focused on "how such conservation and growing of timber can be managed in order to provide continued, durable and sustained use". This marked the birth of the German term *nachhaltend*, later translated to 'sustained' and 'sustainable' in English.

Philosophers like Spinoza, Leibniz, Schelling, Goethe, Herder, and Hegel promoted an idealistic, holistic, and organic worldview, and did not regard the model of sustainability as limited to forest management (Bosselmann 1992, 12; 2008, 20–21; Spindler 2012, 20). Rather, sustainability reflected an appropriate interpretation of life as a whole. Cotta's first essay in 1792 expressed this universal attitude: "In the whole world there is no thing without relationship to something else" (Spindler 2012). That also reflects the creation of the term *oecologie* (from Greek *oikos* for 'house', 'household') by Ernst Haeckel in 1866 in allusion to philosopher Johann Gottfried Herder. Previously, Herder characterised the Earth as our *wohnplatz* ('living space', 'home') and the human role as *haushalten* ('housekeeping') (Spindler 2012).

About the same time, forest academies in Austria-Hungary, Switzerland, France, Russia, Scandinavia, the United Kingdom with its colonies, and finally the United States started to adopt the German prototype of sustainable forestry (Spindler 2012, 21). Consequently, the German word *nachhaltigkeit* was in need of suitable translation. In 1837, Professor Adolphe Parade, the director of the French Forest Academy in Nancy, translated the word as *production soutenu*, revealing its Latin roots as *sustinere* (from *tenere* 'to keep'). Like the English expression 'sustainable', this resembles the notions of enduring, lasting, keeping up, maintaining, carrying on, continuing, and sustaining.

However, during the subsequent era of the Industrial Revolution, the principle of sustainability became increasingly irreconcilable with the ideas of linear progress and indefinitely growing wealth that gained momentum around 1800. Starting in England and finding its way from Western Europe to America, one of the most important changes in the history of humankind had begun (Spindler 2012, 15). It was stimulated by philosophical streams like Newton's model of physics and the mechanistic-atomistic image of exploitation of natural resources, and largely overlooked a consideration of ecological sustainability. Fossil fuels (coal, oil) substituted renewable energy sources like wood and wind. Finally, natural boundaries had to be stretched to match the needs of the demographic change. Corresponding to this development, the idea of local, public and common responsibility was rejected to give way to a private, free enterprise approach, with its premise of granting individuals absolute dispositional powers over their properties, including environmental goods (Spindler 2012). As relations to the land became increasingly marked by self-serving, competing neighbour rights and less by ecological concerns, the individual was raised above nature.

However, development during the Industrial Revolution did not render the idea of sustainability redundant (Spindler 2012, 16). With regard to the present-day global crisis concerning ecological, economic and social structures in equal measure, it is now of greater topicality than ever before. By the early 1980s, sustainability was clearly understood as the antithesis of the growth paradigm. Its core meaning is the preservation of the integrity of ecological systems (Bosselmann 2008, 40–41). There is ample evidence that the Brundtland Commission aimed for sustainable development as ecologically sustainable development and as a counter model to the "more-is-better" growth paradigm of modern economies (ibid 2008, 25–32).[10] However, powerful corporate and state forces prevented sustainable development from becoming such a counter model. Instead, until today, sustainable development has remained a meaningless concept of pursuing environmental, social and economic interests.

The preservation of the integrity of Earth's ecological system has featured in modern environmental law for a long time.

It has been incorporated in many domestic conservation laws (ibid, 63–64; Steinhoff, 2013) and international environmental law, where it first appeared in the 1974 *Great Lakes Water Quality Agreement between Canada and the United States.* [11] Since then, some 23 international environmental treaties and agreements refer to ecological integrity as a general objective like, for example, the preamble[12] and Article 7 of the 1992 Rio Declaration on Environment and Development (*"States shall cooperate in a spirit of global partnership to conserve, protect and restore the health and integrity of the Earth's ecosystem"*) or Article 40 of the Rio+20 outcome document The Future We Want (*"We call for holistic and integrated approaches to sustainable development that will guide humanity to live in harmony with nature and lead to efforts to restore health and integrity of the Earth's ecosystem"*). The 2000 Earth Charter is

---

[10] The strong sustainability model.

[11] Its purpose is "to restore and maintain the chemical, physical and biological integrity of the waters of the Great Lakes Basin Ecosystem" (IJC 1978).

[12] "(W)orking towards international agreements which respect the interests of all and protect the integrity of the global environmental and developmental system".

in its entirety designed around the concept of ecological integrity. For example, principle 5 urges *"all individuals, organizations, businesses, governments, and transnational institution"* to *"[p]rotect and restore the integrity of Earth's ecological systems, with special concern for biological diversity and the natural processes that sustain life"*. Similarly, Article 2 of the 2010 IUCN Draft International Covenant on Environment and Development states: *"Nature as a whole and all life forms warrant respect and are to be safeguarded. The integrity of the Earth's ecological systems shall be maintained and where necessary restored."* This inclusion is significant because the Draft Covenant is a codification of existing environmental law and intended to be a blueprint for an international framework convention.

Applying the usual standards for the recognition of concepts as international law, it would be possible to say that the repeated and consistent references to ecological integrity amount to an emerging fundamental objective or *grundnorm* of international environmental law (Kim & Bosselmann 2013).

A fundamental rule to not harm the integrity of Earth's ecological or planetary systems would be a significant step towards Earth law and a reflection of the need to respect our planetary boundaries. As Michelle Maloney, in her comprehensive Earth jurisprudential analysis, states: "Ecological integrity is both the 'end game' and the starting point. It is the end game because humanity needs to ensure human societies do not interrupt the ecological integrity of ecosystems in their region and nations. It is also the starting point for any regulatory regime for living within our limits we must put the overall health of the Earth first, and fit the human project within its frame." (2014)

In pursuing such an approach, we ought to consider a universal move towards a new global treaty (such as the SOS Treaty), covenant (such as the Earth Charter) or constitution.

5. Towards a Global Constitution?

A global constitution may not be realized for many years to come. Nor may it be self-evident, given that real action mostly takes place at the local level, that is, in communities and cities. On the other hand, the health of the entire planet is at stake. This requires global awareness wherever people live and act ("think globally, act locally"). It is worth pondering, therefore, whether global values can be identified and written into some form of a world constitution. It is certainly within the realm of global environmental constitutionalism to take an interest in the possibility of a universal environmental code or constitution.

In the aftermath of the Second World War, international law was elevated to a new level. The United Nations Charter and the Universal Declaration of Human Rights created a unifying framework for the international community built on dignity and equality for all people. In addition to its purpose of settling conflicts, international law gained the purpose of promoting and reaffirming common values. In this pursuit, the Westphalian state system created the seeds of global civic identity. Somewhere between 1945 and today, humanity entered the "planetary phase of civilization" (Lazlo 2006; Rockefeller 2002). While the notion of a planetary civilization still lacks the global polity (Ougaard 1999) that could legitimize a global constitution or government, it is possible to identify, at least, some constitutionally relevant values and principles.

An early example of such an attempt was the 1948 *Preliminary Draft of a World Constitution* (http://www.worldbeyondborders.org/chicago draft.htm), which was translated into 40 languages. Known also as the "Chicago World Constitution", [13] its first chapter is structured as a "declaration of duties and rights" – not just rights – and contains the following sub-chapter c:

> The four elements of life – earth, water, air, energy – are the common property of the human race. The management and use of such portions thereof as are vested in or assigned to particular ownership, private or corporate or national or regional, of definite or indefinite tenure, of individualist or collectivist economy, shall be subordinated in each and all cases to the inherent interest of the common good.

The concern behind this draft was that international social justice and peace cannot be achieved without giving priority to the common good, in particular the global commons, over private property. Elisabeth Mann Borgese, an early pioneer of international environmental governance, [14] asserts that the Draft World Constitution has significantly influenced theory and the concepts of international environmental law (Mann Borgese

---

[13] Named after its drafting group of humanists, social scientists, philosophers and lawyers around the University of Chicago.

[14] Also known as the "mother of the oceans", Elisabeth Mann Borgese was the organizer of the first conference on ocean governance in 1970, founder of the International Ocean Institute and a highly influential proponent of the common heritage principle with respect to the UN Convention of the Law of the Sea. Retrieved from http://internationaloceaninstitute.dal.ca/emb.htm

1999). Today, we can clearly appreciate the urgency of protecting the global commons (oceans, atmosphere, biosphere) that all people in all nations so fundamentally depend on (Bosselmann 2015).

No other document has articulated this concern more strongly and more inclusively than the Earth Charter. It had its origins in the global ethics movement that started with the UN Charter, the founding of UNESCO (1946) and IUCN (1948), and the Universal Declaration of Human Rights (Bosselmann & Engel 2010, 15–26; Holdgate 1999,51). With its history and "contributions of literally millions of minds around the world" (Bosselmann & Engel 2010, *Foreword*, 8), the Earth Charter is the most inclusive international document to date to define globally shared values and principles. According to Nicholas Robinson, "the binding principles embodied in the Earth Charter can be and are being applied in courts and are found in virtually all national environmental laws" (ibid, 12). Considering further its endorsements by thousands of national and international organizations, including UNESCO and IUCN, and a number of states, and also its general recognition in international law (Bosselmann & Taylor 2005), the Earth Charter meets many of the hallmarks of a model global constitution (Bosselmann & Engel 2010, 239–255; Bosselmann 2009).

6. Conclusion

Can we be optimistic about the prospects of a legal paradigm shift? Earth-centred law mainly exists in a growing body of literature but it is also emerging as a new, albeit rudimentary, legal paradigm. At this juncture, we should combine all our forces to re-imagine environmental law and work towards a SOS Treaty and Earth Systems law. It is a very worthwhile cause – regardless of any optimism or pessimism that we may harbour when thinking about our destiny.

References

Ackerman, B. (1991). *We the People*. Cambridge: Harvard University Press.
Berry, T. (1999). *The Great Work: Our Way into the Future*. New York: Bell Tower Press.
Boyd, D. (2012). *The Environmental Rights Revolution*. Vancouver: UBC.
Bosselmann, K. (1992). *Im Namen der Natur – Der Weg zum ökologischen Rechtsstaat*. Munich: Scherz.

—. (1995). *When Two Worlds Collide: Ecology and Society*. Auckland: RSVP.

Bosselmann, K. & Taylor, P. (2005). The Significance of the Earth Charter in International Law. In Blaze Corcoran, P. (Ed.), *Toward a Sustainable World: The Earth Charter in Action* (pp. 171–173). Amsterdam: KIT Publishers.

Bosselmann, K. (2008). *The Principle of Sustainability: Transforming Law and Governance*. Aldershot: Ashgate.

—. (2009). Earth Charter (2000). In *Max Planck Encyclopedia of Public International Law*. Oxford: Oxford University Press, 4.

—. (2010). Losing the Forest for the Trees: Environmental Reductionism in the Law. *Environmental Laws and Sustainability*, Special Issue of *Sustainability 2*(8), 2424–2448. Retrieved from http://www.mdpi.com/2071-1050/2/8/2424/

Bosselmann, K. & Engel, R. (2010). *The Earth Charter: A Framework for Global Governance*. Amsterdam: KIT Publishers.

Bosselmann, K. (2011a). Earth Democracy: Institutionalizing Ecological Integrity and Sustainability. In Engel, R., Westra, L. & Bosselmann, K. (Eds.), *Democracy, Ecological Integrity and International Law* (pp. 319–330). Cambridge: Cambridge Scholars Publishing.

—. (2011b). A Vulnerable Environment: Contextualizing Law with Sustainability. *Journal of Human Rights and the Environment* 2, 45–63.

—. (2013a). The Rule of Law Grounded in the Earth. In: Westra, L. & Vilela, M. (Eds.), *The Earth Charter, Ecological Integrity and Social Movements* (pp. 3–11). New York: Routledge.

—. (2013b). Grounding the Rule of Law. In Christina Voigt (Ed.), *Rule of Law for Nature: New Dimensions and Ideas in Environmental Law* (pp. 75–93). Cambridge: Cambridge University Press.

—. (2015a). *Earth Governance: Trusteeship for the Global Commons*. Cheltenham: Edward Elgar.

—. (2015b). Global Environmental Constitutionalism: Mapping the Terrain. 21/2 *Widener Law Review, 171-185*.

—. (2015c). Sustainability and the Law: History, Ethical Functions, Current State and Future Prospects of Sustainability in Law and Policy. In Salmon P. & Grinlinton, D. (Eds.), *Environmental Law in New Zealand,* Ch. 3. Wellington: Thomson Reuters.

Bosselmann, K. & Taylor, P. (Eds.) (forthcoming 2016). *Ecological Approaches to Environmental Law*. Cheltenham: Edward Elgar.

Boyle, A. (2007). Human Rights and the Environment: A Reassessment. *Fordham Envt'l L.R.* XVII, 471–511.

—. (2012). Human Rights and the Environment. Where next? *European Journal of International Law,* 23(3), 613–642.

Bruckerhoff, J. (2008). Giving Nature Constitutional Protection: A less anthropocentric interpretation of environmental rights. *Texas L.R.,* 86(3), 615.

Burdon, P. (Ed.) (2011). *Exploring Wild Law: The Philosophy of Earth Jurisprudence.* Adelaide: Wakefield Press.

—. (2014). *Earth Jurisprudence: Private Property and the Environment.* New York: Routledge.

Callies, C. (2001). *Rechtsstaat und Umweltstaat.* Tübingen: Mohr Siebeck.

Cullinan, C. (2003). *Wild Law: A Manifesto for Earth Justice.* Totnes: Green Books.

Ehm, F. (2010). *The Rule of Law: Concept, Guiding Principle and Framework.* European Commission for Democracy through Law (Venice Commission). CDL-UDT011. Retrieved from http://www.venice.coe.int/webforms/documents/default.aspx?pdffile= CDL-UDT%282010%29011-e

Gaines, S. (2014). Reimaging Environmental Law for the 21st Century. *Environmental Law Reporter,* 44(3), 10188.

Grober, U. (2013). *Sustainability: A Cultural History.* Totnes: Green Books.

Holdgate, M. (1999). *The Green Web: A Union for World Conservation.* London: Earthscan.

Illge, L. & Schwarze, R. (2006). *A Matter of Opinion: How Ecological and Neoclassical Environmental Economists Think about Sustainability and Economics.* Berlin: German Institute for Economic Research.

Jakobson, T. (2012). Nordic Ecophilosophy and Critical Realism. In Bhaskar, R. et al (Eds.), *Ecophilosophy in a World of Crisis* (pp. 180–199). New York: Routledge

Jeffords, C. (2011). *Constitutional Environmental Human Rights: A Descriptive Analysis of 142 National Constitutions.* Connecticut: The Human Rights Institute.

Kim, R. & Bosselmann, K. (2013). International Environmental Law in the Anthropocene: Towards a Purposive System of Multilateral Environmental Agreements. *Transnational Environmental Law* 2, 285–309. doi: 10.1017/S2047102513000149.

—. (2015). Operationalizing Sustainable Development: Ecological Integrity as a *Grundnorm* in International Law. *Review of European Community and International Environmental Law, 24(2).* doi: 10.1111/reel.12109.

Kloepfer, M. (Ed.) (1994). *Umweltstaat als Zukunft*. Bonn: Economica.

Kloepfer, M. (2013). Umweltschutz. In *Leitgedanken des Rechts. Festschrift für Paul Kirchof*. In Kube, H. et al. (Eds.), *Leitgedanken des Rechts. Festschrift für Paul Kirchof* (pp.867–869). Heidelberg: CF. Müller.

Laszlo, E. (2006). Paths to Planetary Civilization. *Kosmos* 5, 2.

Law D. & Versteeg, M. (2011). The Evolution and Ideology of Global Constitutionalism. *Calif. L. R. 99*(1163). Retrieved from http://scholarship.law.berkeley.edu/californialawreview/vol99/iss5/1

Maloney, M. (2014). *The Role of Regulation in Reducing Consumption by Individuals and Households in Industrialised Nations*. PhD Thesis. Griffith University, 239.

Mann Borgese, E. (1999). *The Beginnings – The IOI*, 9–13. Malta: International Ocean Institute.

Meadows, D. H., Meadows, D. L., Randers, J. & Behrens III, W. W. (1972). *The Limits to Growth*. New York: Universe Books. Retrieved from http://www.donellameadows.org/the-limits-to-growth-now-available-to-read-online/

Meadows, D. (2012). Limits to Growth, Humanity is Still on the Way to Destroying Itself. *Der Spiegel, 7 December 2012*. Retrieved from http://www.spiegel.de/international/world/limits-to-growth-author-dennis-meadows-says-that-crisis-is-approaching-a-871570.html

Ougaard, M. (1999). *Approaching the Global Polity*. CSGR Working Paper, 42. Coventry: Centre for the Study of Globalisation and Regionalisation.

Peters, A. (2006). Compensatory Constitutionalism: The Function and Potential of Fundamental International Norms and Structures. *Leiden J. Int'l Law* 19, 579–595.

Rockefeller, S. (2002). Building a Global Culture of Peace. *Orion Magazine*, 21(1), 46.

Rockström, J. et al. (2009). Planetary Boundaries: Exploring the Safe Operating Space for Humanity. *Ecology and Society* 14 (2), 32. Retrieved from http://www.ecologyandsociety.org/vol14/iss2/art32/

Slaughter A.-M. & Burke-White, W. (2002). An International Constitutional Moment. *Harvard Int'l L.R.* 43, 1.

Spindler, E. (2012). Geschichte der Nachhaltigkeit. Vom Werden und Wirken eines beliebten Begriffes. In Jenkings, J. & Schröder, R. (Eds.), *Sustainability in Tourism. A Multidisciplinary Approach* (pp. 2–17). Wiesbaden: Gabler. Retrieved from http://www.nachhaltigkeit.info/media/1326279587phpeJPyvC.pdf

Steffen, W. et al. (2015). Planetary Boundaries: Guiding Human Development on a Changing Planet. *Science* (347), 791. doi: 10.1126/science.1259855.

Steinberg, R. (1998). *Der Ökologische Verfassungsstaat.* Frankfurt/M: Suhrkamp.

Steinhoff, G. (2013). Ecological Integrity in Protected Areas: Two Interpretations. *Seattle Journal of Envt'l Law* 3, 155–180.

Tarlock, D. (1994). The Nonequilibrium Paradigm in Ecology and the Partial Unraveling of Environmental Law. *Loy. L.A. L. Rev.*, 27, 1121. Retrieved from http://digitalcommons.lmu.edu/llr/vol27/iss3/22

Taylor, P. (1998). *An Ecological Approach to International Law: The Challenge of Climate Change.* London: Routledge.

The World Justice Project (WJP), *The WJP Rule of Law Index report* (2014). Retrieved from http://worldjusticeproject.org/sites/default/files/files/wjp_rule_of_law_index_2014_report.pdf

Turner, G. (2014). *Is Global Collapse Imminent?* Melbourne: Melbourne Sustainable Society Institute. Retrieved from http://espas.eu/orbis/sites/default/files/generated/document/en/MSSI-ResearchPaper-4_Turner_2014.pdf

UN Report of the Secretary-General. Harmony with Nature, A/69/322/18, August 2014. Retrieved form http://www.un.org/ga/search/view_doc.asp?symbol=A/69/322

Von Carlowitz, H. C. (1713). *Sylvicultura oeconomica. Anweisung zur wilden Baum-Zucht.* Leipzig, Freiberg: TU Bergakademie Freiberg & Akademische Buchhandlung 2000

CHAPTER FIVE

LEGAL TOOLS TO OPERATIONALIZE ANTHROPOCENE ENVIRONMENTAL LAW

ALEXANDRA ARAGÃO[1]

1. Why is the Legal Approach to the Planetary Boundaries Important?

Although often forgotten (Galaz et al 2012)[2], law is a crucial social science to drive the imperatives of the new planetary boundaries paradigm.

To understand why the legal approach to planetary boundaries is important, one must realize that the law is not only a mechanism for conflict resolution but also an inducer of social change. The law poses limits on individual rights, sets mandatory minimal standards, sanctions infractions and is a tool for social change and paradigm shifting. But changing society from the "inside" is a slow and difficult process. It's not easy to change mentalities, beliefs, habits, and lifestyles. Social inertia[3] amounts to a tolerance and perpetuation of social injustice. In times of social crisis – and particularly when it is associated with an ecological crisis – the law can have a revolutionary function, forbidding behaviours, activities or omissions that, although they are generally recognized as unfair, are maintained due to a dangerous cocktail of social inertia, unconsciousness, selfishness, and shortsightedness. In critical moments, law can perform an emancipatory function, triggering sudden social

---

[1] Faculty of Law, Universidade de Coimbra.

[2] For instance, when addressing the subject of integrated scientific research Galaz et al. (2012) don't mention law: "The need for integrated technological, institutional, social and ecological innovations to deal with the problem of global environmental change is well known in literature".

[3] The concept was introduced by Pierre Bordieu when studying the processes of social reproduction.

changes. The abolition of slavery and the recognition of voting rights for women are just two examples. In the environmental field, the Montreal Protocol, an environmental success story,[4] is another obvious example that comes to mind.

Just as equality between people of different races and between men and women became evident two hundred years ago, the need to protect the planet and the Earth System is imposing itself now with growing evidence.

Keeping within the planetary boundaries is a question of long-term survival; recognizing the legally binding character of the safe operating space (Rockström et al. 2009a) is a question of short-term justice. Furthermore, we advocate that operationalizing the planetary boundaries (Rockström et al. 2009b) throughout different scales of justice and across the various dimensions of justice is a legal imperative in the European Union.

Considering that the planetary boundaries can be downscaled, they are essential criteria for assessing fairness in the use of the Earth's resources. As described by Klaus Bosselmann (2008), they are essential to operationalize justice in the relationship between nations, citizens, generations and species.

- Justice between nations – between those with natural resources such as oil, precious metals and stones, but also water, forests, fertile land, and those that don't have any of these assets.
- Justice between citizens – rich and poor have access to very inequitable shares of the Earth's resources.
- Justice between generations – between the present generations, on one hand, continuously exploiting the planet beyond the safe operating space, and future generations, on the other hand, who will inherit a poorer and *malfunctioning* planet.
- Justice in the relationship between species – undoubtedly, the human species consumes a disproportionate amount of resources, threatening the lives of other species.

From global macro-justice to local micro-justice, the planetary boundaries help to visualize inequities and can be used as indicators of fairness in the relations between countries, regions, social groups,

---

[4] For more information, see the concise publication by the United Nations Environment Programme, produced in 2007 for the 20-year celebration of the Montreal Protocol available at
http://ozone.unep.org/Publications/MP_A_Success_in_the_making-E.pdf.

economic activities, and individuals, both present and future, belonging to our species or not.

Given the evidence of injustice in the current use of Earth's resources and the eminence of the imperative of protection of the Earth System, the role of the law is first of all to create duties and then to create rights – the duties of those who consume an unsustainable share of the Earth's resources, the rights of those who don't have access to the resources because they are too expensive, because they are too far away, because they are too damaged, because by the time they want to consume them... they are extinct.

2. Anthropocene Environmental Law

In previous times, human knowledge about the 'functioning' of the Earth System and human capacity to control the Earth's forces were so limited that Man had to make use of strategies like magic, sacred celebrations and rituals to placate outraged volcanoes, storms, floods, and droughts in their struggle to survive the hostile elements. In the Anthropocene, the *status quo* has changed radically. Humans are now the main force shaping and transforming the planet (Crutzen 2002).

Over the last centuries, we have gathered great knowledge about the Earth's biogeochemical processes and have started to understand the complex interrelations between land, air, water, biodiversity, and humans. Therefore, the objective of preserving the Earth System in a certain desired state depends on us more than ever. Specifically, it depends on science and technology but no less on society. Lifestyles influence the human impact on the Earth System just as much as the number of people living on the planet. And lifestyles are more than vague abstract categories used to blame industrialized societies for the state of the world. Lifestyles can be measured and compared using consumption rates, mobility patterns, energy consumption levels, discarding practices, eating habits, and so on.

This change in the *status quo* has legal consequences (Galaz 2014).[5] To clarify our reasoning, we will summarize the argumentative logic in three steps and a conclusion:

1. we are changing the Earth,
2. we know that some changes will have negative effects,

---

[5] For a reflection on the political and institutional implications posed by the Anthropocene, see Galaz (2014).

3. we understand *why* and *how* the changes occur,
4. therefore we have the duty to avoid future negative changes and reverse established ones.

These sequential statements show, in an oversimplified logic, the emergence of a new *Anthropocene Environmental Law*, the set of legal strategies, rules and principles necessary to ensure our permanence in the safe operating space.

The reason why the change in the geological epoch and the scientific evolutions associated with the knowledge and understanding of the Earth processes, determine legal shifts is quite clear. Beyond democratic legitimacy, legal statements must be grounded in sound scientific foundations (Berkowitz 2007). Therefore, it is not surprising that the evolution towards a new scientific paradigm entails the transformation of the whole set of legal tools applicable to products, activities, plans, programmes, and policies affecting the state of the Earth System.

This requirement is clearly expressed in the European Union Constitutional Law: "In preparing its policy on the environment, the Union shall take account of: available scientific and technical data (…)". [6] According to the Treaty, science and technology are the first criteria to take into account when drafting environmental law.

3. Anthropocene Environmental Law versus *Business-as-Usual* Environmental Law

What is the big difference between *Anthropocene Environmental Law* and *Business-as-Usual Environmental Law*?

The difference is the legal strength of the obligations imposed (Tibierge et al. 2009).[7] In *Business-as-Usual Environmental Law*, there were obligations to **make an effort** to prevent environmental damage and to improve the quality of the environment. Environmental protection actions were based on the best available techniques, good practice and due

---

[6] Article 191 n.1 of the Treaty on the Functioning of the European Union.

[7] As explained by Catherine Tibierge, the legal strength of a norm is not only dependent on authority (the issuing legal body, especially the Parliament) or on sanction (the legal form assumed by the norm and the sanctions imposed thereof; criminal statute prescribing life imprisonment, for instance). The legal strength of a norm emanates from legitimacy, persuasion, reception, repetition, validity, rely, effectivity, etc. For a detailed exposition, see Tibierge et al. (2009).

diligence. Criteria like social proportionality and rule of reason commanded the choice of the measures to be adopted.

In *Anthropocene Environmental Law*, the obligation is now to **achieve an outcome**: effective prevention of environmental damage and a real improvement of the quality of the environment. This requires adopting **all the measures necessary** to attain milestones, respect deadlines and deliver results. The criteria for the choice of means to attain the objectives are ecological proportionality and efficacy, that is, the capacity to meet the targets.

What are the grounds for this legal shift?[8] What is the justification for stronger obligations in the Anthropocene?

The justification is two-fold: a) scientific knowledge about the functioning of the complex Earth System processes is increasing, and b) human influence on the status of the complex Earth System processes is growing (Walker, Carpenter, Rockström, Crépin & Peterson 2012).[9]

The fact that we are starting to **understand** the mutual interferences between humans and the planet, that we **know** the consequences of our actions, and that we are **mastering** the processes necessary to avoid those consequences transforms the law based on "best efforts" into a law based on **results**. In other words, mere obligations of means are not sufficient to address the major challenges posed by the Anthropocene. In sum, the new *Anthropocene Environmental Law* is characterised by obligations of results, and this is the big difference.

The stakeholders of the *Anthropocene Environmental Law* – the public sector (international organizations, states, autonomous peoples), the private sector (from large multinational corporations to small and medium-sized enterprises), the third sector (namely, national and international NGOs), and of course, the citizens (both organized and individually) – have a general obligation to attain a certain result: maintaining the Earth System in a Holocene-like state, the only safe operating space we know.

---

[8] The reasoning is similar to the arguments used in the context of medical liability. Normally a doctor would only assume an obligation of means: he endeavours to heal the patient. But considering the evolution of therapeutic techniques, pharma knowledge and chirurgical knowhow, some minor medical interventions become routine and can hardly go wrong. In those cases, the doctor assumes an obligation to *cure* the patient (for further developments in medical law, see Pedro, R. T. (2008)).

[9] Depending on the point of view, humans can be seen as exogenous factors influencing the ecological processes or as endogenous factors just as any other element of nature. On the difference, see Walker, Carpenter, Rockström, Crépin & Peterson (2012).

In the context of the safe operating space, what does an obligation of results mean? It means that it is not enough to adopt some well-intentioned but probably arbitrary environmental protection measures and hope for the best. Of course, measures such as product regulations, cap and trade policies for emissions, environmental impact assessments, environmental tax reforms and environmental education are all very important to keep environmental conditions within the safe operating space. They are the *best available legal techniques* we have, for the moment, to deal with the irreversible anthropogenic changes that are driving us out of the Holocene. But it is not enough to take some − or all − of these environmental measures if at the same time there is no permanent monitoring of whether the effects of the measures correspond to what is necessary to keep humanity within the safe operating space.

The advantage of the planetary boundaries, as scientific studies point out (Rockström et al. 2009b),[10] is defining in absolute terms the thresholds that should not in any case be exceeded. The comparison between the planetary boundaries and the baseline situation, combining all the nine Earth processes, gives us the *coordinates* of the safe operating space.

Through monitoring, we can know whether the measures taken are excessive, sufficient or inadequate. In this case, drastic measures, such as total bans, may be necessary. In fact, when, despite the measures taken, monitoring results show environmental trends that are strongly negative, displayed as steep slopes on some graphs' curves, then percentage reductions may not be enough. In that case, strict prohibitions may be the only proportionate measures.

As a conclusion, monitoring activities and database production, including *ex ante* and *ex post* assessments, prospective studies, trend identification, data modelling, scenario analysis, and probabilistic forecasts, are essential tasks in *Anthropocene Environmental Law*. Monitoring control variables as progress indicators is fundamental to assess the effectivity of the measures adopted to keep the Earth System within the safe operating space.

---

[10] For a deeper understanding of the planetary boundaries theory, see Rockström et al. (2009b) and see also Chapter 2 of this book, written by Will Steffen.

4. Legal Tools to Operationalize Anthropocene Environmental Law

Inevitably, understanding the Earth's processes and knowledge about human interference with the Earth System implies wiser rules and more judicious decision making. The emergence of *Anthropocene Environmental Law* brings along new prerogatives and obligations regarding knowledge: first, sharing existing information; second, producing further information. The right to know and the corresponding duty to inform are two sides of the same coin: transparency. In the Anthropocene, transparency means sharing information that is relevant to understanding the effectivity and fairness of the measures and policies adopted to keep within the safe operating space. Transparency is essential to the strengthening of environmental democracy. It enables citizen participation in public decision making and citizen control of ongoing and future activities, and of omissions that are potentially noxious for the safe operating space. Directly or through associations, organizations or groups, citizens can be collaborators, partners, allies, *watchdogs* or *whistleblowers* of planetary boundary control variables and indicators.

Producing adequate information is another dimension of promoting knowledge in *Anthropocene Environmental Law*. This comprises the duty to regularly obtain relevant data on control variables relating to planetary boundaries and transform them into readable information to support well-informed policies and smarter regulation of activities or omissions. In short, this is called *smart regulation*, a movement that has guided European Union policies for years.[11]

In this context it is important to note that despite representing a new legal approach, knowledge promotion duties and information rights

---

[11] "The European Commission is committed to providing a proportionate and reliable evaluation system as part of its Smart Regulation cycle. Robust and useful analysis critically judging the outcomes of EU intervention is essential. Learning from past experience, recognizing the most efficient and effective ways of operating and developing a flexible and proportionate approach to analysing such actions will improve accountability and make EU intervention stronger, matching actions to priority needs and delivering the necessary high quality results" ("Strengthening the Foundations of Smart Regulation – Improving Evaluation", Communication from the Commission to the European Parliament, the Council, the European Economic and Social Committee and the Committee of the Regions, COM(2013) 686 final, Brussels, 2.10.2013). For further information, see http://ec.europa.eu/smart-regulation/index_en.htm.

inherent to *Anthropocene Environmental Law* can be operationalized through existing legal mechanisms.

There are two international instruments perfectly suited to implementing the advanced obligations imposed by *Anthropocene Environmental Law:* the Aarhus Convention on access to information, participation and access to justice in environmental matters, and the Kiev Protocol on Pollutant Release and Transfer Register.

The Aarhus Convention, based on an inspiring international text dating back to the '80s – the World Charter for Nature, [12] is a binding international agreement between 47 Euroepan parties. The Kiev Protocol, on the other hand, was designed to be a global protocol, open for accession by any sovereign state member of the United Nations. [13]

Both the Aarhus Convention and the Kiev Protocol are prominent materializations of four citizen's rights: the right to know, the right to participate, the right to effective environmental laws, and the right to control, review and challenge. In fact, the Aarhus Convention grants every citizen, association or organization, including NGOs, access to justice (through the courts or any independent and impartial body) to control the right to be informed (Meyer & David 2012, 479), [14] get involved and enforce the laws.

In other words:

- Whenever a request for access to information has not been correctly dealt with, a review procedure is possible to ensure access to written, visual, aural, electronic or any other material form of environmental information.
- Whenever public participation is possible, [15] the legality of any decision, act or omission on proposed activities that may have a significant effect on the environment can be challenged.

---

[12] Adopted and solemnly proclaimed by the United Nations General Assembly in 1982, the World Charter for Nature aims at protecting the "essential ecological processes and life-support systems".

[13] Including those that did not ratify the Aarhus Convention and those that are not members of the United Nations Economic Commission for Europe (http://www.unece.org/).

[14] According to Michel Prieur, access to environmental information is already customary law. In fact, it is prescribed in almost every major international treaty and is regarded by the states as a binding obligation (Meyer & David 2012, 479).

[15] Public participation is possible during the administrative procedures leading to decisions taken by public authorities on proposed activities that may have a significant effect on the environment.

- Whenever provisions of national law relating to the environment have been contravened,[16] acts or omissions by private persons or by public authorities can be challenged.

5. Transparency in the Anthropocene

We have already said that the first and utmost rights to be recognized in the framework of the new planetary boundaries paradigm are those connected to transparency[17] – the right to know the status of the Earth System and the right to understand the influence of actions and omissions, individual and collective, public and private, on this status. Knowing (Faure & Lefevre 1999)[18] what is each country's and each installation's contribution to keeping the planet within the safe operating space, or departing from it, is an essential precondition to taking action, overcoming political reluctance and breaking the social inertia, which are indispensable when facing the challenges posed by the Anthropocene epoch.[19]

Looking closer at the two international environmental agreements mentioned in light of the *Anthropocene Environmental Law,* we will highlight the major norms that can be used to operationalize transparency.

First of all, the Aarhus Convention recognizes "the importance of fully integrating environmental considerations in governmental decision making and the consequent need for public authorities to be in possession of accurate, comprehensive and up-to-date environmental information".[20]

For this purpose, each of the parties to the Convention shall ensure that "public authorities possess and update environmental information which is relevant to their functions"[21] and "publish the facts and analyses of facts

---

[16] This general access to justice is possible regardless of respect or disrespect of access to information or public participation rights.

[17] In the European Union, transparency is a fundamental value, enshrined in the Treaties (Article 15 n.3 §2 and 3) and in the Charter of Fundamental Rights of the European Union (Article 42).

[18] On the crucial role of reporting and information on the promotion of compliance with international environmental law, see Faure & Lefevre (1999).

[19] The importance of "accountability mechanisms", "including mandatory disclosure of accessible, comprehensible and comparable data about corporate and government sustainability performance" to "empower citizens and consumers" is also stressed by the supporters of the *State of the Planet Declaration* adopted at the Planet under Pressure Conference, London, March 2012. Available at http://www.planetunderpressure2012.net/pdf/state_of_planet_declaration.pdf.

[20] Preamble of the Aarhus Convention, 16§.

[21] Article 5, n.1 of the Aarhus Convention.

which it considers relevant and important in framing major environmental policy proposals". [22] This information shall be made progressively available to the public and accessible through telecommunications networks. At least every four years, national reports on the state of the environment shall be produced, published and disseminated, including information on the quality of the environment and on pressures on the environment.[23]

Additionally, the Kiev Protocol determines the duty of the parties[24] to ensure that every year, competent authorities collect information on releases of pollutants from various sources[25] and that the operators of polluting facilities report annually on point source pollutants, detailing releases to air, land and water, as well as waste production and transfer. All the information gathered shall be made available to the public in a user-friendly format through telematics.[26]

Reporting on the status of the environment soon became a widespread practice.[27] Building on the progress achieved by the Aarhus Convention and the Kiev Protocol, the European Environmental Agency published "An Assessment of Assessments" (http://www.eea.europa.eu//public ations/europes-environment-aoa), a comprehensive overview of available sources of environmental information across the European region, in 2011. The purpose was to seek "improved ways of governing environmental knowledge to support the policy process". In other words, "the aim of environmental assessments is to support the framing and implementation of environmental policy and more generally to support the transfer of knowledge and translation and communication across the so-called science-policy interface" (European Environmental Agency 2011). One of

---

[22] Article 5, n.7 (a) of the Aarhus Convention.

[23] Article 5, n.3 and 4 of the Aarhus Convention.

[24] In 2015 there were 33 parties to the Kiev Protocol.

[25] Article 7 n.4 of the Protocol on Pollutant Release and Transfer Register.

[26] Article 4 of the Protocol on Pollutant Release and Transfer Register.

[27] For large undertakings and groups, the disclosure of social and environmental information will be mandatory after 6 December, 2016, the deadline for transposing the directive on disclosure of non-financial and diversity information by certain large undertakings and groups (2014/95/EU of 22 October, 2014). The example of global scale reporting is the global monitoring report prepared in 2009 in accordance with the global monitoring plan for effectiveness evaluation of persistent organic pollutants in the context of the Stockholm Convention. Available at
http://chm.pops.int/Implementation/GlobalMonitoringPlan/MonitoringReports/tabi d/525/Default.aspx.

the conclusions is "the conceptual part of the assessment of assessments process needs to provide clear instructions to participating countries and organizations on the type of literature, reports and documents to be included in the process." We think that the planetary boundaries conceptual framework may shed some light on this problem.

Nevertheless, the search for a conceptual framework is not only a problem of scientific reporting; it is also a problem of legal understanding.

6. The Earth System: An Unidentified Legal Object (ULO)

As a new scientific object is being built – the Earth System and the planetary boundaries in the Anthropocene – we are also witnessing the building of a new legal object. Until now, the Earth System was an *unidentified legal object* – an ULO (Melot & Pélisse 2008).[28] The contours of its legal protection hadn't yet been defined. There were treaties for protecting *some parts* of the object: the oceans,[29] the atmosphere,[30] the biodiversity,[31] and the wetlands[32] but not the whole object taking into account the complex interactions between biosphere, atmosphere, cryosphere, hydrosphere, and the climate system. Besides, existing legal instruments were based on inaccurate scientific assumptions. They were based on linear dynamics and ignored feedbacks, critical transitions, regime shifts, and the risk of human-induced large-scale catastrophic changes (Steffen et al. 2004).

In the last few years, nature scientists have been working hard to recognize the fundamental Earth System processes that are crucial for maintaining the planet in a desired status (the Holocene). Recognizing the

---

[28] Melot and Pélisse (2008) discuss the difficulties in classifying an empirical object as a legal object, and develop the concept of *"unidentified legal objects"*.

[29] The United Nations Convention on the Law of the Sea of 10 December, 1982. Retrieved from
http://www.un.org/depts/los/convention_agreements/convention_overview_conven
tion.htm

[30] The United Nations Framework Convention on Climate Change of 9 May, 1992. Retrieved from http://unfccc.int/resource/docs/convkp/conveng.pdf.

[31] The United Nations Convention on Biological Diversity of 5 June, 1992. Retrieved from https://www.cbd.int/doc/legal/cbd-en.pdf.

[32] The United Nations Convention on Wetlands of International Importance especially as Waterfowl Habitat of 2 February, 1971 (amended in '82 and '87). Retrieved from
http://www.ramsar.org/sites/default/files/documents/library/current_convention_te
xt_e.pdf.

biogeochemical boundaries of the planet through the identification of tipping points and control variables amounts to defining our safe operating space. Promoting human prosperity within the safe operating space is essential to the maintenance of the socio-ecological resilience and the attainment of the global sustainable development goals.[33]

Likewise, lawyers must work together to shape a new legal object: the Earth System. In the new Anthropocene Environmental Law, the object of protection is not just an astronomical object orbiting a star or, to put it simply, **a planet** (the only one known to have conditions that support life, by the way...). The object of legal protection is a planet *with certain biogeochemical features*. We know now, after recent assessments,[34] that these features have been largely produced by human activity (Steffen et al. 2011).

Besides, the object of legal protection is supposed to last, in its current status, for a long time, longer than human life. In this regard, the Earth System is a **heritage**. At first glance it seems clear that the obvious characterisation of the Earth System is as a natural heritage; the Earth is a natural object but, since the Anthropocene, it is also man-made. The current terrestrial status is the direct result of human cultural activity. Consequently, it is a mix of natural and cultural heritage.

Recalling the set of criteria used by UNESCO to select the relevant world heritage sites, the Earth System fits all the criteria required for not only natural but also cultural heritage. According to Article 1 of the UNESCO Convention, "sites" are "works of man or the combined works

---

[33] One of the main outcomes of the Rio+20 Conference was the agreement by member states to launch a process to develop a set of sustainable development goals, building upon the Millennium Development Goals for the period after 2015 [online] http://www.un.org/en/mdg/summit2010/pdf/List%20of%20MDGs%20English.pdf. The sustainable development goals shall be "action-oriented, concise, easy to communicate, limited in number, aspirational, global in nature and universally applicable to all countries while taking into account different national realities, capacities and levels of development and respecting national policies and priorities" (for more information on the *post-2015 process*, see https://sustainabledevelopment.un.org/topics/index.php?menu=1561).

[34] For the influence in the composition of the atmosphere and resulting climate changes, see the various scientific assessments and reports on climate change by the *International Panel for Climate Change*. Retrieved from http://www.ipcc.ch/publications_and_data/publications_and_data_reports.shtml. For the disturbance of ecosystems, see the *Millennium Ecosystem Assessment*. Retrieved from http://www.millenniumassessment.org/en/index.html.

of nature and man, and areas including archaeological sites which are of outstanding universal value from the historical, aesthetic, ethnological or anthropological point of view".

Browsing the UNESCO criteria,[35] it becomes apparent that the Earth System fulfils all the detailed requirements for classification. Drawing upon the words of the Convention, it is not absurd to say that the Earth exhibits a *unique interchange of human values*; it is a *unique testimony to human civilization*; it displays *outstanding landscapes which illustrate significant stages in human history*; it is the only example of a *traditional human settlement*; it contains *superlative natural phenomena or areas of exceptional natural beauty and aesthetic importance*; it is the only *outstanding representation of major stages of Earth's history, including the record of life, significant on-going geological processes in the development of landforms, or significant geomorphic or physiographic features*; it is the only *outstanding representation of significant on-going ecological and biological processes in the evolution and development of terrestrial, fresh water, coastal and marine ecosystems and communities of plants and animals*; it contains the *only natural habitats for in-situ conservation of biological diversity, including those containing threatened species of outstanding universal value from the point of view of science or conservation*; finally, it is directly *associated with events or living traditions, with ideas, or with beliefs, with artistic and literary works of outstanding universal significance*.

The Earth System is, undoubtedly, a "site of outstanding universal natural and cultural value".

7. Conceptual Adaptation

As a consequence of the scientific evolution towards the planetary boundaries paradigm, some long-standing legal concepts have to be reconsidered and reformulated in the new framework of Anthropocene Environmental Law. This conceptual adaptation is particularly important for some operational concepts relating to thresholds and desired states.

---

[35] For a full description of the ten criteria, see http://whc.unesco.org/en/criteria/. The operational guidelines for implementation of the World Heritage Convention are available at http://whc.unesco.org/pg.cfm?cid=57

7.1 "Emission Limit Values" and "High Level of Protection of the Environment"

Take concepts like "emission limit values" and "high level of protection of the environment", for example. Both concepts were developed and enshrined in environmental laws long before the advent of the planetary boundaries theories. Nevertheless, they can be very useful tools for the legal implementation of the planetary boundaries in the new Anthropocene Environmental Law provided they are correctly understood and updated to reflect the planetary boundaries.

The concept of "emission limit values" applies to direct emissions of certain pollutants[36] from point sources to the environment. In the European Union, the concept of "emission limit values" is a cornerstone of the directive on industrial emissions.[37] In the words of the directive, "emission limit values" are *general binding rules* adopted with the intention of being used directly to set permit conditions.[38] These values apply to the end of the pipe [39] and should never be exceeded... except in exceptional circumstances[40] where temporary derogations may be granted.[41]

"Emission limit values" are usually defined taking into account the best available techniques used for preventing or reducing pollution. And

---

[36] Such as sulphur dioxide, oxides of nitrogen, carbon monoxide, volatile organic compounds, metals and their compounds, dust, asbestos, chlorine, fluorine, arsenic, cyanides, polychlorinated dibenzodioxins, organohalogen compounds, organophosphorus compounds, organotin compounds, cyanides, biocides, etc.

[37] Directive 2010/75/UE of the European Parliament and of the Council of 24 November, 2010. According to the directive, 'emission' means "the direct or indirect release of substances, vibrations, heat or noise from individual or diffuse sources in the installation into air, water or land" (article 3 n.4); and 'emission limit value' means "the mass, expressed in terms of certain specific parameters, concentration and/or level of an emission, which may not be exceeded during one or more periods of time" (article 3 n.5).

[38] Article 3 n.8.

[39] Article 15 n.1: "The emission limit values for polluting substances shall apply at the point where the emissions leave the installation, and any dilution prior to that point shall be disregarded when determining those values".

[40] Namely for the testing and use of emerging techniques (article 15 n.5). An emerging technique is a novel technique for an industrial activity that, if commercially developed, could provide either a higher general level of protection of the environment or at least the same level of protection of the environment and higher cost savings than existing best available techniques" (article 3 n.14).

[41] Article 15 n.5.

the best techniques are those that are "most effective in achieving a high general level of protection of the environment as a whole".[42]

This is the point where these two concepts meet.

The principle of the high level of protection has a very strong presence in European environmental law.[43] The high level of environmental protection principle (HLEP) is present in the Treaty on European Union,[44] the Treaty on the Functioning of the European Union[45] and the Charter of Fundamental Rights of the European Union.[46] In secondary law, the Industrial Emissions Directive is the most visible expression of this principle, being reaffirmed five times in the preamble and seven times in the articles of the directive. In Europe, ecological protection is an indisputable Union imperative. Consequently, it is not legitimate to question if the environment should be protected but only *who*, *when* and *how* to protect it. The environmental principles provide the answer: the polluter-pays principle answers the question *who*; the precaution principle answers the question *when*; and the high level of environmental protection principle answers the question of *how* to protect the environment.

The high level of environmental protection principle does not provide criteria for attaining an *absolutely high* level of protection but only a *relatively high* one. This means that this principle requires that every decision be considered in its context. What is expected is that the decision maker compares two or more options corresponding to different levels of protection. The high level of environmental protection principle helps in

---

[42] The "best available techniques" means the most effective and advanced stage in the development of activities and their methods of operation that indicate the practical suitability of particular techniques for providing the basis for emission limit values and other permit conditions designed to prevent and, where that is not practicable, to reduce emissions and the impact on the environment as a whole (article 3 n.10).

[43] In the European Union law, the requirement for a high level of protection also applies to other important values besides the environment. This is the case of education and human health (Article 9 of the Treaty on the Functioning of the European Union), security (Article 67(3) of the Treaty on the Functioning of the European Union), public health (Article 168 of the Treaty on the Functioning of the European Union and 35 of the Charter of Fundamental Rights of the European Union) and consumers (Article 169 of the Treaty on the Functioning of the European Union and 38 of the Charter of Fundamental Rights of the European Union).

[44] Article 3(3).

[45] Articles 114 and 191(2).

[46] Article 37.

comparing techniques, methods and results, ensuring the choice of the strongest environmental protection.

Far from being a vague and open principle, the high level of environmental protection principle is a true standard that can provide concrete decision guidelines on the solution that best protects the environment *macroscopically.*[47]

The adaptation of these two legal concepts to the planetary boundaries framework involves changing the processes used to define the "emission limit values". The reference point is not what we can possibly do, considering the latest technological advances, to attain a high level of protection with regard to some pollutants. The reference point is now what *must be done* (through technology and innovations[48] but also *at the expense of* lifestyles and consumption patterns, and *despite* market laws, freedom of initiative and protection of property) to make sure we keep within the safe operating space considering the systemic interferences and feedback between the different pollutants and the nine planetary boundaries. This is the new definition of the highest level of environmental protection in the Anthropocene.

---

[47] The first references to the macroscope were due to Eugene Thomas and Howard Odum in 1971. Later, in 1975, the same idea was developed in a very suggestive way by Joël de Rosnay in his book entitled *The Macroscope* (pp. 6 and 7): "The macroscope is (...) a symbolic instrument made of a number of methods and techniques borrowed from very different disciplines. (...) The macroscope can be considered the symbol of a new way of seeing, understanding, and acting. Let us use the macroscope to direct a new look at nature, society, and man and to try to identify new rules of education and action. (...) The macroscope filters details and amplifies that which links things together. It is not used to make things larger or smaller but to observe what is at once too great, too slow, and too complex for our eyes (human society, for example, is a gigantic organism that is totally invisible to us). Formerly, in trying to comprehend a complex system, we sought the simplest units that explained matter and life: the molecule, the atom, elementary particles. Today, in relation to society, we are the particles" [online] http://www.appreciatingsystems.com/wp-content/uploads/2011/05/The-Macroscope .pdf). In the legal context, it was François Ost who mentioned the macroscope as an imaginary optical instrument that gives lawyers the right perspective to look at the phenomena of the natural world for purposes of regulation (Ost, François (1995). *La Nature Hors la Loi - L' écologie à l' épreuve du droit*, Paris: Éditions La Découverte, 93).

[48] Emerging techniques.

7.2 "Environmental Quality Standards" and "Favourable Conservation Status"

While the concepts of "emission limit values" and "high level of protection of the environment" are used in industrial law to regulate the exercise of certain noxious activities, the concepts of "environmental quality standards" and "favourable conservation status" are used in laws relating to natural resources and environmental receptors such as elements of fauna, flora, water, soil, and air.

As before, these concepts have to be re-examined and re-adjusted to the new framework.

It is clear from the legal regime of industrial emissions that "environmental quality standards" prevail over "emission limit values" and best available techniques.

> Where an environmental quality standard requires stricter conditions than those achievable by the use of the best available techniques, additional measures shall be included in the permit, without prejudice to other measures which may be taken to comply with environmental quality standards.[49]

This is the ultimate evidence that we have moved from obligations of effort to duties of result. It doesn't matter whether the owner of an installation is using cutting edge technology; what matters is the outcome – the status of the environmental receptors revealed by the parameters subject to environmental monitoring.

In European Union water law, the core objective is to achieve a good ecological status. "Ecological status" is an expression of the quality of the structure and functioning of aquatic ecosystems associated with surface waters. In defining the ecological status of the water bodies, an array of biogeochemical parameters have to be taken into account: biological elements; composition, abundance and biomass of phytoplankton; composition and abundance of other aquatic flora; composition and abundance of benthic invertebrate fauna; composition, abundance and age structure of fish fauna; hydromorphological elements supporting the biological elements; hydrological regime; quantity and dynamics of water flow; residence time; connection to the groundwater body; morphological conditions; depth and width variation; quantity, structure and substrate of the bed; structure of the shore; chemical and physico-chemical elements

---

[49] Article 18 of the Industrial Emissions Directive.

supporting the biological elements; transparency; thermal conditions; oxygenation conditions; salinity; acidification status; nutrient conditions; specific pollutants; pollution by all priority substances identified as being discharged into the body of water; pollution by other substances identified as being discharged in significant quantities into the body of water; quantity, structure and substrate of the bed; structure of the riparian/intertidal zone; continuity; tidal regime; freshwater flow; wave exposure; and direction of dominant currents.

In nature conservation law, the concept of conservation status performs the same functions as the concept of environmental quality standards: it is the expression of the desired status of the natural resource in consideration.

In the European directive on the conservation of natural habitats and of wild fauna and flora,[50] the conservation status of a natural habitat means the sum of the influences acting on a natural habitat and its typical species that may affect its long-term natural distribution, structure and functions as well as the long-term survival of its typical species within a defined territory.[51] On the other hand, the conservation status of a species means the sum of the influences acting on the species concerned that may affect the long-term distribution and abundance of its populations in a defined territory.[52]

The conservation status of a natural habitat will be taken as favourable when three criteria are met: its natural range and the areas it covers within that range are stable or increasing; the specific structure and functions necessary for its long-term maintenance exist and are likely to continue to exist for the foreseeable future; and the conservation status of its typical species is favourable.[53]

As for species, the conservation status will be taken as favourable when population dynamics data on the species concerned indicate that it is maintaining itself on a long-term basis as a viable component of its natural habitats, the natural range of the species is neither being reduced nor is likely to be reduced for the foreseeable future, and there is, and will probably continue to be, a sufficiently large habitat to maintain its populations on a long-term basis.[54]

Using the planetary boundary for biodiversity and biofunctionality, downscaled first to the European Union level and thereafter to the national

---

[50] Council Directive 92/43/EEC of 21 May 1992.

[51] Article 1 (e) §1.

[52] Article 1 (i) §1.

[53] Article 1 (e) §2.

[54] Article 1 (i) §2.

level, the European concept of favourable conservation status can be fine-tuned and adjusted to the global level requirements of the safe operating space.

8. Conclusion

In the European Union, the Environment Action Programme to 2020[55] – "Living well, within the limits of our planet" – is the first supranational legal instrument incorporating the new scientific paradigm. The Action Programme requires "coordinating, sharing and promoting research efforts at Union and Member State level with regard to addressing key environmental knowledge gaps, including the risks of crossing environmental tipping points and planetary boundaries".

From now on, maintaining *business-as-usual*[56] *environmental law* and tolerance towards overshooting planetary boundaries shall be deemed illegal; precaution and prevention to avoid exceeding dangerous thresholds shall be mandatory; if ordinary measures are insufficient to keep within the safe operating space, then extraordinary measures shall be adopted.

This was precisely the reasoning behind the European Union Court of Justice ruling of November 2014 in the "Client Earth" case: "where a Member State [such as the UK] has failed to comply with the requirements of the directive (...) [on air pollution] (...) and has not applied for a postponement of the deadline (...), it is for the national court having jurisdiction, should a case be brought before it, to take, with regard to the national authority, any necessary measure, such as an order in the appropriate terms, so that the authority establishes the plan required by the directive in accordance with the conditions laid down by the latter".[57] Going even further, the Supreme Court of the United Kingdom ruled that this is not an issue to be left at the mercy of the political will of

---

[55] Decision n. 1386/2013/EU of the European Parliament and of the Council of 20 November, 2013, laying down the Seventh European Union Environment Action Programme.

[56] "We have become a force of nature, but individually we continue to be vulnerable. Business as usual is not an option. The time for action is now" (*State of the Planet Declaration* adopted at the Planet under Pressure Conference, London, March 2012, by the co-chairs Lidia Brito and Mark Stafford Smith, supported by the conference Scientific Organizing Committee). Available at http://www.planetunderpressure2012.net/pdf/state_of_planet_declaration.pdf.

[57] Case C-404/13 of the 19th November 2014.

governments. There is a "need for immediate action" and new plans must be delivered not later than 31 December 2015.[58]

The same line of thought was endorsed in the Netherlands in a recent and still more ambitious judicial decision.[59] In June 2015, the Hague District Court ordered the Dutch state "to limit the joint volume of Dutch annual greenhouse gas emissions, or have them limited, so that this volume will have reduced by at least 25% at the end of 2020 compared to the level of the year 1990". As thoroughly demonstrated by the Court, these targets are not mere political obligations dependent on reciprocal fulfilment by other states. Furthermore, they aren't mere programmatic norms requiring previous legal implementation. The emission targets are strict legal obligations enforceable in a Court of Law.

The time of the *Anthropocene Environmental Law* has arrived.

References

Berkowitz, R. (2007). Democratic Legitimacy and the Scientific Foundation of Modern Law. *Theoretical Inquiries in Law*, 8.1., 91–115.

Bosselmann, K. (2008). *The Principle of Sustainability. Transforming Law and Governance.* Aldershot: Ashgate.

Crutzen, P. J. (2002). Geology of Mankind. *Nature*, 415, 23. Retrieved from
http://www.geo.utexas.edu/courses/387h/PAPERS/Crutzen2002.pdf.

European Environmental Agency (2011). *An Assessment of Assessments*, Copenhagen, 24.

Faure, M. & Lefevre, J. (1999). Compliance with International Environmental Agreements. In Vig, Norman J. & Axelrod, Regina S. (Eds.) *The Global Environment. Institutions, Law and Policy*. London: Earthscan.

Galaz, V. et al. (2012). 'Planetary Boundaries' – Exploring the Challenges for Global Environmental Governance. *Current Opinion in Environmental Sustainability*, 4, 1-8. Retrieved from
http://community.eldis.org/.5ad50647/Galaz%20et%20al%202012%20COSUST.pdf

Galaz, V. (2014). *Global Environmental Governance, Technology and Politics. The Anthropocene Gap.* Cheltenham: Edward Elgar.

---

[58] https://www.supremecourt.uk/decided-cases/docs/UKSC_2012_0179_Press Summary.pdf
[59] Case C/09/456689 / HA ZA 13-1396, judgement of 24 June, 2015.

Melot, R. & Pélisse, J. (2008). Prendre la mesure du droit : enjeux de l'observation statistique pour la sociologie juridique. *Droit et société,* 2(69-70), 331-346. Retrieved from http://www.cairn.info/revue-droit-et-societe-2008-2-page-331.htm

Meyer, N. & David, D. (2012). *L'intégration de la coutume dans l'élaboration de la norme environnementale: éléments d'ici et d'ailleurs.* Brussels: Bruylant.

Pedro, R.T. (2008). *A responsabilidade civil do médico: reflexões sobre a noção da perda de chance e a tutela do doente lesado.* Coimbra: Coimbra Editora.

Rockström, J., Steffen, W., Noone, K., Persson, Å., Chapin, F. S., Lambin, E. F., et al. (2009a). A Safe Operating Space for Humanity. *Nature,* 461(7263), 472. doi:10.1038/461472a.

Rockström, J., Steffen, W., Noone, K., Persson, Å., Chapin, F. S., Lambin, E., et al. (2009b). Planetary Boundaries: Exploring the Safe Operating Space for Humanity. *Ecology and Society, 14*(2), 32. Retrieved from http://www.ecologyandsociety.org/vol14/iss2/art32/

Steffen, W., Andreae, M. O., Bolin, B., Cox, P. M., Crutzen, P. J., Cubasch, U. et al. (2004). Abrupt Changes: the Achilles' Heels of the Earth System. *Environment: Science and Policy for Sustainable Development,* 46, 3, 8–20.

Steffen, W., Peterson, A., Deutsch, L., Zalasiewicz, J., Williams, M., Richardson, K. et al. (2011). The Anthropocene: From Global Change to Planetary Stewardship. *Ambio,* November, 739–761. Retrieved from http://www.ncbi.nlm.nih.gov/pmc/articles/PMC3357752/

Tibierge, C. et al. (2009). *La force normative. Naissance d'un concept.* Paris: LGDJ.

Walker, B. H., Carpenter, S. R., Rockström, J., Crépin, A., & Peterson, G. D. (2012). Drivers, "Slow" Variables, "Fast" Variables, Shocks, and Resilience. *Ecology and Society, 17*(3), art. 30. Retrieved from http://www.ecologyandsociety.org/vol17/iss3/art30/

CHAPTER SIX

THE COMMON HERITAGE: CONSTRUCTIVE UTOPIANISM

PRUE TAYLOR[1]

1. Introduction

Other chapters in this book have argued that we are faced with two fundamental realities. First, the complex integrated Earth System, upon which all life depends, is under threat from human activities. Of the nine planetary boundaries identified, four have been transgressed, creating varying degrees of risk. Of these four, two (climate change and biosphere integrity) are 'core planetary boundaries' due to their combined importance and inter-relationship. The combined impact of these four transgressions is to push the Earth System (ES) into a state in which life, including human life, is imperilled. In short, we have moved beyond the safe operating space (SOS) for human existence. This important work demonstrates, in scientific terms, what we learned from the 'Spaceship Earth' image; the Earth is an interconnected living system upon which all humanity (and all other life) depends. However, it teaches us something else; humanity is now destabilising the ES and "beginning to undermine our own life-support system" (Steffen, Chapter 1). Therefore we need a coherent ES-focused governance system, that is, one that respects this biophysical reality and manages human behaviour accordingly (Steffen, Chapter 1).

The second fundamental reality is that our current political and legal world order is wholly inadequate and unable to cope. We have been struggling for many decades within the current Westphalian system of

---

[1] University of Auckland.

sovereign states using traditional legal principles in an ad hoc manner. The resulting governance system is increasingly showing its inadequacies. A recent analysis, for example, described international environmental law as immature, underdeveloped and ineffective (Francioni 2014). Despite this, discussions at the Rio +20 Conference carefully sidestepped or ignored calls for major changes to our system of global (or state-centred) governance that would focus on planetary boundaries and potentially challenge the power of sovereign states (Serrao-Neumann 2014). This reflects the fact that the global economic growth and development agenda, which causes so much ecological harm, continues to trump ecological values.

These twin (interrelated) realities create the prospect of a grim future. There are, however, some bright lights. In the political/legal context, the inadequacies of our governance systems are becoming increasingly clear and many more commentators are forthright in their criticism and repudiation. Critiques now abound – from those that focus on the ethical and normative limitations of legal principles to those that question the doctrines upon which they are based. Others point out more fundamental problems such as the absence of a *grundnorm* that articulates a moral and legal imperative to guide and transform the law in a similar manner to respect for human dignity (in the case of human rights) (Kim & Bosselmann 2013; Bosselmann, Chapter 4). These critiques are assisted by a more sophisticated understanding of biophysical systems and are part of an emerging human consciousness or awareness of the human-nature relationship and our responsibility for collective well-being. More generally, in the last 50 years, a myriad of social movements have emerged, which, to varying degrees, pose significant challenges (moral, political, social and economic) to the status quo in the combined pursuit of ecological and social justice.

It is not the purpose of this chapter to traverse these critiques and social movements but rather to suggest that the ground is now becoming more fertile for pursuing a bold strategy of 'constructive utopianism'. This term is borrowed from Thomas Mann, who used it to distinguish between 'escapist' or 'blasphemous' utopianism and describe efforts to prepare the way for a 'universal, renovating law' that is consistent with reality and truth (Mann Borgese 1999a). Constructive utopianism describes a strategy to bridge the growing abyss between the emerging reality and truth of destructive human impact on the ES, and our tendency to cling to past forms of political and legal organization that are inadequate and increasingly repudiated. This chapter focuses on one aspect of such a strategy – the advancement of an ethical and legal concept for governance of human activity as it impacts upon the ES, leaving other chapters to focus on other critical aspects of protecting and restoring the SOS. Its central argument is that the common heritage of mankind (CHM) is possessed of certain fundamental characteristics that make it uniquely suited to this critical governance task.

This chapter begins with a short overview of the history of CHM in the context of oceans governance. This is used to help highlight its key elements. It then addresses some of the central controversies that have inhibited its use, together with aspects that need further refinement. This legal discussion is then complemented by a short review of some key themes from the modern commons discourse. This will assist in gaining an understanding of the potential transformative power of the common heritage concept. The commons discourse creates an important connection between a broader cultural, social and political perception or awareness of the ES as a 'commons' and the qualities of commons-based governance. Commons-based governance differs in many respects from the traditional global governance that relies upon nation-states and international organizations.

Before beginning, a word on terminology is needed. In legal literature, the common heritage concept often uses the word 'mankind' despite the fact that a more appropriate word would now be 'humankind' or 'humanity'. Furthermore, it should be noted that CHM, despite the use of 'mankind' or 'humanity', is not inherently an anthropocentric concept. As I have argued elsewhere, it would be more appropriately referred to as the common heritage *of life* (Taylor 1998). However, for the purposes of this chapter, 'common heritage of mankind' and its abbreviation, 'CHM' have been used to avoid any confusion between this text and the legal literature referred to.

2. History of CHM in Context of Oceans Governance

The CHM principle has a long history as a legal concept. In a treaty context, it was first used in the 1967 Outer Space Treaty and then again in the 1979 Moon Treaty. However, one of its most important (and infamous) uses was in the development of an international oceans governance regime that culminated in the 1982 Law of the Sea Convention (LOS).

In 1967, Arvid Pardo (a Maltese diplomat and international lawyer) stood before the UN and argued that the seabed and ocean floor, beyond the limits of national jurisdiction, should be considered the common heritage of mankind. As such, it should be subject to an international management regime for its use and long-term environmental protection.

Pardo's concern was that continued unmanaged use of the world's oceans would become a serious threat to international peace and security due to the environmental impact of new technologies, the militarization of the seafloor and expanding state claims to jurisdiction over large parts of the oceans. He was also deeply concerned about the connection with growing economic and social disparity. Developed states had a clear economic and technological advantage in claiming and exploiting the ocean's resources, adding to existing inequalities and threatening peace and security. His vision was that any future mining on the ocean's seabed be fully internationalized, with revenue providing an independent revenue source for the UN and a source of wealth for developing states (Pardo, 1967).

This innovative proposal led to the adoption of the 1970 UN Declaration of Principles Governing the Seabed (setting out the legal principles needed to implement the CHM) and created the necessary international momentum for the negotiation of LOS. This was (and is) no ordinary legal convention. It was intended to be a 'constitution for the oceans', setting out a comprehensive and universal legal order agreed to by consensus (Beesley 2004; Tuerk 2010).

Part XI of LOS is key to the legal implementation of CHM. It defines the 'Area' as the 'seabed and ocean floor, and the subsoil thereof, beyond the limits of national jurisdiction'. The Area and its resources (e.g., minerals) are the CHM, leaving other parts of the ocean system to be governed by other legal principles (Article 136). No claim or exercise of sovereignty or sovereign rights over any part of the Area (or its resources) or appropriation by any state, natural or juridical person, shall be recognized (Article 137). All rights to the Area's resources are vested in 'mankind', with the International Seabed Authority (ISA) established to act on behalf of (and for the benefit of) mankind (Article 140). The ISA must ensure the equitable sharing of benefits arising from activities (e.g., economic and technological benefits from mining) conducted in the Area, taking into particular account the needs and interests of developing states and others. Key tasks include promoting marine scientific research, transferring technology to developing states, and protecting the environment from harm – the latter task being one of the ISA's main functions (Articles 143-145). The state parties are all members of the ISA and are regarded as having to act through it. The enterprise was created to carry out operational activities in the Area (Articles 158, 166, 170).

The combined effect of these articles was to create a unique commons management regime, the main elements of which are explained in more detail below. However, under LOS, this regime only applied to a small part of the whole ocean environment, namely the 'Area', that is, the deep seabed, beyond the limits of national jurisdiction and its mineral resources. In short, it did not apply CHM to the whole ocean environment as an integrated fluid global ecological system. Despite its limited scope, the CHM regime in Part XI proved so controversial that the United States initially refused to sign LOS due to a difference of opinion on the use of the Area and its resources to benefit mankind as a whole (Beesley 2004). Developing states argued that the only way to ensure equitable benefit sharing, taking into account their needs, was via a global entity with exclusive mineral exploitation rights. Some developed states viewed this as a form of distributive justice that was hostile to commercial investment and contrary to market-oriented approaches (Tuerk 2010). LOS eventually came into force 12 years later, following the 1994 Implementation Agreement that substantially reduced the distributive justice elements of the mining regime in favour of greater protection of commercial exploitation interests (Tuerk 2010; Anand 1997).

By the end of negotiations in 1982, Pardo expressed grave disappointment in what had been achieved (Mann Borgese 2000b). A combination of political and economic factors greatly restricted the scope of CHM to mineral resources on the deep seabed. While the LOS history proved to be divisive and disappointing, as will be discussed below, it was not a failure for CHM but rather an important beginning. Its specific recognition within LOS, together with other considerations, contributes to its ongoing evolution and recognition beyond the history of LOS (from 1970–1994).

3. Key Elements of a CHM Regime

What does it mean to declare a space or resources to be CHM in international law? There is no concise and fully agreed-upon definition of CHM. Its elements depend on the space/resources to which it is applied and the details of the regime applying it. However, there is ample legal commentary supporting the following (Baslar 1997; Wolfrum 2008; Tuerk 2010; Birnie 2009):

- the space/resources are part of the international common heritage (patrimony) and therefore *belong to all humanity in common*. This means they cannot be owned, enclosed or disposed of (i.e., appropriated) by any state/s or other entity. As a commons they can be used, but not owned, either as private or common property or via the claim of sovereign rights;

- the use of the common heritage shall be carried out in accordance with a system of cooperative management for the benefit of all humanity (common good). This has been interpreted as creating a type of 'trust' relationship, with states acting as trustees for the benefit of all humanity (i.e., for the common good, not for the exclusive benefit of states/private entities), including future generations, taking into account the particular needs and interests of developing states (inter and intra-generational equity);
- there shall be active and equitable sharing of benefits derived from the use of the CHM;
- it shall be reserved for peaceful purposes; and
- it shall be transmitted to future generations in a substantially unimpaired condition (requiring protection of ecological integrity).

Taken together, the significant contribution of CHM (in the oceans context) was that it was specifically intended to overcome the problems associated other legal regimes: extending claims of state sovereignty, common property and freedom of the high seas. Sovereignty and common property both imply legal rights of use and abuse (*jus utendi et abutendi*). Freedom of the high seas implies an open-access (or first-in, first-served) regime, according to which all are free to degrade and exploit (Tuerk 2010). These legal regimes serve the rights and interests of only a few members of the international community in a manner that is inconsistent with "the ever-more urgent need for cooperation in addressing world problems, and for environmental sensitivity and sustainable cooperative development of world resources" (Pardo 1993, 96).

CHM replaces these traditional approaches of international law with a new conceptual option, based on a duty or responsibility to share a commons for the benefit of all (not just states). This is a very different and more equitable legal approach intended to designate an entity as a global commons (and therefore legal object), subject to an international trusteeship regime for its long-term use and protection. CHM has been described as "one of the most developed applications of trusteeship or fiduciary relationship in an environmental context" (Birnie 2009, 198). It has also been described as the second-most revolutionary concept in international law, the first being the UN Charter's limits on the right of states to wage war (Scovazzi 2015).

The potential contained within the key elements of CHM has ensured that it remains central to the efforts of international environmental lawyers to advance legal development.

Pardo summed up the essence of the CHM concept in these words:

Traditionally, international law has been essentially concerned with the regulation of relations between states. In ocean space, however, the time has come to recognize as a basic principle of international law the overriding common interest of mankind in the preservation of the quality of the marine environment and in the rational and equitable development of resources lying beyond national jurisdiction. *This does not imply disregard of the interest of individual states, but rather the recognition of the fact that in the long term these interests can be protected only within the framework of a stable international regime of close co-operation between states."* (Pardo 1975,176-emphasis added)

While Pardo had the foresight to conceive of the oceans as a shared commons and to develop a commons-based management regime based on the CHM concept, as will be seen below the same logic now applies to the ES.

4. CHM – A Moral Concept

The CHM is much more than a legal principle; it is also an ancient moral or ethical concept. Pardo focused on its legal articulation and implementation but others, including Elisabeth Mann Borgese and Father Peter Serracino Inglott, traced and developed its ethical foundations (Taylor and Stroud 2013; Taylor 1998). The historical origins and equivalents of the concept can be traced to Islamic law, African customary law and Asian non-theist traditions, including pre-Christian Roman law (Mann Borgese 2002).

In essence, CHM embraces a moral force that unifies humanity and is capable of generating an integrated "view of ourselves in our environment that is both new and old and that departs from uniquely Eurocentric, Western tradition and attempts to blend Western scientific values with Eastern philosophical values" (Mann Borgese 1986, 131). At its core is the notion of sustaining the basis or foundations of life, as a precious gift of inheritance (patrimony), for the benefit of all. It expresses concern and responsibility for the 'other' that encompasses both human interactions (between present and future generations) *and* the human-nature relationship. This includes elements of social equity in recognition of the interdependence between ecological degradation and social inequity. However, at its core is *collective human responsibility* for the ecological commons over the 'rights' of some to its resources. Mann Borgese describes CHM, in the context of LOS, as institutionalizing a 'philosophy of nature' (Mann Borgese 1986, 132).

An understanding of the moral foundations of CHM is critical for a number of reasons. First, as Noyes points out, this is important to its acceptance (Noyes 2012). Second, international legal principles can be vague because of the legal processes by which they develop, leaving their content and interpretation vulnerable to intentional (and unintentional) distortion over time. This can be mitigated, to some degree, by a clearer understanding of their ethical foundations. There is a growing acceptance that this "turn to [the relevance of] ethics" is a legitimate part of legal process and is (in fact) necessary to counter the rigidity of legal positivism (Peters 2014, 548). Third, this deeper appreciation of CHM is helpful to understanding the potential scope of its application, far beyond the narrow context of LOS (and other treaties). In 1993, Pardo commented that due to the work of a number of scholars, CHM is now mentioned in connection with all areas beyond the limits of national jurisdiction, including Antarctica, the moon and outer space. Furthermore, some writers consider that CHM should "form the basis of international law on [other] matters concerning humanity as a whole, such as the environment, climate, technology and food resources" (Pardo 1993, 68). As Pardo noted, these proposals suggest that the CHM concept is useful in "organizing new forms of international cooperation in matters that are not directly related to specific areas of the Earth...[including] climate and the environment" (Pardo 1989, 9–10). Recent research on the application of CHM in legal literature identifies its use (by academics) in the contexts of outer space, climate, biodiversity, the human genome, shared water resources, and marine living resources (Taylor and Stroud 2013).

Indeed, Elisabeth Mann Borgese saw the potential of CHM as a moral and legal concept for governance of a "new world order". She stated many times that the deep oceans, which have been declared the common heritage of mankind, are our "great laboratory" for the making of a new world order (1999b). Her view is partly linked to her understanding of the oceans as a microcosm of the whole biosphere. It is also linked to her long involvement in a Draft World Constitution, written by a group of eminent persons in 1947/48 (Mann Borgese 1999a). The first chapter is a declaration of duties and rights. It states: "The four elements of life – earth, water, air, energy – are the common property of the human race. The management and use of such portions thereof as are vested in or assigned to particular ownership ... *shall be subordinated in each and all cases to the inherent interest of the common good*" (http://www.world beyondborders.org/chicagodraft.htm). As noted in Chapter 4, the primary concern behind this Draft World Constitution was that international social justice and peace could not be achieved without giving priority to the common good.

Despite the frustrations of LOS, Pardo noted: "The ethical and moral implications of the adoption of the common heritage concept, even with regard to an undefined area, are a breath of fresh air in the perhaps excessively traditional international legal literature" (1993, 68).

Of course, the law alone cannot transform the human-nature relationship. Ethically informed legal concepts, like CHM, can only play a supporting role in societal transformation. The limited use of CHM by states since LOS is perhaps an indication, at a societal and political level, that the necessary 'philosophical settings' are not yet in place for CHM's broader acceptance and use (Mann Borgese 1986). This observation in no way precludes them from emerging (Bosselmann 1995).

5. Some Important Controversies

Controversy surrounds many elements of CHM because it challenges the current traditional legal and governance regimes that apply to natural and physical resources and spaces of global significance. Furthermore, the precedent established for oceans governance creates the potential for CHM to be applied more extensively in acknowledgement of the interdependence of planetary processes and the scale of human impact upon them. However, controversy surrounds many elements of CHM because it challenges the current traditional legal and governance regimes that apply to natural and physical resources and spaces of global significance.

To date, the controversies surrounding CHM have inhibited its use (in treaty regimes) beyond LOS. Most significantly, it was rejected as a concept to guide UN treaty regimes on global climate and biological diversity in favour of the weaker and more general 'common concern' concept (Taylor 2012). This section briefly considers some of these controversies, focusing on those most relevant in the context of ES and the management of the SOS. This helps us to distinguish between what is a core element of the principle of CHM and what is an incident of its use in the particular context of LOS. It also helps us identify those aspects of CHM that require further development or refinement.

The territorial obsession: As noted above, a significant limitation of the LOS regime was that CHM only applied to a small part of the oceans (the deep seabed and its resources outside national jurisdiction). As a result, it was applied in isolation from the sea column and space above, excluded marine living resources, and did not apply to the ocean space and resources *within* national jurisdiction. Thus, CHM did not apply to the entire ocean environment as a complex and interconnected ecological whole. This created an ecological nonsense that has left much of the oceans vulnerable to traditional notions of state sovereignty, common property and freedom of the high seas. Two current issues of oceans governance are illustrative. First, the exclusion of marine living resources from the CHM has resulted in lengthy UN negotiations. There is currently no agreement on an international regime for marine living resources beyond the limits of national jurisdiction. They therefore remain vulnerable to exploitation via the open-access approach of 'freedom of the high seas'. Second, remaining uncertainty about the outer limits of the continental shelf has allowed states to extend their claims to sovereign rights, resulting in a gradual encroachment upon the size of the Area. There is no international jurisdiction for any state or entity to stop this incremental encroachment on the CHM (Hafner 2011; Treves 2011; Franckx 2010).

The historic use of CHM by LOS is perpetuated in legal discussion. As a result, CHM is commonly used to distinguish areas under national jurisdiction (or control) from those that are common spaces (i.e., *beyond* national jurisdiction) with its use limited to common spaces. This application of CHM is largely consistent with traditional international law because it does not interfere with state sovereignty (i.e., the unilateral right of states to make decisions for their own benefit) as exercised both *within* a state's territory and areas under national jurisdiction.

However, this traditional legal approach fails to deal with a growing range of possible non-spatial applications of the CHM. These include common resources (both tangible and intangible, natural or cultural) such as cultural heritage, genetic resources (including the human genome) and digital domains, and the so-called 'global commons', being components of the Earth's ecological system such as the global atmosphere, biological diversity and the oceans. What all these possible manifestations of the CHM share is that they are inherently of vital importance to all life, including humanity. Therefore they need to be shared and co-operatively governed (i.e., protected and restored) in a manner that transcends the territorial obsession of states (and its legal corollary of state sovereignty) and has as its primary objective responsibility for the common good of all, including future generations.

The ES and planetary boundaries, around which this book centres, together with the identification and measuring of an SOS, take these non-spatial manifestations of the CHM an important step further. This work helps us visualize and conceptualize ecological processes as integrated components of the ES – an integrated (yet complex) whole. This has the potential to help us move beyond the current fragmented approach of governance and law, which deals with key planetary processes as separate parts (e.g., climate system, biological diversity, oceans and soils) or uses indeterminate labels (such as the 'global environment') and creates different legal regimes based upon political boundaries. As explained in more detail in other chapters, this conceptualization of the ES, as an integrated whole, would enable us to identify it as the object of a legal regime.

However, given the past legal use of CHM, the question is: does the territorial obsession of international law prevent the ES being recognized as the CHM? A proper understanding of the history of CHM (beyond LOS) would suggest that it does not.

Arvid Pardo was aware of the problems associated with the limited application of CHM under LOS. He sought to avoid these by proposing a draft ocean space treaty in 1971 that "attempted to show how the common heritage concept could be implemented in the marine environment as a whole" (1993, 67). Accordingly, CHM would apply without regard to the pre-existing jurisdictional status of any particular area. However, CHM would be applied in a different way in respect of areas *within national jurisdiction*. States would retain the legal power to control and regulate but this sovereign authority would be subject to limitations specifically designed to protect the interests of all humanity. This was an attempt to reject *unfettered* state sovereignty (Tuerk 2010) or, as Pardo put it, "[a] new legal order had to be created in the oceans based on a new principle which constrained both sovereignty and freedom in the common interest" (1992).

Two very important points follow from this.

First, CHM is an attempt to transform state sovereignty as exercised both *internally and externally* in respect of shared ecological systems. As mentioned above, the trusteeship aspects of CHM cast nations as trustees with fiduciary obligations or responsibilities. Applied to shared ecological systems, this would require states to protect and restore ecological systems and manage their use for the benefit of all. Thus, CHM attempts to redefine state sovereignty rather than conflict with it. However, for this aspect of CHM to be truly transformative, it must be implemented in a way that requires and enforces a quality of cooperation that goes well beyond traditional notions of international cooperation, which continue (implicitly and explicitly) to prioritize national interests. There is a fundamental need for transparent, participatory and trusted processes for creating coordinating and enforceable international standards that demand the "commitment of every state [to actively] engage in the promotion and protection of environmental quality as an essential public good" (Francioni 2012, 456). This will require a critical rethink of state sovereignty in terms of the authority to make and enforce the law and use natural resources, wherever they are. Most significantly, it will require ecological values to take priority over current exploitative paradigms of economic growth and development together with a radical rethink about social justice and control of supranational corporate interests. Anything less will fail to unseat the status quo of our current state-centric world.

Second, it is often argued that CHM cannot apply to spaces and common resources *within* a state's national jurisdiction because this would be contrary to the LOS principle of *non-appropriation*. While this principle was critical to protect what remained of the high seas from ongoing sovereign claims and privatization, it is not a requirement of CHM in all circumstances. This is clear from Pardo's application of CHM to the entire ocean environment (see above). It is also clear from his suggestion that the content of CHM should be applied pragmatically in relation to international needs. In his view, 'world resources' should not be conceived of in a static sense (Mann Borgese 2000, xxvii).

Kiss approaches the issue of *non-appropriation* by pointing out that the common heritage concept is used successfully in respect of the world's valued cultural and natural heritage by a number of international conventions, including the 1972 Convention for the Protection of the World's Cultural and Natural Heritage. This heritage is often within the jurisdiction of one state and therefore appropriated. Indeed, much is in private ownership. However, in these circumstances, the core of CHM is that the heritage must be transmitted from present to future generations. Therefore, the essential criterion of CHM is responsible non-destructive uses and good management in the interests of all humanity – "in essence a trust" (Kiss, p.433). CHM is, therefore, a concept that is much more flexible in its application than is often understood. Kiss uses the history of CHM in the natural and cultural heritage context to conclude that there is now a strong sense that a common heritage exists within the territory of states, "even if its implications have not been clearly established" (Kiss, p.435 and Sand 2014).

As the PB work so aptly illustrates, what occurs within every state's territory has, over time and space, a cumulative impact on shared planetary processes and the ES as a whole. The concept of the SOS helps us transcend the territorial obsession of international law by demonstrating that territorial distinctions are now obsolete. Any appeals to national interests and sovereignty, as a defence against stringent ecological commitments, are potentially dangerous and misguided in an interdependent (life-support) system. Furthermore, in the long term, such appeals may undermine the welfare of national populations and be revealed as contrary to national interests. Nevertheless, the ability of CHM to reach inside a nation's jurisdiction – and challenge these perceptions – is simultaneously one of its most revolutionary and controversial aspects.

Had Pardo's 1971 proposal for an ocean space treaty succeeded, it would have resulted in a significant *re*claiming of the oceans as an interdependent global commons. Despite the failure of this proposal, the use of CHM in the 1970 Declaration and in LOS has opened two small cracks "in the massive wall of opposition to international acceptance of the common heritage concept as a basic principle of international law" (Pardo 1993, 69).

The question of 'property': The relationship between CHM and property concepts is highly significant and related to the issue of territoriality discussed above. CHM has (on occasion) been misconstrued or misunderstood as a 'common property' concept or, in the case of the deep seabed, as internationalizing (even socializing) the ownership of natural resources. In the first case, this has led to undue emphasis on its potential use as a means to acquire intellectual property rights over genetic resources (in the case of biological diversity); in the latter case, to undue emphasis on equitable utilization and benefit-sharing from resource exploitation. In short, states have focused on the supposed 'property' elements of CHM for their own purposes and consistent with their own economic paradigms. These interpretations have left CHM vulnerable to the criticism that it is of limited use when the priority needs to be respectful treatment of ecological systems, long-term protection and restoration and equitable use.

What has been forgotten (or conveniently overlooked) is that CHM was intended as a *non*-property concept. In 1970, Arvid Pardo explained that the word 'property' (in the case of CHM) was deliberately avoided because it implies the legal rights of use and misuse (*jus utendi et abutendi*). "Property implies and gives excessive emphasis to just one aspect: resource exploitation and benefit therefrom" (Mann Borgese 2000, xxvii). The consequences of CHM as a non-property concept are highly significant (i.e., belonging to all but owned by none).

First, it prevents any form of appropriation (or enclosure) of a commons either by states or private entities (e.g., corporations). This can range from territorialisation to privatization, to creeping 'green jurisdiction' in the name of environmental conservation (Sand 2007, 529).

If the CHM belongs to all humanity, it can be used for the benefit of all but owned by none.

Second, it puts emphasis on careful common management to facilitate long-term use by all humanity (not exclusively states or corporations). Economic value from use can be an element but value is primarily expressed in non-monetary terms, that is, in a shared and relational context, in which use is morally, socially and ecologically bound. In other words, the overriding priority is long-term shared use value for all, not short-term exchange value for a few. Viewed in this way, the concept of 'benefit sharing' can be understood in terms of a wide range of values inherent in healthy ecological systems (see discussion below).

Third, it does not conflict with state sovereignty in respect of shared spaces and ecological systems *within* a state's national jurisdiction. States would still have the legal authority to control and regulate but this would be subject to careful limitations designed to protect the *overriding* interests of all. As previously noted, this casts states in the role of trustees, with fiduciary obligations to protect and enhance ecological systems for the common good of all. Many ideas exist for articulating a changing role for the state (internally and externally), including guardianship, public trust doctrine, stewardship, custodianship, and the eco-constitutional state (Bosselmann 2015). CHM is generally considered to take a trusteeship approach. In the view of Peter Sand, sovereignty 'bounded' in this way has the potential to enhance the democratic legitimacy of the nation-state rather than undermine it (2004, 58–59).

Fourth, as a non-property concept, CHM is capable of articulating an important distinction that has significant consequences in both theory and practice. It embraces a positive vision of ecological systems belonging to *everyone*, giving rise to collective responsibilities as well as use rights. This contrasts with a rather negative vision of ecological systems as belonging to *no one* and therefore left vulnerable to the tragedy of the commons or hidden agendas to enclose or propertize.

Benefit sharing: As noted above, the use of CHM in LOS entailed a complex and controversial regime for the equitable sharing of benefits (financial and technological) from the mining of resources. This has opened CHM up to the criticism that it is only a concept for resource exploitation and distribution. This has been linked to weakened international support for CHM (Kiss, p.437–38).

Again, Kiss and others question whether this is a key element of CHM. Once the essential characteristics of CHM are understood – non-destructive use and good management in the interest of all humanity, including future generations – then the term for the benefit of humanity can be "interpreted in a generous way to include aesthetic, cultural and scientific benefits as well as economic revenues" (Kiss, p. 438). Indeed, precedents for these alternative forms of 'benefit'-sharing exist. LOS itself refers to the sharing of scientific knowledge as a benefit for all. Recently, robust environmental protection was acknowledged as being for the benefit of all humanity in the context of mining in the area (ITLOS, Advisory Opinion, 2011). Indeed, environmental protection, as a benefit for humanity (and all life) and an objective of a CHM regime, seems to be one of the least contentious elements of CHM (Wolfrum 2008). LOS also provides that archaeological and historic objects found in the area must be preserved or disposed of for 'the benefit of mankind as a whole' (Article 149). As one commentator notes, uses of a public character (e.g., research and exhibition) are given priority over uses for private interest (e.g., trade and personal gain), which "are given little weight, if any" (Scovazzi 2014).

In the context of the ES, benefit sharing would have to be explicitly stated to prioritize protection and restoration. This could include setting aside ecological systems (or parts thereof) for periods of non-use (Laitos 2012). Any language that opened the door to trade-offs between these imperatives and economic gain or the illusion of 'balancing' must be avoided. However, benefit sharing would also have to be expressed in a manner that adequately and fairly addresses the critical social equity issues integral to human activity and its impact on the ES.

Subject status under international law? The traditional view is that states are the primary subjects of international law. As a result, only states can directly benefit from, acquire obligations under, and enforce international law. While the CHM concept may require states (either themselves or through an international organization) to act as trustees, without subject status for humanity (including future generations) or some representative of humanity as a collective, sovereign states retain the monopoly power to pursue national interests and subjugate the common good.

While some commentaries suggest that CHM creates 'humanity' as a new subject for international law, others reject this idea (Fuse 1998, 95 and Wolfrum 2008, para 28). Pardo seems to have foreseen the need to accept humanity and future generations as a subject (Fuse 1998, 95). In this way CHM creates an important opportunity to put the *demos* into international law, thereby rectifying a significant democratic deficit. However, to fully operationalize this element of CHM, robust institutional structures and mechanisms for participation and representation are required to give a direct and powerful voice for the interests of present and future generations. Unfortunately, this was not achieved by the LOS regime. The ISA (which administers the CHM) is constituted and governed exclusively by states. No opportunity exists for the direct voice of humanity within this regime. Furthermore, the ISA has limited jurisdiction (itself) to protect the area and therefore common rights and interests (Treves 2010). However, in a recent development, the role of the ISA to act in the interests of all humanity (by ensuring adequate environmental protection standards for any mining in the area) was given significant judicial acknowledgement (Advisory Opinion, para 230).

The issue of subject status is implicit in suggestions that the CHM should be institutionalized in the form of a trusteeship council. Malta, for example, proposed that the existing UN Trusteeship Council be transformed to hold the principle of CHM in sacred trust and to "act as the conscience of the United Nations and the guardian of future generations" (Mann Borgese 2000a; de Marco and Bartolo 2013). The idea of a transformed UN Trusteeship Council is considered further in Chapter 11 of this book.

While CHM raises the issue of subject status, the answers must be found within the broader reform of international law and the communitarian values that must emerge to drive this reform (Cassese 2012). In the ecological context, we should not overlook the argument made by those who advocate rights for nature; the implication being that nature itself could/should have subject status under international law.

Enforcement is one (among many) important weakness of the current international environmental law. In general, states avoid binding legal obligations that can be enforced via liability and compliance regimes. Furthermore, the development of *erga omnes* obligations (those of a special character, owed by one state to all other states and to the international community as a whole), together with the necessary legal standing to enforce these obligations, has been very limited. Enforcement is still largely locked within the paradigm of reciprocity, which a state or states may (or may not) elect to enforce. As a consequence, it is likely that little (if any) consideration will be given to the protection of the collective interests of the international community (Francioni 2012, 455). Given this fundamental weakness, enforcement of obligations in respect of the CHM would require something more than what states are currently willing to provide. Institutions with the necessary jurisdiction, together with legal subjects/representatives with adequate legal standing, need to be developed.

A utopian ideal? As described above, the CHM requires cooperation in a manner that (i) transcends territorial obsession, (ii) gives priority to common interests over national self-interests, (iii) discharges responsibility for common interests, and (iv) recognizes that states are not the only legitimate source of authority for determining the content of law and its implementation/enforcement. Given the serious challenges that these elements pose for traditional international law, CHM has been described as a 'utopian ideal'.

This label ('utopian ideal') has often been used to pillory or diminish the potential and status of CHM as a realistic legal and political concept acceptable to states. This tendency could well be part of an effort to frustrate the transformative potential of CHM. On the other hand, the label may be taken as an important reminder about the sources and processes by which international law develops.

The traditional 'positivist' view is that international law comprises only those norms or rules specifically agreed to by states as an exercise of their free consent. This view leaves humanity at the mercy of the national political and economic interests often used as a justification for totally inadequate levels of international cooperation and commitment. The use of these agendas to block and limit climate change commitments is a powerful example of this.

An alternative view is that international law is *also* comprised of fundamental norms or principles intended to harmonize human behaviour with universal ethical concepts and values. In some cases, these norms may have attained social legitimacy and crystalized as legal norms. In other cases, the exact status and quality of these norms will be uncertain. To some degree, this view of international law draws upon natural law theory. However, more recently, prominent international jurists have argued that it is the legitimate role of legal scholars to actively pursue a utopian agenda *if* an appropriate process is followed. Antonio Cassese, for example, explores this process and describes it as *critical positivism* (2011, 258). This involves (in part) an ethical analysis that recognizes the great importance of ethical values and tries to use them to both critique existing law and argue persuasively about what the law 'ought' to be and how to get there (Peters 2013). This is very different from arguing that a legal concept is the law simply because it ought to be so from an ethical standpoint. In the view of Anne Peters, Cassese's critical positivism gives us a strategy to weave humanism into legal reasoning (2013, 552). In the words of Cassese, legal scholars may "suggest ideas and advance solutions without harbouring too many illusions" as the power to resolve the problems of the world community currently remains in the hands of politicians, diplomats and military leaders (2011, 271). Peters characterises Cassese's approach as a programme of *realistic* as opposed to illusionary utopia "and argues that it is emphatically the province of legal scholars" (2013, 552; Cassese 2012).

This was exactly the careful process of legal reasoning followed by Pardo and many others. In a 1993 article, Pardo noted that in a strict (positivist) legal and political sense, CHM had only been adopted with regard to the seabed and its resources. Nevertheless, taking into account its ethical and moral implications, and despite the "pertinacious opposition of many developed countries …, the common heritage concept has *the potential to become a fundamental principle of international law; not because I say so but because in the contemporary world, global co-operation for the common good in the seas and elsewhere must prevail over competition and wasteful use of resources*" (Pardo, p.68, emphasis added).

Alex Kiss takes a similar approach in his 1985 article "The common heritage of mankind: utopia or reality?" He identifies the core of CHM and distinguishes it from some of the non-essential criteria that have created misunderstandings and limited its adoption by states. Noting the ebbs and flows of CHM's acceptance, he argues that it is a materialization of the common interests of the international community. "The central idea is that of a trust which is to be exercised in the common interest of mankind either by international bodies, by groups of states, or by individual states under some form of supervision by the international community …" (Kiss, p. 439).

While the approaches of Pardo and Kiss are consistent with the process of realistic utopianism, they could equally be considered consistent with 'constructive utopianism'. As previously noted, this term was coined by Thomas Mann (father of Elisabeth Mann Borgese) to describe a strategy for bridging the abyss between our tendency to "cling with stupid tenacity to what has been surpassed by time, to what is inadequate and clearly repudiated" and the truth (goals of the spirit) and reality (that which adheres to facts) (Mann Borgese 1999a, 216). If we bring CHM's ethical foundations together with its legal potential, it is clearly a concept that could transform the current Westphalian system of independent self-interested states. It articulates the type of global cooperation, in pursuit of the common good, that is required to protect and restore the planetary processes that comprise the ES and maintain an SOS.

The moral force and legal potential of CHM are, in part, evidenced by its failure to go away. Legal literature continues to elaborate on CHM (Taylor & Stroud 2013) and some international negotiations have kept it on the table despite the reluctance of many other states to use it (Scovazzi 2013).

Thus far, discussion has utilized legal reasoning to advance the argument that CHM has the potential to be a legal concept for guiding management of humanity activity upon the ES. This chapter now turns to consider the modern commons discourse. This discourse is helpful in deepening our understanding of the potential transformative power of the CHM concept. More specifically, it could (at a normative level) contribute to "recouping the original promise of the environmental movement, that is, *the conceptualization and the legal treatment of the natural environment* as a [common good] to be administered in the interest of all and of the generations to come" (Francioni 2012, 455).

6. The Commons and Common*ing*

In recent years there has been a discernable *re*discovery of the importance of the commons (Bollier 2014). The commons has always been a key component of human culture and society, and has remained important for indigenous and communal societies. The rediscovery applies primarily to industrialized societies and is a response to the realization that there are serious limitations (ecological and social) to forms of governance that depend heavily on the market, the state or (when working in unison) the market-state. Commons discourse offers important critiques of these forms of governance in relation to the commons.

First, these governance approaches frequently result in the enclosure of the commons. This process has a long and often violent history that continues via new forms of expropriation, privatization and commercialization of shared resources – often for private gain. It is achieved through a spectrum of exclusive or preferential governance regimes, including the acquisition of sovereign rights, private property rights, exclusive licences, and pollution rights. These modern forms of enclosure are one of the great *un*acknowledged problems of our time.

Second, enclosure is (or results in) dispossession. It is a move away from resources 'belonging' to everyone and being available for the benefit of all to property, ownership and commodification. The former ('belonging' to all) is often informed and upheld by a rich social, cultural and legal context. The latter ('property') creates legal rights and economic priorities, and creates producers, consumers and hierarchies of 'stakeholders'.

Combined, enclosure and dispossession are legal strategies that hide the commons from public view (Mattei 2012).

Modern commons scholarship is diverse and does not limit itself to critique (Ostrom 1990, Bollier & Helfrich 2012). It also engages in developing understanding of what a commons is and how it can be governed in a positive and constituting manner. This work has two important components. It reawakens us to the existence of a commons (those things that are and should remain for the benefit of all) and helps us redevelop a sense of the common good. These are critical aspects of *re*claiming the commons. This is crucial because we can only begin to protect what we see and what we value (perceive) from the pressures of enclosure and dispossession. It also makes us aware that market mechanisms and state regulation are not the only means by which society can manage the human relationship with the ES (Ostrom 1990, Bollier 2014). Further, it reawakens us to the fundamental reality that individual benefit is dependent upon the collective good.

Some key features, drawn from the work of commons scholar David Bollier, are summarized here (Bollier 2014):

- There is no master inventory of what is (or is not) a commons. A commons arises when a community decides to govern or manage a resource in a collective manner, with special regard to the sustainability of the resource and equitable access or use. A commons can be tangible or intangible, natural or cultural resources (including digital domains) and may exist at multiple and interrelated scales – local, regional, national, global.
- A commons is not solely a resource. It is also a paradigm that combines a resource with a defined community and social protocols (social practices, values and norms) to manage a resource. In Linebaugh's opinion, the commons is largely about these social protocols, that is, there is no commons without common*ing* (Bollier 2014). No template exists but key components include collective benefit (while also often providing for individual well-being), responsibility, participation, transparency, accountability, and trusteeship. The success of common*ing* is not guaranteed but is necessary to prevent a slide back into the tragedy of the (open-access) commons (Hardin 1968). In this regard, the work of the late Elinor Ostrom, in identifying several factors critical to the success of governance regimes for common pool resources (CPRs), is highly influential (Ostrom 1990).
- The governance of a commons may embrace economic values but economic values often remain peripheral or are only one

component of a broader range of non-economic values that are often relational in character.

• Contemporary challenges for commons scholarship include finding new legal and institutional forms and social practices for (i) governing ourselves in respect of diverse and complex ecological systems at larger scales (i.e., beyond local and regional to embrace national and global) to ensure their ecological integrity; and (ii) aligning multiple levels of political (and legal) jurisdiction with ecological realities and priorities (Ostrom 1990).

In short, commons scholarship draws upon past experiences of common*ing* with the objective of creating new institutional and legal structures and forms fit for contemporary ecological and social challenges. It places overarching emphasis on providing for collective benefit as a necessary precondition to provide for the individual prosperity of all humanity (present and future). Commons scholarship reminds us that alternative (and potentially transformative) forms of governance and law are possible, which return authority and responsibility to communities of people and do not swing between the poles of private vs public, or result in a slide back to the tragedy of the open-access commons (Mattei 2012). Moreover, commons regimes provide for a diverse range of values beyond dominant economic exchange values. Both the critique and the solutions provided by commons scholarship will be significant for the redesign of governance and law to meet the global ecological decline (Weston and Bollier 2013, Westra 2011).

When the essence of CHM is understood within the context of the commons discourse, it is clearly ideally suited as a guiding legal principle (norm). By conceptualizing the ES as a commons, CHM identifies the ES as a legal object and requires a management regime that is a real alternative to the current tragedy of the open-access commons. It challenges states, as the sole source of authority, to determine the more detailed legal framework necessary to ensure management of PBs for the benefit of all. But it also requires a rethink about states as the sole source of responsibility for respecting and protecting for the benefit of all. Crucially, it requires states to act as environmental trustees, with moral and legal responsibility to act in the interests of all humanity (including their own citizens and future generations) both within and outside state jurisdiction and according to global (coordinating) standards that prioritize ecological protection and restoration.

In summary, CHM provides a guiding legal principle for a new form of commons-based governance. However, due to its history in treaty negotiations, many key elements will require careful elaboration and refinement. For example, it is not inherently an anthropocentric concept despite its terminology (Taylor 1998) and its moral underpinnings still require deeper investigation and further articulation (Taylor 2013). The non-property and non-territorial aspects are still not adequately understood (Baslar 1997). These aspects of CHM are critical to prevent backsliding into a property concept and unintentional (or intentional) misinterpretation. Effective means of participation and representation for beneficiaries (present and future) and mechanisms to hold states accountable must also be developed. To be meaningful, this will require significant advances in current law on 'subject status'. Closer consideration of the concept of benefit will assist in resolving the tensions between states and utilitarian and non-utilitarian values. Dealing with the role of supranational corporations and institutional arrangements will require innovative thinking. Social equity must be better understood as an integral element. These significant issues aside, CHM is unique in its ability to create a sense of moral solidarity. It appeals to the human communitarian desire to care for, share and use what is common to all. For these reasons, CHM is linked to a renewed interest in cosmopolitanism, global constitutionalism and global ecological citizenship in addition to the commons discourse.

7. Conclusion

This chapter has argued that CHM is a unique concept with considerable potential. However, it requires us to be willing to organize ourselves and act in a fundamentally different manner, according to a values framework that places our shared planetary processes at the very centre of concern. Building this willingness will require the convergence of multiple social and cultural movements acting consistently to achieve the change they advocate. But the task is much greater than this. The concept of the ES creates a basis for transforming our perception of reality and our ability to conceive of new forms of governance. To deliver on this transformation, we must also create a global polity capable of working for the global collective benefit.

If we (humanity) fail in our endeavours, there is a real risk that unilateral systems, based on state and corporate self-interest, will act to further enclose and propertize more and more of the commons (Hafner 2011). Our task is to advance strategies of constructive (or realistic) utopianism and remain alert to regressive trends. As Arvid Pardo reminded us: "It will be up to all of us to frustrate [designs to thwart CHM] and to open deeper and wider cracks in traditional international law until, in the eternal cycle, a new global order emerges from the ruins of the old, better to serve all humanity" (1993, 69).

Arvid Pardo and Elisabeth Mann Borgese were visionaries. They saw CHM as an ethical and legal concept capable of transforming global governance and solving the interrelated problems of ecological degradation, social inequality and conflict in an interdependent world. This new order will not be easy to achieve. "It will require profound changes in the ways we deal with each other and with nature." However, CHM is the seed. "Like life itself, the new order started in the deep ocean, which has been declared to be the 'common heritage of mankind' and is expanding over the seas and ocean to coastal zones, until it embraces the whole biosphere in 'the majesty of the oceanic circle'" (Mann Borgese 2000a,1).

References

Anand, R.P. (1997). The Common Heritage of Mankind: Mutilation of an Ideal. *The Indian Journal of International Law*, *37*(1), 1–18.

Baslar, K. (1997). *The Concept of the Common Heritage of Mankind in International Law*. The Hague: Kluwer Law International.

Beesley, A. (2004). Grotius and the New Law. In A. Chircop and M. McConnell (Eds.) *Ocean Yearbook*, Vol 18, 98–116.

Birnie, B. et al (Eds.) (2009). *International Law and the Environment*. Oxford, UK: Oxford University Press.

Bollier, D. (2014). *Think Like a Commoner: A Short Introduction to the Life of the Commons*. British Columbia: New Society Publishers.

Bollier, D. & Helfrich, S. (2012) (Eds). *The Wealth of the Commons: A World Beyond Market & State*. Florence, MA: Levellers Press.

Bosselmann, K. (1995). *When Two Worlds Collide*. New Zealand: RSVP Press.

—. (2015). *Earth Governance: Trusteeship for the Global Commons*. Cheltenham: Edward Elgar.

Bosselmann, K., & Taylor, P. (Eds) (forthcoming 2016). *Ecological Approaches to Environmental Law*. Cheltenham: Edward Elgar.

Cassese, A. (Ed.) (2011). *Five Masters of International Law: Conversations with R-J Dupuy, E Jimenez de Arechaga, R Jennings, L Henkin and O Schachter*. Oxford: Hart Publishing.

—. (Ed.) (2012). *Realizing Utopia: The Future of International Law*. Oxford: Oxford University Press.

Francioni, F. (2012). Realism, Utopia, and the Future of International Environmental Law. In A. Cassese (Ed.), *Realizing Utopia: The Future of International Law* (pp. 442–460). Oxford: Oxford University Press.

—. (2014). International Common Goods: An Epilogue. In A. F. Vrdoljak & F. Lenzerini (Eds.), *International Law for Common Goods: Normative Perspectives on Human Rights, Culture and Nature* (pp. 443–448). Oxford: Hart Publishing.

Franckx, E. (2010). The International Seabed Authority and the Common Heritage of Mankind: The Need for States to Establish the Outer Limits of their Continental Shelf. *The International Journal of Marine and Coastal Law, 25*, 543–567.

Fuse, T. (1998). Common Heritage of Mankind in the 21st Century. In R. Rajagopalan (Ed.), *Proceedings of Pacem in Maribus XXV* (pp.93–105). Malta: International Oceans Institute, Foundation of International Studies Valletta.

Hardin, G. (1968). The Tragedy of the Commons. *Science, 162(3859)*, 1243–1248. doi: 10.1126/science.162.3859.1243.

International Programme on the State of the Oceans. *State of the Oceans Report 2013*. Retrieved from http://www.stateoftheocean.org/research.cfm.

Hafner, G. (2011). The Division of the Commons? The Myth of the Commons: Divide or Perish. In H. Hestermeyer (et al) (Eds.), *Law of the Sea in Dialogue* (pp.91–111). Berlin: Springer.

Kiss, A. (1985). The Common Heritage of Mankind: Utopia or Reality? *International Journal, 40(3)*, Law in the International Community (Summer, 1985), (pp. 423–441).

Kim, R.E. and Bosselmann, K. (2013). International Environmental Law in the Anthropocene: Towards a Purposive System of Multilateral Environmental Agreements. *Transnational Environmental Law, 2(02)*, 285–309.

Laitos, J.G. (2012). *The Right of Nonuse*. New York: Oxford University Press.

Mann Borgese, E. (1986). *The Future of the Oceans: A Report to the Club of Rome*. Montreal: Harvest House.

—. (1999a). The Years of my Life (The Nexus Lecture). Republished in H. Pils & K Kuehn (Eds.), *Elisabeth Mann Borgese und das Drama der Meere* (2012) (p.206–226). Munich: Lighthouse Foundation.

—. (1999b). *The Oceanic Circle: Governing the Seas as a Global Resource*. Report to the Club of Rome. Tokyo: UN University Press.

—. (2000a). The Oceanic Circle. In Mann Borgese et al. (Eds.), *Ocean Yearbook* (14th ed.), (pp. 1-15).

—. (2000b). Arvid Pardo (1914–1999): In Memoriam, Mann Borgese et al. (Eds.), *Ocean Yearbook* (14th ed), pp. xix–xxxviii.

—. (2002). The Common Heritage of Mankind: From Non-living to Living Resources and Beyond. In N. Ando (et al) (Eds.), *Liber Amicorum Judge Shigeru Oda* (pp.1313–1334). Netherlands: Kluwer International Law.

De Marco, G. and Bartolo, M. (1997). *A Second Generation United Nations: For Peace and Freedom in the 21ˢᵗ Century*. Oxon: Routledge.

Mattei, U. (2012). First Thoughts for a Phenomenology of the Commons. In Bollier, D. and Helfrich, S. (Eds), *The Wealth of the Commons: A World Beyond Market & State* (pp.37– 44). Florence, MA: Levellers Press.

Noyes, J.E. (2011). The Common Heritage of Mankind: Past, Present, and Future. *Denver Journal of International Law & Policy* 447–471.

Ostrom, E. (1990). *Governing the Commons: The Evolution of Institutions for Collective Action*. Cambridge: Cambridge University Press.

Pardo, A. (1967). Address to the 22nd Session of the General Assembly of the United Nations, UN GAOR, 22ₙ𝒹 sess., UN Doc. A/6695 (18 August, 1967).

—. (1975). *The Common Heritage; Selected Papers on Oceans and World Order 1967-1974*. Valletta: Malta University Press.

—. (1989). Speech: 27 June, 1989, Pacem in Maribus-XVII (unpublished).

—. (1992). From Mare Liberum to the Common Heritage of Mankind. Speech delivered to the Maritime Museum. Malta: (unpublished).

—. (1993). The Origins of the 1976 Malta Initiative. *International Insights, 9(2),* 65–69.

Peters, A. (2013). Realizing Utopia as a Scholarly Endeavour. *The European Journal of International Law, 24(2),* 533–552.

Prieur, M. & Garver, G. (2012). Non-regression in Environmental Protection: A New Tool for Implementing the Rio Principles. *Future Perfect, Rio+20* (pp.30–31). UK: Tudor Rose Pub.

Rockström, J. (et al) (2009). Planetary Boundaries: Exploring the Safe Operating Space for Humanity. *Ecology and Society, 14*(2), 32. Retrieved from http://www.ecologyandsociety.org/vol14/iss2/art32/

Sand, P. H. (2004). Sovereignty Bounded: Public Trusteeship for Common Pool Resources? *Global Environmental Politics, 4,* 47–71.

—. (2007). Public Trusteeship for the Oceans. In T. M. Ndiaye & R. Wolfrum (Eds.), *Law of the Sea, Environmental Law and Settlement of Disputes* (pp.521–544). Leiden, Netherlands: Koninklijke Brill.

—. (2014). The Concept of Public Trusteeship in the Transboundary Governance of Biodiversity. In Kotze, L. and Marauhn (Eds.), *Transboundary Governance of Biodiversity* (pp.34–64). Leiden: Koninklijke Brill NV.

Scovazzi, T. (2013). The Exploitation of Genetic Resources in Areas beyond National Jurisdiction. In L. Westra (et al) (Eds.), *Confronting Ecological Collapse: Ecological Integrity for Law, Policy and Human Rights* (pp. 47–64). New York: Routledge.

—. (2014). Underwater Cultural Heritage as an International Common Good. In A. F. Vrdoljak & F. Lenzerini (Eds.), *International Law for Common Goods: Normative Perspectives on Human Rights, Culture and Nature* (pp. 175–230). Oxford: Hart Publishing.

—. (2015). Common Heritage of Mankind: A Bibliography of Legal Writings. *The International Journal of Marine and Coastal Law*, 30(2), 391–394.

Serrao-Neumann, S. (2014). Emerging Planetary Boundaries and the Sustainability Perspective. In W. Steele (et al) (Eds.), *Planning across Borders in a Climate of Change* (pp.177–188). London: Routledge.

Taylor, P.E. (1998). *An Ecological Approach to International Law: The Challenge of Climate Change*. London: Routledge.

—. (2012). The Common Heritage Principle and Public Health: Honouring Our Legacy. In Westra (et al) (Eds.), *Human Health and Ecological Integrity: Ethics, Law and Human Rights* (pp.41–55). London: Routledge.

—. (2013). The Future of the Common Heritage of Mankind: Intersections with Public Trust Doctrine. In Westra, L. (Eds.), *Confronting Ecological Collapse: Ecological Integrity for Law, Policy and Human Rights* (pp. 32–40). London: Routledge.

Taylor, P.E. & Stroud, L. (2013). *Common Heritage of Mankind – A Bibliography of Legal Writing*. Malta: Foundation de Malte.

Taylor, P.E. (2014). The Earth Charter, the Commons and the Common Heritage of Mankind Principle. In Westra, L. and Vilela, M. (Eds.), *The Earth Charter, Ecological Integrity and Social Movements* (pp.12–23). London: Routledge.

Treves, T. (2011). Judicial Action for the Common Heritage. In H. Hestermeyer (et al) (Eds.), *Law of the Sea in Dialogue* (pp.113–133). Berlin: Springer.

Tuerk, H. (2010). The Idea of Common Heritage of Mankind. In Gutiérrez, M. (Ed.), *Serving the Rule of International Maritime Law* (pp.157–175). Oxfordshire, UK: Routledge.

Westerlund, S. (2008). Theory for Sustainable Development: Towards or Against? In Bugge, H.C. & Voigt, C. (Eds.), *Sustainable Development in International and National Law* (pp.49–66). Netherlands: Europa Law Pub.

Weston, B. H. & Bollier, D. (2013). *Green Governance: Ecological Survival, Human Rights and the Law of the Commons.* UK: Cambridge University Press.

Westra, L. (2011). *Human Rights: The "Commons" and the Collective.* Vancouver, BC: University of British Columbia Press.

Wolfrum, R. (2008). Common Heritage of Mankind. *Max Planck Encyclopedia of Public International Law.* Retrieved from http://www.mpepil.com.

Zalasiewicz, J., Williams, M., Haywood, A. & Ellis, M. (2011). *The Anthropocene: A New Epoch of Geological Time?* Phil. Trans. R. Soc. A, 369. doi: 10.1098/rsta.2010.0339.

International Documents

Seabed Disputes Chamber of the International Tribunal for the Law of the Sea, Responsibilities and Obligations of States Sponsoring Persons and Entities with Respect to Activities in the Area, Advisory Opinion (Feb. 1, 2011).

United Nations Convention on the Law of the Sea (concluded 10 December, 1982, entered into force 16 November, 1994) 1833 UNTS 397.

Agreement Governing the Activities of States on the Moon and Other Celestial Bodies (adopted 5 December, 1979, entered into force 11 July, 1984) 1363 UNTS 3.

Convention for the Protection of the World Cultural and Natural Heritage (adopted 16 November, 1972, entered into force 17 December, 1975) 1037 UNTS 151.

United Nations General Assembly Resolution 2749 (XXV) Declaration of Principles Governing the Seabed and the Ocean Floor, and the Subsoil Thereof, beyond the Limits of National Jurisdiction, UN GAOR, 25th Sess., Supp. No 28, 24 UN Doc. A/8028 (1970).

Treaty on Principles Governing the Activities of States in the Exploration and Use of Outer Space, including the Moon and other Celestial Bodies (signed 27 January, 1967, entered into force 10 October, 1967) 610 UNTS 205.

CHAPTER SEVEN

A NEW OBJECT OF LAW:
ATTEMPT FOR A LEGAL CONSTRUCTION

PAULO MAGALHÃES[1]

Let's not pretend that things will change if we keep doing the same things. A crisis can be a real blessing to any person, to any nation for all crises bring progress. Creativity is born from anguish, just like the day is born from the dark night. It's in crisis that inventiveness is born, as well as discoveries are made and big strategies are created. He who overcomes crisis overcomes himself without getting overcome. He who blames his failure on a crisis neglects his own talent and is more interested in problems than in solutions. Incompetence is the true crisis. The greatest inconvenience of people and nations is the laziness with which they attempt to find the solutions to their problems. There's no challenge without a crisis. Without challenges, life becomes a routine, a slow agony. There's no merit without crisis. It's in the crisis where we can show the very best in us. Without a crisis, any wind becomes a tender touch. To speak about a crisis is to promote it. Not to speak about it is to exalt conformism. Let us work hard instead. Let us stop, once and for all, the menacing crisis that represents the tragedy of not being willing to overcome it.

—Albert Einstein

1. A Theoretical Gap

According to Nietzsche, "There are no facts, only interpretations". This means that knowledge of facts is no substitute for their comprehension.

The exponential increase in the knowledge about the Earth System does not necessarily mean we understand it in all its dimensions,

---

[1] Interdisciplinary Centre of Social Sciences CICS.NOVA - Faculdade de Ciências Sociais e Humanas - Universidade Nova de Lisboa.

particularly in terms of all the consequences this new reality entails. Still, albeit somewhat unconsciously, the increasing ability to intervene and change the state of the Earth System as a whole is moving us from the role of passive spectators towards actors capable of changing the plot itself. "We are now in the driving seat" (Rockström 2014), but it seems that despite having access to the command centre, we don't have the social organization to define who and how to use the "central computer" (Matos 2015)[2] that would allow us to conduct our own behaviour in respect of Spaceship Earth (Fuller 1969).

Even if from a technological perspective we are able to overcome and manipulate Spaceship Earth at all levels, the crew doesn't have the internal organization that allows collective action to handle its operation. We have never been so vulnerable with respect to the level of social organization.

In nature, where more remains hidden than is revealed, the unexplainable "whole" that surrounds us has been delineated by sets of rites, myths, beliefs and concepts that established order amongst ideas and named the unnameable: *Mother Nature, Mother Earth, the Great Machine, goddess Gaia, the law of nature, living space, ecological space, life-support system.* They are all forms for what we today call the Earth System.

Throughout the history of science, properties and behaviours of different components of the Earth System have been analysed on different physical, material, and biological levels. However, the higher, more intangible and diffuse levels of interconnection and global systemic integration remained in our mental sphere, hidden as the true *terra incognita*. Even if laboratory analyses allow us to interpret the unseen and incorporeal character of natural phenomena, a problem arises with the attempt to comprehend them on a global scale, integrated within the true system, the "whole". For example, carbon dioxide (CO_2) and its role in the biochemical process of photosynthesis are well known but its effects at higher concentrations in the atmosphere and the consequences of its interaction with other elements were perceived only recently. Neither the "global" nor the "whole" fits in any laboratory or suits the process of delimitation and precision required by legal norms.

First, human activity operates at the lower level of the Earth System (material, physical, biological), that is, at the level of exploitation of resources and ecological infrastructure. It not only disturbs the dynamics and interdependencies at the level of activity but also at a higher level of the Earth System, provoking chemical changes in the atmosphere and

---

[2] See Chapter 3 of this book, written by Clóvis de Matos.

hydrosphere, initiating a process of manipulation of the pattern of order. So, for the first time, anthropogenic impacts affected the Earth System as a whole, regardless of whether they happened at only the lower level of the Earth System. The unified and interdependent character, and the properties of the global system, began to unravel through the feedback from the higher levels of integration of the Earth System. That initiated an interpretation of the laws of the "whole" that could not be understood from the behaviour of its components only.

> In fact, the 'whole' is organized from the molecule up to the biosphere, and at each level of integration, characteristics emerge which cannot be analysed based only on mechanisms that explain lower levels of integration. This phenomenon, known as *emergence*, corresponds to the appearance of new characteristics at combined levels and which do not exist at the level of its constituting elements. (Filipe, Coelho & Ferreira 2007)

The characteristic behaviour of the whole cannot be derived, even in theory, from the most complete possible knowledge of the behaviour of its components, whether considered individually or in other combined proportions or organizations.

> *Emergence* can also be seen as a *process* in which "spontaneous" order is displayed from within the system. It is when different elements are allowed to combine that they form patterns and interactions between them. When they lose their established rational order, entering into a situation of unstructured chaos, a new structure may emerge. (Miller & Swinney 2001)

The Earth System is a complex one within which there are different levels of functioning and interaction. The pattern resulting from millennia of slow interactions between the various components of the Earth System produced a biogeophisical structure corresponding to a single period of climate stability: the Holocene. This spontaneous *emergence* of an order produced emergent phenomena that contributed equally to the consolidation of the pattern of well-buffered stability that works inside an "envelope of natural variability" (Steffen et al. 2004, 336). These reciprocal interactions of teleconnections, retroactions and feedbacks led to a complex and dialectical system, which resulted in a favourable condition for the development of human civilizations.

The number of such phenomena is immense, and only by an analysis of the interconnections on a global scale can we begin to lift the veil of their incredible complexity. One of the most interesting phenomena, in that by its domino effect it could be a determining factor in maintaining the current state of the Earth System, is the transport of dust between the Sahara and Amazon (NASA & Garner 2015). From the Sahara desert and, with more intensity, the Bodélé Depression in Chad, an ancient lake rock bed composed of dead microorganisms loaded with phosphorus, around 182 million tons (the equivalent of 689,290 semi-trucks' full) of dust are transported each year by the wind, travelling 1600 miles across the Atlantic, though some drops to the surface or is flushed from the sky by rain.

Near the eastern coast of South America, at longitude 35W, 132 million tons remain in the air, and 27.7 million tons (enough to fill 104,908 semi-trucks) fall to the surface over the Amazon basin. It fertilises the basin decisively, maintaining that dense green mass that, in turn, with its 600 billion trees and an extraordinary sophisticated process, pumps 20 billion tons of water daily into the atmosphere (larger trees pump about 1000 litres/day of water), and injects 17 billion cubic metres of water containing a high concentration of organic matter into the ocean (one-fifth of all the fresh water that reaches the oceans). Amazingly, deserts are crucial to life in the oceans and global climate regulation. With this dialectic chain of systemic *emergences*, we realize the interdependent whole of the entire system. In its higher level of integration, as stated by Hongbin Yu,[3] "This is a small world ... we're all connected together" (Grey 2015).

Only recently has visualizing this example become possible, allowing us to comprehend the unimaginable potential chain of interconnections and teleconnections on which we depend, and that we are influencing by inducing changes in the preconditions that maintain the status of the system.

The changes in some of the initial pattern of stability in the system corresponding with the Holocene period, for example, the increase in CO_2 concentrations (and consequent changes in heat accumulation, global thermodynamics, and feedbacks produced by climate change), allowed us to "open the book" on the dynamics and interdependencies that occur at the higher level of the Earth System.

---

[3] Hongbin Yu, an atmospheric scientist at the University of Maryland who works at NASA's Goddard Space Flight Center in Greenbelt, Maryland, is lead author of the study about dust transport, with data collected by a lidar instrument on NASA's Cloud-Aerosol Lidar and Infrared Pathfinder Satellite Observation, or CALIPSO, satellite from 2007 through 2013.

The Great Acceleration[4] by the human enterprise started in the middle of the twentieth century with an increase in the exploitation of resources and ecological infrastructures – "The speeding up of just about everything after the Second World War ... sometimes called the Great Acceleration... human population has tripled, but the global economy and material consumption have grown many times faster" (Hibbard et al. 2006). It created such fundamental changes in the state and functioning of the Earth System that it is designated as the end date for the Holocene period and the start date for the Anthropocene.

The *tsunami* caused by the changes in the dynamic natural pattern is overwhelming social and economic systems to such an extent that it calls for a questioning and re-evaluation of many of the fundamental ideas upon which the Great Acceleration was built. Although urgent, we have not yet been able to go the required distance to perform a critical analysis of these facts, their scientific interpretation, and their implications for international relations and the social, political and economic realms.

Although restricted to an academic level, the discussion on the de-territorialised and globalised reality in which we now live has created a situation in which everything is being questioned. Garcia (2010), in her analysis about the fragmentation of state sovereignty, identified many authors who address this issue:

> There are authors who question whether we need to abandon the concept of the State (Heiko Faber), those that claim that the Modern State has ceased to exist (Wolfgang Reinhold), those who ask "why do we still talk of the State?" (Peter Saladin), or those who claim that there is an incompatibility between globalisation and sovereign States (Thomas Vesting). There are even those who assert that the national State no longer guarantees peace, freedom, security, protection of human rights and the environment (Julianne Kokott).

Ruggie (1993) argues that

> scholars of international relations are not very good ... at studying the possibility of fundamental discontinuity in the international system; that is, at addressing the question of whether the modern system of States may be yielding in some instances to post-modern forms of congaing political space. We lack even an adequate vocabulary; and what we cannot describe, we cannot explain.

---

[4] See Chapter 2 of this book, written by Will Steffen

In a fully globalised world, connected through biophysical interactions between people and nations at social and economic levels, several fundamental premises of the Westphalian system of sovereign states have changed. The change is so deep that even words until today unquestionable in the description of these situations, such as the word "international", have become obsolete in the attempt to capture the totality of social relations that cross the boundaries of states.

> The growing importance of non-State actors involved in social interactions beyond State boundaries, regional and global structures, and the improvement in the efficiency of international norms, resulted in terms such as "transnationalism" and "globalism". These new terms are responses to the inadequacy of the term 'international' to depict observed empirical phenomena, making the 'international' an unsatisfactory analytical (or indeed epistemological) category to describe global society. Thus understood, the 'international' might be seen as a description of social structures that have lost much of their relevance in the wake of increasing de-nationalisation through trans-nationalisation or globalisation. (Albert 2007)

Disturbances we create in the pattern of Holocene stability, combined with the new technologies available, make visible the higher level of integration of the Earth System. The awareness of this new reality and the knowledge of the consequences created the new globalised context, where everything changes. It is even normal to resort to "problem words" (Morin 2007) and not "solution words", as in the case of the word "complexity". In this sense, several authors resort to "complex sovereignty" (Magalhães 2007; Pauly & Grande 2007, 48–67) to define what otherwise could not be named in the confrontation between the evolution of social-ecological reality and the concept of sovereignty.

Edgar Morin (1990) explains in his "complex thought" that "complexity cannot be reduced to a single master word, law or simple idea. In other words, the complex cannot be reduced to a law or idea of complexity. It cannot be something easy to define, thereby taking the place of simplicity". In other words, calling complexity "complex" does not solve the problem with which we are confronted.

Even on the short human temporal scale, the Great Acceleration was short and recent. Its feedbacks carry with them impertinent and subversive questions that pressure the existing social system and its assumptions. Answering them implies a radical change/evolution in theoretical perspectives.

The facts exist: the Earth System functions as an interdependent "global whole" in the way it has always functioned in its different states throughout its history – what does not yet exist is a theory able to first represent the world beyond the nation-state and then allocate a *place* to what is the higher level of integration of the Earth System. Since there is no interpretation capable of representing this global reality within our system of social organization, we continue to act as if that reality does not exist.

Nietzsche, therefore, is correct in his statement, the point here being that the legitimacy of interpretation lies in its capacity to explain reality; in other words, its ability to reflect and understand the actual situation in the world. As Camilleri and Falk (1992) very well explain,

> The legitimacy of a discourse resides in the explanatory power of reality, so that legitimacy erodes to the extent that its inadequacy to reflect the real situation in the world increases. In every area where the discourse of sovereignty has lost its ability to accurately portray the facts, it is precisely at the gap between theorization of reality and the actual reality of the ecological dynamic of the biosphere that this loss of legitimacy becomes clear.

Without a theory able to interpret the facts raised by the global and interdependent reality of the Earth System, we will continue to live an illusion that tries to fit new facts into an old interpretation.

In this context, it is no surprise that the majority of the reactions to environmental disruption caused by the Great Acceleration are limited to interventions in the periphery of the social system. We classified this "looking-for period" as the first generation of environmental law, with modest intervention in human relationships, that is, we relied on long lists of prohibitions without intervening in the primary drivers of the system or properly understanding the huge theoretical challenge.

Even without the scientific information needed to unravel some of the contours of the new circumstances that impose themselves on law, Amaral (1994) understood the structural and systemic nature of the challenge being faced.

> Environmental law is a primary branch of law, born not to regulate the relations amongst humans but to try to insert discipline in the relationship between humans and nature. ... before the eyes of humanity, a new era has been unravelling, we may actually even be entering into a new civilization. ... It is why this new civilization has begun to generate its Law – a new type of Law. Environmental Law is not just another specialised and technical branch, but requires a whole new philosophy that shapes the way we look at Law.

2. The Legal Nebula

Defining the outlines of reality upon which to build environmental law is conditioned by the possibility of knowing *what is to be protected*; in other words, by the ability to define and delimit the *quid* to be put under the scope (protection) of the law.

The transmutation of the "environment" from a slightly relevant social interest into an authentic legal good, with a value *per se*, added a profound new meaning: The "environment" shall be protected as a value by itself, and not as it was previously – that is, merely the causal path of damage.

Previously, for law, damage to the environment only existed when it caused damage to people or goods. With the new formulation, damage is perceived

> as disturbance of an autonomous and unitary legal interest it allows, immediately, to draw – based on axiological ordering of the subject of injury – the distinction between damage to the environment as a legal good [ecological damage] and the damage caused to people and property by environmental disturbances (environmental damage, *Umweltschäden*, *Milieuschäden*). (Cunhal 2002)

The autonomy of the environment as a legal good, with a value *per se*, is one of the major conceptual achievements made along the path of its legal protection. Despite several national and international legal systems adopting this recognition, during this *looking-for* period, there was no scientific knowledge available that would enable us to understand the facts, the *quid*, with which jurists were faced. This lack of knowledge and the impossibility of defining the environmental good within existing paradigms made these new questions impertinent. "*The subversive impulse of environmental law*" was what Canotilho (2009) called this structural incompatibility. In our view, the subversion of law by the environment is based on three fundamental scale preconditions:

- the global scale of the good intended to be captured under the scope of law, and the impossibility of establishing any kind of material or abstract legal division of the "environmental good" (geographic scale)
- the cumulative and intergenerational character of the damages and benefits caused in this "environmental good" (time scale)
- the restrictive and limiting approach of environmental law towards an economic system conceived on unlimited growth on a planet with limited resources (economic/ecological scale)

On the way to representing the environment as a legal good, states found they needed to capture and create a narrative able to interpret something that had always had a local and a global dimension, diffuse and indeterminate. Some states searched the "whole" within their own boundaries and eventually arrived at an understanding of the *unitary character* of the environment. Departing from the principle of territoriality of norms and political power, it appears that this unitary character referred to a national context even though there was already an empirical perception that this unit referred in fact to the larger *whole*, the global. But due to a lack of legal representation of the true scale of the legal good in question, the "environment" had to adapt itself to political borders.

The attempt to define the global on a local scale quickly became ineffective. In the National Environmental Performance Report on Planetary Boundaries of the Swedish Environmental Protection Agency (Nykvist, Persson, Moberg, Persson, Cornell, & Rockström 2013), it is stated that "Sweden is exposed to environmental impacts from other countries which affect Sweden's ability to achieve these environmental quality objectives. At the same time, Swedish consumption and production have an impact on environmental performance in other countries". International organizations such as the EU recognize this global dependency: "Even though we have never used our natural resources with so much efficiency as we do at present, we are still degrading our essential resources ... in Europe as well as in the rest of the world, and in the environmental field, borders do not exist" (SOER 2015).

These structural genetic defects gave rise to a process of relativism and de-legitimization of the legal good. The result was a dysfunctional congenital degeneration:

a) the legal weight of "ecological footprints" turned out to be unsupportable by the *jus utendi, fruendi et abutendi* of property and sovereignty (Canotilho 2009)
b) the cumulative character and global spread of harm over the course of various generations, and protection of rights without subjects (namely future generations)
c) the causal link between the acts that harm the systemic character of the environmental damage and affect all the Earth System, whose effects only reveal themselves much later
d) the global dispersion of benefits of ecosystem services
e) the idea of polygonal relations extended to a global scale, within a context of plural responsibility
f) the *tipping points* resulting from the accumulation of damage caused over the course of various generations

g) *interconnections* between different territorial components divided
   by abstract political frontiers
h) the imposition of limits and environmental obligations as
   generators of unequal competing conditions on a global scale
i) the legitimacy problem of instituting legal proceedings, civil
   society or class actions

All things considered, there was more than enough reason to reject this
first generation branch of environmental law. Incompatibility with the
assumptions of the system gave rise to a phenomenon referred to in
specialised literature as *Vollzug Defizit,* the "implementation deficit"
(Hucke & Wollmann 1998), or *enforcement deficit*. It came to characterise
environmental law due to a) an exponential proliferation of norms and
standards; b) the manipulated application with intent to restrict its scope;
c) the systemic deferral while awaiting regulation; and d) outright failure
to apply norms. Prieur (1991) considered it a "diffuse form of
deregulation" while Charbonneau (1998) speaks of a de-legitimization of
environmental law and Carbonnier raises the hypothesis of No-Law.

But as paradoxical as it may seem, even when rejected, this *quid*
referent to a *healthiness environment* did in fact invoke a qualitative
change in the fundamental goals of states. That is so because it did not
cease to represent a value superior to those the law aims to protect from an
individual or collective point of view.

This deep material foundation, as a vital dimension of life and the
human species, is not just a constitutionally guaranteed right in about 125
constitutions (Bosselmann 2015);[5] it is even being considered a hypothesis
that would lead to the emergence of a new type of state, a *post-social state*
(Silva 1989), or a successor to the *welfare state*, an *environmental law*
state (Rangel 1994).

The entry of the environment into the *core* fundamental objectives and
tasks of the states as a collective legal good and/or fundamental right of
each individual citizen also raised procedural questions of legitimacy in
court or when participating in administrative procedures.

Various states (mainly Portuguese-speaking countries), challenged by a
reality not reflected in their spatial dimension, sought to develop a theory
through "problem words" that were better able to portray the diluted and
diffuse reality that conditioned them. The "theory of diffuse interests" at
the basis of *class action* (in Portuguese *Ação Popular)* teaches us that
when legal goods are involved, such as the environment, consumption or

---

[5] See Chapter 4 of this book, written by Klaus Bosselmann.

quality of life, "they belong to all of us and can never be allocated exclusively to any subject. It means that the diffuse interests include at the same time a collective and individual dimension, neither being merely collective, nor merely individual" (Sousa 1998). Cappelletti (1975) expresses the other side of the coin: they belong "to everyone and no one".

But the all-encompassing scale of *diffuse interests*, once again, cannot be limited to a single community belonging to a particular state but only to humanity as a collective in the trans-spatial dimension, such as "the entire human race, being the combination of all human beings that inhabit the planet" (Santos 2001), and in a trans-temporal dimension, in the sense of the "collective *ad infinitum*, including all human beings that will succeed the current living generation at a given time" (Malhotra 1998). Each generation thus becomes "a link in an endless chain of generations that collectively forms a community, a human family" (Agius 1998). This has led to a doctrine that defends the emergence of a new subject in international law: humanity; a true *"revolution in social and legal thought"* (ibid).

The combination of the "whole" and "everyone" may be the biggest challenge that the law will face this century. The uncertainty exists not only around the good intended to come under the law's protection but also around the identification of the holders of this diffuse good, therefore the nebula broadens to the international dimension.

The UN General Assembly Resolution 43/53 Protection of Global Climate for Present and Future Generations of Mankind of 6 December, 1988, with a combination of lack of political will and an absence of suitable concepts to define a fundamental resource, states that "climate change on Earth and its adverse effects are a common concern of mankind". This solution has roots in concepts such as *common interest, global commons, intergenerational equity, responsibility or rights, common ecological heritage of humankind, life-support system and "the awareness that the problems of ocean space are closely interrelated and need to be considered as a whole"* (UNCLOS 1982).[6] They all share the difficulty of defining their form in a precise manner.

So we arrive at a point where all contradictions and paradoxes of the legal nebula are possible, especially when "problem words" blend into "concern words" through indeterminate, merely descriptive, neutral and open concepts. It can easily lead to the "whole" being synonymous for

---

[6] UNCLOS (1982). *United Nations Convention on the Law of the Sea*. Retrieved from:
http://www.un.org/depts/los/convention_agreements/texts/unclos/unclos_e.pdf

nothing and nobody. "International law itself was (and to a certain extent remains) ill-equipped to address state activities affecting negatively an intangible natural resource which spans across and beyond the national territories of states" (Borg 2009).

3. The "Whole" Problem

The reality of the "whole" disappears in the political map of state boundaries. However, if the "whole" exists in a higher level of functioning and integration of the Earth System, is it or is it not possible to represent this new reality beyond the states?

Starting from the first two elements that gave rise to structural incompatibility, geographic scale and time scale, which carried with them the subversion introduced into the law by the "environment", and recent developments in our knowledge of the functioning of the Earth System, we will work on a possible evolution of these still embryonic and inefficient formulations of *legal concerns* from an actual vague and indeterminate formula into an operational legal instrument, giving shape to rights and duties.

Expressions such as *"life-sustaining systems of the biosphere"* (United Nations 1992), *"conservation of climate as part of the common heritage of mankind"* (United Nations 1988), or *"the problems of the ocean space are closely interrelated and need to be considered as a whole"* (UNCLOS 1982) presented in different texts of international law are themselves attempts to approach the biogeophysical foundations at the basis of the emergence of life and the conditions that allowed the development of human civilization. It is clear that these merely descriptive concepts are not rooted in a set of criteria that offer the possibility of measurement or delimitation that would allow us to define a legal object; that is, to define the *concept and its amplitude*, distinguishing it for all other legal goods but also matching the unitary global reality of the "environment".

The word *system* in the term *life-sustaining systems of the biosphere* points back to the empirical idea of a combination of various interrelated and interacting components, out of which emerges a whole that is more than the sum of its components. However, this reference to general concepts, without proceeding to a description of criteria that could be used to delimit a physical space in which the system operates or the mention of an indicator that provides us with information on the system state, once again reveals how unspecified concepts rule the environmental nebula.

The phrase *conservation of climate as part of the common heritage of mankind*, although referring to the initial proposal of the Maltese initiative and included as such in the text of this resolution of the UN General Assembly, does not refer to a specific and particular good but rather to a set of interconnected goods that shape a system with a specific functionality inherited from Mother Nature. This heritage is the integration of the geophysical properties of the planet with the living biosphere that forms a single global system as the result of an evolutionary process of interaction.

Even the expression *whole* carries with it a systemic idea. As in the preamble of UNCLOS (1982), where the necessity to manage "ocean space" is recognized, it refers not to the geographical and political space made up by the sum of the different areas of state jurisdiction and high seas but rather to the necessity to elaborate on problems related to the use of the oceans as a whole, taking into account the *ocean environment as an integrated fluid ecological system*. Though still empirical in nature, the perception exists that all these concepts direct us towards the notion of a *system*. The question of how we can build a legal concept relating to a system not tied to any territorial delimitation, since in environmental matters the system is global, remains unanswered.

What are these *life-sustaining systems of the biosphere*, the biosphere being an object that is not confined to any sovereignty, existing both in and outside all sovereignties? We can all perceive it intuitively but we cannot touch or appropriate it, even though it is profoundly related to and dependent on the physical nature placed under the jurisdiction of the different states of the planet. What is *ocean space as a whole,* which apparently transcends every sea, ocean or jurisdiction but does not materialize in a geographical dimension? What is this *natural heritage* that belongs to the time *continuum* of all successive generations, carrying with it interests shared with the unborn, and which should not be mixed with the territorial space that belongs to the people amongst whom they will be born?

The first jump into the unknown will focus on the dysfunctional relationship between the reductionist physicist, or biological approach of law towards nature, and the intangible biogeophysical realities that determine the state and functioning of the Earth System.

It seems to us that the key to establishing order in our interpretation, as we construct legal abstractions in regard to nature, lies in the recognition of different analytical levels. As Soromenho-Marques (2006) observes in relation to the immaterial heritage, it also matters here:

> To avoid reductionism of a physicist or biological nature, we should today avoid the repetition of an old debate that ran through the 17th and 18th centuries on the nature of matter, as the Newtonian theory of the Universe

was presented. During this period, the Cartesians rejected the theory of gravitational force as they considered it "miraculous". For them, the category of material force should always be characterised by direct transmission through physical contact. We cannot make the same mistake concerning the heritage. In fact there exist other types of heritage beyond those that can be seen or touched.

In this search for the environmental legal good, the law has already had to face realities that go beyond our sensory capacity and had to broaden the notion of system and ecosystem functions, which have already been recognized in some legal orders, particularly the European Union (Comissão Europeia, 2000). Although these evolutions are attempts to theorize reality and produce a more adequate representation of the systemic character of environmental goods, we do not yet have a concept able to represent the true scale of these biogeophysical interconnections that extended human relations on a global scale.

We find ourselves in a stalemate. On one hand, if we advance with the search for this environmental legal good within the geographical limits of states, we obtain an *ecological nonsense*,[7] inevitably amputated and dysfunctional. On the other hand, if we approach the Earth System on its true scale of biogeophysical relationships, we will collide with the geographic delimitation of sovereignties and the lack of the political and legal existence of the entire Earth System, and therefore arrive at a completely dysfunctional relationship between the Earth System and the social system.

Awareness of the different internal dynamic levels of the Earth System and its dependence on the *core drivers* at the origin of a *structural pattern* that produced a unique period of climatic stability in the history of the planet (the Holocene) could determine the name and define what kind of environmental legal good we are looking for. The possibility to accurately represent facts and reconstitute, legitimize and thereby make sovereignty evolve, as has happened along the course of history, will only become viable if we cease to hide the reality of these intangible relations.

The intangible heritage contributes to the understanding of the critical crossroads of contemporary humanity, shedding light on the human condition, and on some of the possible paths for their redemption. (Soromenho-Marques 2006)

---

[7] See Chapter 6 of this book, written by Prue Taylor.

4. The Software/Hardware Relation

Defining and delimiting the *quid* to be placed under the scope of law will require the construction of legal abstractions in accordance with the known reality of nature, and finding solutions that harmonise representations of nature with those of the social system.

The fact that this planet, as opposed to many others, is not just a sphere of rocks and an atmosphere offers us a solid point of departure for our reflection. Our planet, orbiting around the sun at a distance of 149 million kilometres in an orbit called the habitable zone,[8] created the necessary physical conditions for an active water cycle to exist, which includes the three – solid, liquid and gaseous – phases. This water cycle enabled the development of an incredibly complex biosphere, forming patterns of organization and global integration through combined internal interaction. Together these patterns form a meta-system.

The need to understand this global reality led to an evolution in life sciences, which integrated different areas of scientific knowledge, creating a contrast with the reductionist tendencies of the Cartesian perspective. This process eventually resulted in the concept of the Earth System that came to mean "the suite of interacting physical, chemical, and biological global-scale cycles (often called biogeochemical cycles) and energy fluxes which provide the conditions necessary for life on the planet" (Oldfield & Steffen 2004).

Being in dialectical interaction with the biotic and abiotic infrastructures, these processes function as a set of intangible operational instructions with properties that determine the ways in which the Earth System self-organizes and regulates itself, and can be designated as the "programme" of the Earth System. In a brilliant theoretical analogy, Soromenho-Marques (2006) clarifies the relationship between tangible and intangible heritage: "I believe that in an ultramodern analogy we can read this relationship in the same way that *software* and *hardware* relate to each other." This analogy could in fact be equally valid at revealing the relation between the tangible infrastructure (*res corporals*) of the planet and the intangible system (*res incorporales*) of physical laws, thermodynamics or biochemistry, forming in their combination an authentic piece of software containing the operational instructions that determine the functioning state of the Earth System.

---

[8] See Chapter 3 of this book, written by Clóvis Matos.

The Earth System is a very real and constant presence in our lives. However, since we cannot see or touch it, it was thought to be infinitely abstract until recent technological evolutions made it visual through images captured from space. It thus became an open book that has since dazzled us with its high degree of interaction.

The feedback we are getting on the state of the system and current technological developments allow us to read this "book of instructions" across different scientific areas. "For the first time in history, humans have knowledge at their disposal to exert a power over nature, over life and death, allowing us to gain control over what would previously escape our reach, being considered a certain fatality or causal chain of events" (Silva 2002).

At the same time, this potential opened up a new field of opportunities and dangers. In the case of genetic information, the law was called upon to intervene, imposing rules and limits to human-making (bio-law), and information of the human genome was considered the heritage of mankind, even though in symbolic meaning only (UNESCO 1997).

This example shows that the recognition of objects of intangible or immaterial character is not new to legal sciences. Other examples are cultural heritage, recognized through UNESCO's Intangible Cultural Heritage (UNESCO 2003), the intangible value of companies in commercial law and the intellectual property rights and authorship through statements that establish the independence between author's rights and the material support of a work. Despite problems of definition and delimitation, the importance of the values intended to be protected have always justified the search for new solutions.

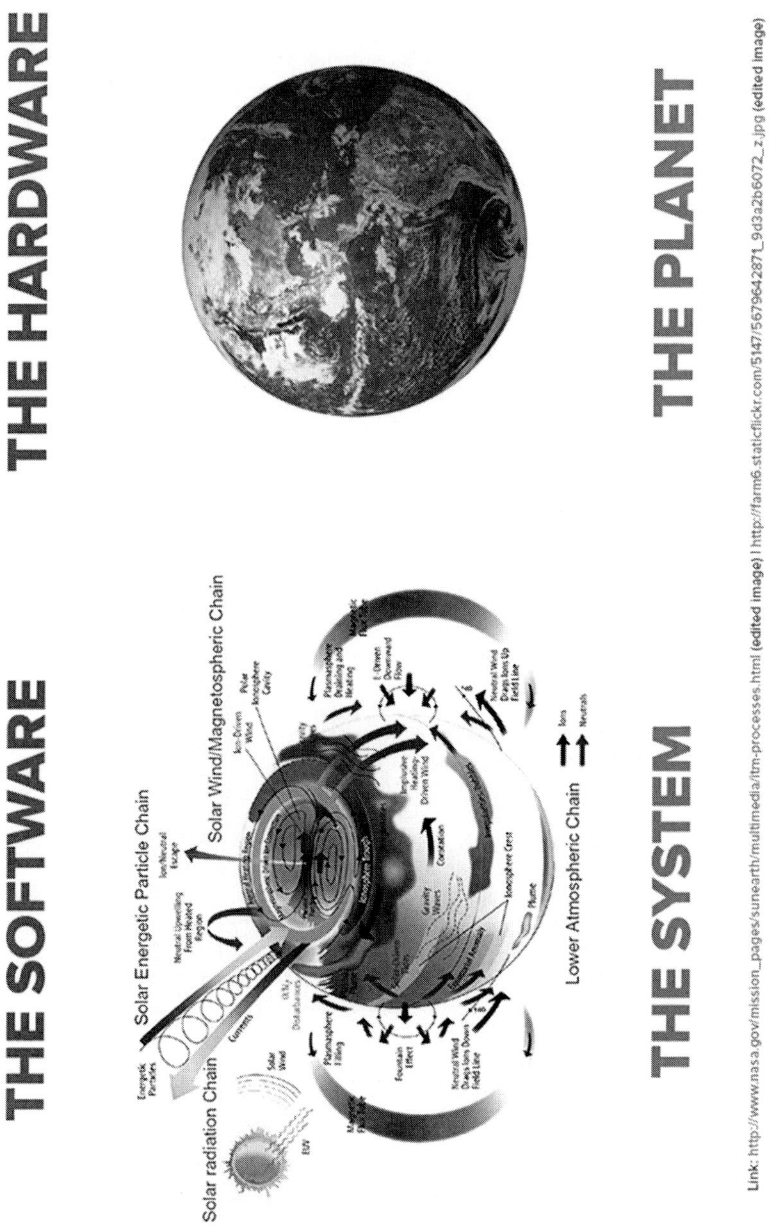

Image 1. The hardware/software relation and the Earth System/planet relation

According to Oldfield and Steffen (2004), the Earth System consists of an interactive atmosphere, ocean, biosphere, cryosphere, and lithosphere that together form a complete and unified system, with characteristics defined as follows.

It deals with a materially closed system that has a primary external energy source, the sun.

- The major dynamic components of the Earth System are a suite of interlinked physical, chemical and biological processes that cycle (transport and transform) materials and energy in complex dynamic ways within the System. The forcings and feedbacks within the System are at least as important to the functioning of the System as are the external drivers.
- Biological/ecological processes are an integral part of the functioning of the Earth System and not just the recipients of changes in the dynamics of a chemical system. Living organisms are active participants, not simply passive respondents. Human beings, their societies and their activities are an integral component of the Earth System, and are not outside forces perturbing an otherwise natural system. There are many modes of natural variability and instabilities within the System as well as anthropologically driven changes. By definition, both types of variability are part of the dynamics of the Earth System. They are often impossible to separate completely and they interact in complex and sometimes mutually reinforcing ways.
- Time scales considered in Earth System science vary according to the questions being asked. Many global environmental change issues consider time scales of decades to a century or two. However, a basic understanding of Earth System dynamics demands consideration of much longer time scales in order to capture longer-term variability of the System, to understand the fundamental dynamics of the System, and to place into context the current suite of rapid global-scale changes occurring within the System. Thus environmental and prognostic modelling approaches are both central to Earth System science.

Now, as we examine this definition of the Earth System and the enumeration of its characteristics from the perspective of law, it seems that many of the problems associated with the definition of legal environmental objects at state level have their origin within these characteristics. The same difficulties are faced by international law. These difficulties converge in the first two preconditions (geographic scale and time scale) that motivate the subversive character of environmental law as follows:

- At the state level, the environment was understood as "an autonomous and unitary legal good". As such, it became a synonym for diffuse and indefinable, thus rendering the protection of this good dysfunctional.
- At the international level, the compartmentalised approach that considered and analysed only the distinct components of the Earth System concealed phenomena of interaction and emergence.

The dysfunction between the current knowledge of the Earth System and the law finds support in the post-2015 Development Agenda of the United Nations, and within the formulation of the sustainable development goals (SDG). This UN strategy puts an emphasis on "the need for a coherent global framework to integrate existing laws that would cover these international areas" (UN 2013). While international treaties and conventions relative to global common goods do exist, the United Nations recognizes that "the frameworks are fractured, and not comprehensive enough to include modern conservation principles or assessments" (UN 2013).

5. A Space Without Territory

The concept or the most adequate international law term (Shelton 2009) to describe the characteristics outlined by Oldfield and Steffen from a legal perspective is the common concern of humankind (CCH), which emerged with regard to the climate in the UNGA 43/53 (1988) resolution. Although this concept is still just a phrase or term that should be understood in a broad sense, therefore being inapt to serve as operational or normative support for an international environment regime, Dina Shelton knew to appreciate the notable innovation of this term and the profound implications of its premises. According to Shelton (2009), the concept introduces two fundamental innovations into international law: the first relates to the fact that this concept does not make any reference to states; the second being the absence of any reference to a geographically delimited area, even though it is associated with other concepts such as the global commons areas – the high seas, Antarctica, the seabed, and outer space – where the common heritage of mankind is applied. "Common concerns are different because they are not spatial, belonging to a specific area, but can occur within or outside sovereign territory" (Shelton 2009).

In the opening speech of the second meeting of the Group of Legal Experts to examine the concept of the *common concern of mankind* in relation to global environmental issues in Geneva 1991, Mostafa K. Tolba, the director of UNEP at that time, asserted:

> It is very important that the concept of common concern of mankind is further elaborated to make its contents and scope understandable and clear; it is also important to make sure how this concept can be interpreted in the terms of rights and obligations of States in the process of its implementation. It is understandable that, since it is a new concept in international law and international relations, it will develop further in the near future and its interpretation given today, will evolve.

With these statements, the central idea of this concept – that its birth is only its own evolution – is retained. It was born as a quasi-concept, a future project, a proclamation of the need to find an idea for an unsolved problem. In other words, since its appearance, the common concern is valuable for the novelty it was, and for what it might still be and represent. It is certain about 30 years on that the UN resolution on the common concern was a way round a possible legal status for "the unique nature of climate which is not restricted to the global commons but spans also across areas subject to national jurisdiction" (Borg 2007). The climate continues to be orphaned not of a definition but of a legal framework for its existence.

In the report of this meeting (UNEP Secretariat, 1991), it was said:

> During the general discussion on the concept of common concern of mankind, the experts reiterated that the concept still has no legal consequences in terms of rights and duties. It was stressed that the concept should not infringe the sovereign right of States and, in this context, a point was raised whether it is desirable to narrow down the scope of the concept and its application and confine it to global environmental issues which may cause significant adverse effects upon the environment. It was re-emphasized that the common concern concept was not meant to substitute the concept of common heritage. There was a general understanding that at the current stage the common concern of mankind may serve as guiding principle rather than legal rule.

He identified the following aspects of the concept of common concern of mankind that require further consideration and elaboration by legal experts:

- possible implications of the concept for specific obligations in the relevant international treaties
- implication for the human right to a healthy environment

-   implication with respect to the issues of equitable burden sharing and fair compensation

Although it is made clear here that the CCH was not intended to replace the CHM, the need for this statement and its reinforcement justifies and substantiates the deep connection between the two concepts and their common origin. By listing the issues that need further consideration, we consider that there is a common denominator among the original objectives of the CHM and the future project implementation of CCH.

Both concepts are the result of the same initial boost of looking for an international management regime with the goal of long-term environmental protection through new structures of politics and governance beyond states without infringing on the sovereign rights of states. For all purposes, the CCH is an embryonic form of the non-territorial dimension of the CHM that never came into being, although that was the motivation and source of the initial boost. In this sense, the CCH represents a latent new legal theory, a united and interdependent global reality seeking its roots in the ancient moral or ethical concepts that unify humanity in the nature of the planet it inhabits.

But, unlike the CHM, which still had some "specific areas of the Earth", remnants of the geographical divisions, to anchor its existence, the global nature and *res incorporales* character of the CCH led to a permanently postponed future. This lack of definition and evolution *sine die* is matched only by the initial project of Arvid Pardo, which suggests that the CHM concept is useful in "organizing new forms international cooperation in matters that are not directly related to specific areas of the Earth (…) [including] climate and the environment" (Pardo 1989).

The resolution UNGA 43/53 (1988), as Borg (2007) recognizes, "identifies the legal status of an 'intangible' common resource (climate) that spans the global commons". It is with the absence of a theory capable of representing the intangibility of nature and recognizing legally a good that is both inside and outside of all states that we can summarize our inability to accurately portray the reality around us.

Therefore, expounding on the statements of the experts, the CCH is not really a substitute of CHM that was compressed and mutilated to fit the territoriality of the borders of states but rather an attempt to fulfil the original objectives of the CHM itself.

Still, the comments made by Shelton about this *quasi-concept* may yet prove extremely useful in the search for a legal environmental good when the absence of spatial character turns into a *living space*, as paradoxical as that may seem. "The environment is not an abstraction but represents a *living space*, the quality of life and the very health of human beings, including generations unborn" (Shelton 2009). This statement is in tune with space as a concept in the global context as considered by theorists on international relations: "Although globalisation theorists differ on whether globalisation marks a distinct rupture in modernity, they do agree that the separation of *space* from *place* is a basic characteristic of modernity that continues but accentuated form under globalising processes" (Coleman 2007).

6. A Safe Space Without Territory

One of the dimensions of complex sovereignty is its openness towards finding new concepts able to represent new *loci* in a transnational or global space. Thereby it presents an alternative to the exclusive perspective of *space* as a territory, distinguishing between *space* with its worldwide operation and *place*. For Giddens (1990),

> The advent of modernity increasingly tears space away from place by fostering relations between 'absent' others, locationally distant from any given situation of face-to-face interaction... What structures the locale is not simply that which is present on the scene; the 'visible form' of the local conceals the distant relations which determine its nature.

And for Dirlik (2001), "Space in this sense refers to products".

This interesting development, where the spatial geographic representation is absorbed by the "functional" dimension of life, offers a *functional space* that is in accordance with Shelton's *living space* as a space system with the function of supporting life.

> On the other hand, the primarily spatial representation of the figure of sovereignty is relaxed, particularly when newly emerging forms of political authority are read to entail not only a spatial but also a functional reconfiguration. Such emerging forms are also read as the increasing importance of functional over spatial understandings of political authority. (Albert 2007)

The non-territorial and intangible character of the climate and the function of maintaining a stable climate meet this vision of a functional space. This new context is still going through a process of assimilation and conceptual adaptation. We should emphasise that the *living space* referred to by Shelton (2009) is not just the climate system but the whole life-support system of which the climate system is just one part.

To clarify these concepts and introduce some order into our interpretation, we recur once again to Oldfield and Steffen (2005).

> The term *climate system* is also used in connection with global change, and is encompassed within the Earth System. Climate usually refers to the aggregation of all components of weather – precipitation, temperature, cloudiness, for example – averaged over a long period of time, usually decades, centuries, or longer. The processes which contribute to climate comprise the climate system, and they are closely connected to biogeochemical cycles. However, there are some important differences between climate change and global change:
>
> - Many important features of biogeochemical cycles can have significant impacts on Earth System functioning without any direct change in the climate system. Examples include the direct effects of changing atmospheric CO_2 concentration on carbonate chemistry and hence on calcification rates in the ocean and also the sharp depletion of stratospheric ozone from the injection of chlorofluorocarbons in the atmosphere.
> - Many interactions between biology and chemistry can have profound impacts on ecological systems, and hence feedbacks to Earth System functioning, without any change in the climate system. Examples include the impact of nitrogen deposition on the biological diversity of terrestrial ecosystems and the effect of non-climate driven changes in terrestrial and marine biosphere emission of trace gases and hence to the chemistry of the atmosphere.
> - Human societies and their activities are usually not considered to be a direct part of the climate system, although their activities certainly impact on important processes in the climate system (e.g., greenhouse gas emissions).

The scale of the *living space* underlying the CCH would have to be the whole Earth System itself. This means, apart from the various *spaces* such as climate, biodiversity and oceans, we need an integrated and integrating approach. Considering that the UN recognizes the lack of a systems approach to environmental problems, and that the *common concern* is the only *term in international law* capable of drawing a systemic reality that exists both in and outside of sovereignties, we need to evolve towards a concept that is able to define the *living space.* Although there has already been consensus over the existence of a certain ecological global *living space*, there was no information available to define and delimit it.

With the exponential development of Earth System sciences in the last 25 years, and the evolution of Earth observations from space, much of what was concealed from our senses has turned into a reality that we can observe in real time as external spectators. By combining all the information of the spatial "big picture" with the information collected from the lower level of the system, for example, through climate palaeontology, it has become possible to reconstruct a history of the atmosphere and the whole Earth System. Knowing the historical behaviour of the Earth System is crucial to understanding the value of the Holocene to humankind, it could have a central role in the definition of the new legal object that lacks protection.

Over the long course of history of our planet, many different chemical compositions of the atmosphere and the oceans have given origin to different levels of heat accumulation, energetic equilibrium and states of the Earth System. Knowing the history of chemical structures and the different resulting combinations of element interaction allowed us to understand the true unique conditions that characterised the period of climatic stability in the last 11,700 years called the Holocene.

As we have seen in previous chapters, chemical alterations and the destruction of ecological infrastructures as a result from the Great Acceleration are pushing the Earth out of the stable domain of the Holocene – the only state of the Earth System that we know for certain is capable of supporting advanced human civilizations – and threatening to undermine our prosperity. The scientific community has attempted to respond to the challenge of understanding and measuring this *living space* by developing the concept of planetary boundaries (Steffen et al. 2015; Rockström et al. 2009). These boundaries are based on the intrinsic "hard-wired" properties of the Earth System itself. They define a combination of indicators that describe the state of the Earth System.

With access to the information in the "software", we have gained the ability to define and measure our *living space*. The paradoxical system of problem words that defined concerns as legal concepts now have a table where the vital factors are properly listed, with every factor assigned a safe zone, with a minimum and maximum that we must not transgress. And this is being done on a scale upon which we all truly depend – the global scale. So, the *living space,* an intangible and non-territorial space of the CCH, will coincide with this well-defined state of the Holocene, denominated by the scientific community as the *safe operating space of humankind*.

In conceptual terms, this *living space* operated by the *safe operating space of humankind* is consistent with the separation performed by international relations theorists between *space* and *place*.

If we are able to distinguish the planet, with its 510 million square kilometres, from the Earth System and its different possible states, we can start to imagine alternative concepts of global coordination without affecting the constituent elements of sovereignty. In fact, within a context of systemic dependency of all sovereignties upon the same *living space*, the separation of this functional and intangible space of life from the physical space of the planet and its sovereignties may even be the theoretical foundation for the development of solutions.

This new conception of a safe operating space for humankind should in turn lead to a new juridical conception of the Earth System that corresponds better with the new scientific knowledge, notwithstanding the uncertainties that will always exist.

Considering that space technology allowed this intangible nature to become perceivable by our senses, and the concept of planetary boundaries offered us the "genetic code" of the functioning of Spaceship Earth, we now have an obligation to organize ourselves and learn to steer collectively. In fact, the only thing that is truly within our reach is managing and governing ourselves in respect of our interactions with the Earth System. The creation of functional spaces without territory, thereby being global, may constitute a fixed point, an element of stability, upon which we may base a new approach and build an organization. In this sense, the possible construction of a new autonomous legal good as a converging point of a looking-for process should focus on the evolution of this combination of processes with shared origins and goals, continuing the search for the stabilisation of a *space* to be invented.

7. From a Space of Concerns to a Heritage

The concept of CHM as a legal one is one of the most revolutionary and radical developments in the last 50 years of international law. Since its emergence, it became clear that no other concept, notion, principle or doctrine provoked such intense debate and controversy as did the possibility of attributing a heritage to both present and future humanity. Its revolutionary and subversive character stems from the philosophical concept of "humanity", which raises questions about legal regimes of resources that are crucial for the maintenance of the *living space* for and by present and future generations.

Since the application and implementation of the CHM required critical re-evaluation of many principles and doctrines of classical international law, this adverse context inevitably resulted in an inadequate implementation.[9] Put otherwise, the application of the model as originally

---

[9] See Chapter 6 of this book, written by Prue Taylor.

proposed by Arvid Pardo (1976), without the recognition of the different existing integration levels of the Earth System (unknown at that time), led to a confrontation between an intellectually valid philosophical principle that recognized the ocean as a heritage of mankind and the lower system level where the model of political and territorial fragmentation reigns.

As the current legal order only acknowledged some of the separate and individual components of the Earth System and not the healthiness of the system as a whole at its higher level, the CHM concept was inevitably pulled towards the only existing lower level. At this point, a confrontation became unavoidable. It is true that the oceans possess a territorial dimension but the presence of a functional biochemical dimension that determines their quality is no less of a truth. This dimension, incompatible with the legal abstractions of political borders, is inevitably global.

In geographical terms, a dead and acidified ocean may continue to be the object of jurisdictional divisions of sovereign powers but it may not serve as an existing life support to marine life and humanity as a whole. It was this functional and qualitative oceanic system that Arvid Pardo was referring to when he launched the concept of the heritage of mankind in 1967.

As there was no legal distinction between the system and the place where the system would operate, the CHM was limited to existing concepts, imprisoned within the territorial dimension of place, becoming confined to leftover parts of state appropriations lying outside state borders.

It was the only possible approach; and, in fact, it still is. However, soon enough a conflict was revealed between the interests and the territorial claims of states, rendering the approach inoperable for goods that cannot be geographically defined, such as the climate. This is why the vital good, a stable climate from which humanity has only been able to receive the benefits in the last 10,000 years, has so far remained a concern or a state of mind, reduced to a narrow concept of atmospheric pollution to be managed on a territorial basis.

Amongst existing legal frameworks, it is difficult to embed and create a non-territory, or a territory at a global scale with intangible characteristics that escape the existing models of physical and biological nature. The only reason the CHM has survived, even though it subverts the model of political-territorial fragmentation, is due to the initial formulations proving to be philosophically valid and ethically undeniable. Actually, there exists a growing understanding that we are at the limits of international law and we need a radical advancement, and CHM and its CCH substitutes and ineffective derivatives are concepts that could open the door.

8. Holocene State as a Heritage Protected by Law

The process that gave birth to the period of the Holocene, unique in terms of climatic stability in the history of the Earth, was a phenomenon of spontaneous *emergence* from the combination of certain elements and their proportions, and which in their reciprocal interactions formed a pattern, giving rise to a combined organizational "order". This natural process should be embraced by humanity as one of the greatest gifts it received from nature as it was exactly these conditions that allowed for the development of human civilizations and all the species of the planet that share the same ecological needs.

We are not able to protect this phenomenon of emergence or teleconnections but we can protect the biogeophysical structures and processes of the state of the Earth System that assure its maintenance. These biogeophysical structures and their internal relative concentrations of gases are gifts to humanity that resulted from millions of years of interactions at Earth's history scale. These intangible conditions have the highest value for humankind. They are a true *grundnorm,* where other values, already legally protected, and a system of organization should establish their *locus*, their basis of stability.

According to Rakhyun and Bosselmann (2013),

> This context, the planetary boundaries framework, scientifically suggests the existence of a foundational environmental principle or grundnorm, which, for the purpose of our research, can be defined as a basic norm to bind any governmental power. This understanding differs from Kelsen's definition, and is closer to Kant's argument that any positive law must be grounded in a 'natural' norm of general acceptance and reasonableness (Vernunft) to prevent pure arbitrariness. The existence of an environmental grundnorm, therefore, rests on the assumption that respecting planetary boundaries is a dictate of reason (Gebot der Vernunft) and general acceptance (allgemeine Gültigkeit). Conceptually, a grundnorm exists independently of a legal system, but underpins legal reasoning in the form of an inference rule.

In this sense we can argue that the *specific state of the Earth System* corresponding to the geological period of the Holocene carries the meaning of heritage as something we need to conserve in everyone's interest. It enables the recognition of a *new value* to be legally protected as an international autonomous legal good. "Heritage is one idea. It is a philosophical idea, a legal concept, as is something that we need to conserve" (Sobrino 2012).

The evolution of the international community, the vital value of this specific state of the Earth System, and the heritage dimension derived from the need to transmit it to future generations enable the recognition of something higher in scale than a concern or an interest that should be legally protected as an autonomous legal good.

The evolution of a *living space "concern"* towards a common intangible natural heritage of humankind as an authentic autonomous legal good seems a crucial conceptual advance for the organization of human relations, which have broadened to a global scale. With the scientific "safe operating space", the legal concept of the *living space* could have a value that can be measured.

As Sobrino (2012) stated,

> I think this idea, to being more than an idea, must institutionalize itself (...) If we combine the idea of heritage with the idea of an international authority and place relative competences on it – not many are needed, apart from certain ones to establish a multilateral framework for action – I think that would resolve many of the current tensions.

The legal concept of heritage can be the *locus* for that vital good, the *living intangible space* represented by the *safe operating space,* and at the same time the support for a global organization.

What is certain is that a purely formal legal approach towards the current notion of the CHM will exclude the maintenance of this Earth System state within the biogeophysical characteristics of the Holocene. The protection of a specific state of the Earth System can only be legally framed by proceeding with an axiological and teleological interpretation on the basis of the legal consecration of the CHM and its substitute or derived concepts.

Arvid Pardo's vision, the origin of the concept of CHM, involved the perception of the "ocean environment as an integrated fluid ecological system" and the concern "that continued, unmanaged use of the world's oceans would become a serious threat to international peace and security from the environmental impact of new technologies, the militarization of the seafloor and expanding state claims to jurisdiction over large parts of the oceans".[10]

---

[10] See Chapter 6 of this book, written by Prue Taylor.

To realize these objectives through the legal regime of the CHM involves distinguishing the system concept and its *intrinsic intangible quality* from the territorial and geographical approach of already existing legal concepts. But as Taylor & Stroud (2012) state, "Arvid Pardo (and others) considered the CHM regime flexible enough to adapt to the emerging challenges, the discovery of new resources and values, such as scientific research".

Departing from this approach, unrealized due to theoretical and practical impossibilities at the time, we will try to adjust the initial intentions of the CHM to the current criteria for the intrinsic unit of the Earth System. While the artificial separation between oceans, climate and biodiversity may be necessary for reasons of task organization, this lower level of operation should not conceal the need for intervention in the protection of biogeophysical conditions at the higher-level integration of the Earth System. This intervention can be put into practice through application of international standards on the quality of the Earth System state realized by the approach of the planetary boundaries.

Nonetheless, it is of interest to understand that all the substitutes and derived concepts gravitating around the CHM seek to plant a seed for the development of a normative framework that offers an alternative to governing the global common goods, and not only the areas and resources beyond its jurisdictions. So, in order for the CHM to become an operational/normative concept, its object needed to be deterritorialised and made to coincide with the initial concepts and premises formulated by Arvid Pardo.

The entire range of more or less indeterminate concepts pursue the same unique end, the reason for their existence being the absence of instruments that could somehow constitute an object of intellectual representation of reality, in this case the Earth System as a whole, within a specific state that supports the *living space*. It is therefore crucial to understand in detail the differences between the concept of CHM and the CCH derived from it. Based on the proposal of Murillo (2008), we will compare them with recent knowledge regarding the safe operating space for humankind and how they may be re-framed so as to correspond to recent scientific evolutions.

TERRITORIAL SCOPE	**CHM**	Areas beyond national jurisdiction and its resources
	CCH	A wider scope – applied in the intangible higher level, both beyond national jurisdiction but also within the jurisdiction of states
SUBJECT SCOPE	**CHM**	The main focus is related to the geographical areas beyond national jurisdiction and its resources.
	CCH	Focused in *functional intangible spaces* that are a "concern" to humanity as whole. At present, the matters are climate change, species in danger and conservation of biodiversity. The intrinsic intangible ecological quality does not exist autonomously on the geographical space therefore the CCH continues without a clear and precise definition, liable to generate rights and duties.
DISTRIBUTIVE SCOPE	**CHM**	Equitable sharing of benefits
	CCH	Equitable sharing of burdens – cooperation and problem solving

Table 1. Differences between Common Heritage of Mankind (CHM) and Common Concern of Humankind (CCH)

From analysis of different perspectives of the approach that considers the Earth System as a unique systemic whole with intrinsic limits regarding its state, we are able to identify the following advantages and disadvantages.

TERRITORIAL SCOPE	The CCH offers a more adequate response to the characteristics of the Earth System both in and outside sovereignties but it has the disadvantage of not having a *locus,* unlike the CHM, so it cannot be attached to a space on which an organization can be built.
SUBJECT SCOPE	The CHM carries the advantage of being able to delimit the area or resource in question, while the CCH has a problem with the intangibility of the object.
DISTRIBUTIVE SCOPE	From the perspective of the Earth System, damages and benefits, caused and produced upon the Earth System as a whole, are shared.

Table 2. Comparative Analysis of Common Heritage of Mankind and Common Concern of Humankind

In summary, we can say that while one has a locus and does not possess an appropriate territorial scope, the other has the appropriate territorial scope but does not have a locus. In regard to the distributive scope, the sum of both may adequately address the characteristics of globally shared damages and benefits at the level of the Earth System.

In this sense, the combination of some of the characteristics of both concepts may bring the necessary advances in law and international relations with the objective of constructing an institutional architecture more adapted to the environmental living space in response to a collective concern of humanity.

9. An Evolutional Legal Living Space

Both concepts of *living space* of the CCH and the *safe operating space of humankind* maintain the common characteristic of being intangible non-territorial spaces regarding the biogeophisical conditions of a specific state of the Earth System that supported favourable conditions for human life on Earth. However, their origins are different – one is legal, the other scientific. This primordial nature is found on the level of the meta-heritage or constituent heritage (Soromenho-Marques 2006), an intangible natural heritage that is the fundamental basis for the intelligibility of all other types of tangible natural heritage already known. It is represented by the processes of life or the major circulatory element flows, which in a previous analogy was referred to as the software relationship of the Earth System.

As a concept, 'state', which is profoundly rooted within territorial space, does not include the *global software* that supports the life system on Earth. The 'safe operating space for humankind', as the best available integrated piece of scientific information with the capacity to elaborate on emerging phenomena in a systemic way, may constitute a keystone of this announced evolution. The question then becomes whether this scientific instrument is sufficient to represent the multiple realities of the Earth System as a whole and in an immutable way.

Although there is still uncertainty regarding the quantification of limits and the existence of planetary limits, they are clear and entirely consistent with the science of complex systems. As we cannot "aspire to an immutability of physical biological and chemical elements" (Canotilho 1991), it will be necessary to operate permanently on an evolutionary flexibility. The ecological paradigm is characterised by complex processes, which inevitably engender uncertainty. "It is up to the law to transform this ecological uncertainty into a social certainty" (Morand 1995).

In this sense, this *living space* will always be a scientific representation of a dynamic system. Therefore, the instrument used for its interpretation will also need to be flexible, dynamic and evolving, allowing a dialogue between the human species and the Earth System that we are part of. The creation of a new international intangible space, while founded in an ever-developing science, will have to be founded on a socially constructed "value" that will guarantee its existence independent of scientific evolutions on the Earth System.

The important thing will be the concept that there is an intangible *living space*, both in and outside sovereignties. Considering present scientific knowledge, this corresponds to the safe operating space of the Holocene, but the concrete definition of limits and elements to be taken into account within this socially constructed space will evolve along the line of continuous, evolutionary and dynamic knowledge of the Earth System.

Once again, as Morin (1990) states, complex thought "has no intent to replace the ambition of simple thinking, which is to control and dominate the real. It is a thought experiment that is capable of handling the real, and negotiating and entering into dialogue with it".

The key will be to find an instrument that represents the known reality of the Earth System, allowing us to enter into dialogue with it.

10. Applying CHM to the Earth System

From the initial intentions and derived concepts that evolved from the CHM concept will result a new legal object based on the fundamental separation between the *res incorporales* relative to the intangible dimension, qualitative and functional, of the Earth System (higher level of integration), and the *res corporals,* referring to the territorial spaces (land, oceans and aerial space, i.e., the lower level of integration) in which these functions and qualities develop.

In this sense, we advance a proposal for an evolution incorporating the combined elements for an axiological interpretation of CHM applied to the Earth System:

- The biogeophysical structure of the Holocene period is part of the international common heritage (patrimony) and therefore *belongs to all humanity in common.* This means it cannot be owned, enclosed or disposed of (i.e., appropriated) by any state/s or entity. As a commons it can be used, but not owned, either as private or common property or via the claim of sovereign rights.
- The use of the common heritage framework shall be carried out in accordance with a system of cooperative management for the benefit of all humanity (or common good). This has been interpreted as creating a type of trust relationship, with states acting as trustees for the benefit of all humanity (i.e., for the common good, not for the exclusive benefit of states/private entities) including future generations, taking into account the particular needs and interests of developing states (intra-generational equity).
- There exists a permanent sharing of damage and benefits realized over the state of the Earth System. It will be necessary to construct an accounting system in order to account for the contributions of each state towards the desired state of the Earth System, and next develop an equitable system of derived compensations for the different uses of the CHM.

- A global entity should be created with exclusive functions in coordination with compensations and the development of projects for the maintenance of this common heritage of mankind.

TERRITORIAL SCOPE	**Scope**	The Earth System as a whole – applied both beyond and within the jurisdiction of states
	Form of Representation	The higher level of Earth System integration; the intangible nature; the well-defined status of the Earth System corresponding to the geological age of the Holocene
SUBJECT SCOPE	**Scope**	Representation of a functional *living space* for humanity as whole, in a trans-temporal dimension; the *safe operating space of humankind*
	Form of Representation	Planetary Boundaries Framework
DISTRIBUTIVE SCOPE	**Scope**	Equitable sharing of benefits and burdens through a system of compensations – ECOBALANCE
	Form of Representation	An aggregated metric with the ability to represent the positive and negative impacts realized upon the Earth System

Table 3. Features of a possible evolution of CHM/CCH to a Common Intangible Natural Heritage of Humankind

This possible pathway of the natural heritage, from the "materially and geographically definable" to the "immaterial and intangible", is similar to the consolidation of cultural heritage. The importance of cultural heritage was consecrated in UNESCO's Convention Concerning the Protection of World Cultural and Natural Heritage in 1972, but 30 years later it was acknowledged that cultural heritage cannot be limited to what can be seen or touched so immaterial heritage was included in the Convention for the Safeguarding of Intangible Cultural Heritage in 2003.

The time has now come for intangible nature to be recognized as a vital resource for all humankind – a common intangible natural heritage of humankind.

11. Conclusion

It is now clear that international law is not yet equipped to handle the ecological goods that exist simultaneously in and outside of all states. There exists a structural, theoretical flaw in the approach taken to date to the global "whole". The starting point on how reality has been framed is not what by, its nature and characteristics, is truly common but the remaining part of the appropriation. The global commons have always been (and continue to be) understood as geographical spaces that exist only outside the political borders of states. The global, diffuse and intangible character of a vital good such as a stable climate, existing both within and outside all states, with the effects of the damage caused extending over several generations, have served to transform this traditional approach into an ecological nonsense. The dysfunctionality of existing legal instruments has not only long since been recognised, but has also triggered several attempts to build concepts, which, however, are soon found to be inoperative, with no legal consequences in terms of rights and duties.

A major advance was recently made towards unravelling the nebulous arguments composed of legally vague and undefined concepts disseminated in national and international legal texts. This advance was made possible because of our increasing understanding of the Earth System, in particular the possibility of measuring and monitoring its state and functioning through the Planetary Boundaries approach. This framework, which aims to define a planetary safe operating space within which humanity can survive and thrive, is based on a scientific understanding of the structure and functioning of the Earth System, and of the risks that destabilisation of the system creates for human well-being.

The discovery and definition of the "Safe Operating Space of Humankind" as a favourable state of the Earth System (with interacting ocean, atmosphere, cryosphere and land components) corresponding to a biogeophysical space, and therefore as a qualitative and non-geographic space, requires a reorientation of how the Earth System has been seen until today. In this sense, the Common Home of Humankind should not be understood as a planet with 510 million square km^2, but should rather be represented by a specific favorable state of the Earth System, using as a baseline the geological period of the last 11,700 years, the Holocene. Therefore, the necessary evolution of as yet undetermined legal concepts such the Common Concern of Humankind should have as its foundation this new known reality.

Setting sustainability targets (e.g., the Sustainable Development Goals) requires the identification of minimum thresholds beyond which human impact on the Earth System is unsustainable, and the adoption of a systemic approach reflecting the complex interactions that characterise the Earth and its human sub-systems. The Common Home of Humankind, as a social construct, should above all also be a legal construct, and should therefore be based on legal solutions to represent this global natural reality.

This new natural intangible heritage should be the *locus* on which to construct a system for the management and maintenance of Earth System use. Upon establishing rules applying to the use of the Earth System, we are also securing the minimum conditions for the dignity of future generations. But before undertaking institutional reform, we need a concept that allows for a solution that will fill the gap between the theory underlying the organization of international institutions and the reality of Earth System dynamics.

This is a structural prerequisite to building the equity and trust needed for collective action. In this sense, it will be a structural instrument for the application of human rights.

I would like to thank Prue Taylor, Viriato Soromenho-Marques and Pedro Magalhães for the revisions, comments, discussions and suggestions that led to the achievement of this chapter.

References

Agius, A. (1998). Obligations of Justice towards Future Generations: A Revolution in Social and Legal Thought. In E. Agius & S. Busuttil (Eds.), *Future Generations and International Law* (p. 7). London: Earthscan Publications.

Albert, M. (2007). Restructuring World Society: The Contribution of Modern Systems Theory. In L. W. Pauly & E. Grande (Eds.), *Complex Sovereignty: Reconstituting Political Authority in the Twenty-first Century* (pp. 48–67).Toronto: University of Toronto Press.

Amaral, F. (1994). *Apresentação, Direito do Ambiente*. Lisboa: Instituto Nacional da Administração.

Borg, S. (2007). *Climate Change as a Common Concern of Humankind, Twenty Years Later... From UNGA to UNSC.* IUCN Academy of Environmental Law, "Towards an Integrated Climate Change and Energy Policy in the European Union". University of Malta. Retrieved from: http://www.iucnael.org

Borg, S. (2009). *Key Note Speech* at the unveiling ceremony of the Climate Change Initiative Monument, University of Malta, 21 April. Retrieved from:
https://www.um.edu.mt/newsoncampus/features/?a=62770

Camilleri, J. & Falk, J. (1992). *The End of Sovereignty? The Politics of a Shrinking and Fragmenting World.* Aldershot: Edward Elgar Publishers.

Canotilho, J. J. G. (1991). Procedimento Administrativo e Defesa do Ambiente. *Revista de Legislação e de Jurisprudência,* anos 123 e 124. Coimbra: Coimbra Editora.

—. (2009). *Sobre o Condomínio da Terra.* Porto: Earth Condominium Publications. Retrieved from:
http://condominio.webfactional.com/media/cms_page_media/18/CAN
OTILHO%20sobre%20o%20Condominio%20da%20Terra.pdf

Cappelletti, M. (1975). Formazioni socialli e interessi di grupo davanti ala giustizia civile. *Riv. Dir. Proc.,* 30, 372.

Charbonneau, S. (1988). *La Nature du Droit de la Prévention des Risques Techniques.* Paris: Revue Française de Droit Administratif.

Coleman, W. D. (2007). Globality and Transnational Policy-making in Agriculture: Complexity, Contradictions and Conflict. In E. Grande & L. W. Pauly (Eds.), *Complex Sovereignty, Reconstituting Political Authority in the Twenty-first Century.* Toronto: University Toronto Press.

Comissão Europeia (2000). Gestão dos Sítios Natura 2000: As disposições do artigo 6° da Directiva "Habitats" 92/43/CEE. Luxenburgo: Servuço de Publicações Oficiais das Comunidades Europreias: Retrieved from: http://ec.europa.eu/environment/nature/natura2000/management/docs/a
rt6/provision_of_art6_pt.pdf

Cunhal, S. J. (2002). *Responsabilidade Civil por Danos Ecológicos.* Coimbra: Cadernos CEDOUA, Universidade de Coimbra.

Dirlik, A. (2001). Place-based Imagination: Globalism and the Politics of Place. In A. Dirlik & R. Prazniak (Eds.), *Places and Politics in an Age of Globalisation* (pp. 15–51). Lanham, MD: Rowman and Littlefield.

Filipe, J. A., Coelho, M., & Ferreira, M. A. M. (2007). *O Drama dos Recursos Comuns – À procura de soluções para os ecossistemas em perigo.* Lisboa: Edições Sílabo.

Fuller, R. B. (1969). *Operating Manual for Spaceship Earth.* Southern Illinois: University Press.

Garcia, M. G. (2010). *Aspectos Éticos da Responsabilidade Ambiental, Actas do Colóquio, Responsabilidade Civil por Danos Ambientais* (pp. 15). Retrieved from: http://www.icjp.pt/sites/default/files/media/icjp_ebook_responsabilida decivilpordanoambiental_isbn2.pdf

Garner, R. (Ed.) (2015). NASA, Satellite Tracks Saharan Dust to Amazon in 3-D. Greenbelt, Maryland: NASA's Goddard Space Flight Center. Retrieved from http://www.nasa.gov/content/goddard/nasa-satellite-reveals-how-much-saharan-dust-feeds-amazon-s-plants/#.VPIBrMYyEy4

Gray, E. (2015). NASA Satellite Reveals How Much Saharan Dust Feeds Amazon's Plants. Greenbelt, Maryland: NASA's Earth Science News Team. Retrieved from: http://www.nasa.gov/content/goddard/nasa-satellite-reveals-how-much-saharan-dust-feeds-amazon-s-plants

Giddens, A. (1990). *The Consequences of Modernity.* Cambridge. England: Polity Press.

Hibbard, K. A., Crutzen, P. J., Lambin, E. F., Liverman, D., Mantua, N. J., McNeill, J. R., Messerli, B., & Steffen, W. (2006). Decadal Interactions of Humans and the Environment. In R. Costanza, L. Graumlich, & W. Steffen (Eds.), *Integrated History and Future of People on Earth* (pp. 341–375). Boston, MA: MIT Press.

Hucke, J. & Wollmann, H. (1998). *Vollzug des Umweltrechts.* Handworterbuch des Umweltreches (Dir. Kimminich/Von Lersner/Ström). Berlin.

Lourenço, E. (1999). *Portugal como Destino Seguido de Mitologia da Saudade.* Lisboa: Gradiva

Magalhães, P. (2007*). Earth Condominium – From the Climate Change to a New Juridic Conception of the Planet.* Coimbra: Edições Almedina.

Malhotra, A. (1998). A Commentary on the Status of Future Generations as a Subject of International Law. In E. Agius & S. Busuttil (Eds.), *Future Generations and International Law* (p. 41). London: Earthscan Publications.

Miller, I. & Swinney, G. (2001). *Chaos Theory and Complex Dynamical Systems: Its Emergence in Human Consciousness and Healing.* Retrieved from http://www.oocities.org/iona_m/ChaosTheory/CTintro.html

Morand, A (1995). La Coordination Materèrielle: De Pesée des Intérêts à l'Ecologisation du Droit. In *Le Droit de l'Environnement dans la*

Pratique (p. 212). Quoted by François Ost, *A Natureza à Margem da Lei, A Ecologia à Prova do Direito*. Lisboa: Instituto Piaget.

Morin, E. (1990). *Introduction à la Pensée Complexe*. Paris: ESF Éditeur.

Murillo, J. (2008). Common Concern of Humankind and its Implications in International Environmental Law. *Macquarie Journal of International and Comparative Environmental Law*, 5(2), 133.

Nykvist, B., Persson, A., Moberg, F., Persson, L., Cornell, S., & Rockström, J. (2013). *National Environmental Performance on Planetary Boundaries*. Swedish Environmental Protection Agency Report. Stockholm: Naturvardsverket. Retrieved from: http://www.naturvardsverket.se/Nerladdningssida/?fileType=pdf&download Url=/Documents/publikationer6400/978-91-620-6576-8.pdf

Oldfield, F. & Steffen, W. (2004). Box 1.1–The Earth System. In W. Steffen, A. Sanderson, P. D. Tyson. (Eds.), *Global Change and the Earth System: A Planet under Pressure* (p. 7). Berlin, Heidelberg, New York: Springer-Verlag.

Pardo, A. (1976). *The Common Heritage. Selected Papers on Oceans and World Order, 1967–1974*. Malta.O.I: Occasional Papers, nº 3.

Pauly, L. W. & Grande, E. (2007). *Complex Sovereignty: Reconstituting Political Authority in the Twenty-First Century*. Toronto: University of Toronto Press.

Prieur, M. (1987). La Déréglamentation en matière d'Environment. *Révue Juridique de L'Environment (RJE), 3*, 320.

Rakhyun, E. K. & Bosselmann, K. (2013). International Environmental Law in the Anthropocene: Towards a Purposive System of Multilateral Environmental Agreements. *Transnational Environmental Law*, 2, 285–309. doi:10.1017/S2047102513000149

Rangel, P. C. (1994*). Concertação, programação e Direito do Ambiente*. Coimbra: Coimbra Editora.

Rockström, J., Steffen, W., Noone, K., et al. (2009b). Planetary Boundaries: Exploring the Safe Operating Space for Humanity. *Ecology and Society 14*(2), 32. Retrieved from http://www.ecologyandsociety.org/vol14/iss2/art32/

Rockström, J. (2014). *Planetary Boundaries and Human Opportunities: The Quest for Safe and Just Development on a Resilient Planet*. Open Online Course offered by the SRC in partnership with SDSN. Edu. November 17, 2014 – February 3, 2015. Retrieved from https://www.sdsnedu.org/learn/planetary-boundaries-and-human-opportunities-past-course-fall-2014

Ruggie, J. G. (1993). Territoriality and Beyond: Problematizing Modernity in International Relations. *International Organization, 47*(1), 139–174. The *MIT Press*. Retrieved from http://www.jstor.org/stable/2706885

Santos, V. M. (2001). *A Humanidade e o Seu Património, Reflexões Contextuais sobre Conceptualidade Evolutiva e Dinâmica Operatória das Relações Internacionais*. Lisboa: Instituto Superior de Ciências Sociais e Políticas.

Shelton, D. (2009). Common Concern of Humanity. *Iustum Aequum Salutar, 1,* 33–40. Retrieved from http://epa.oszk.hu/02400/02445/00012/pdf/EPA02445_ias_2009_1_03 3-040.pdf

Silva, V. P. (1989). *Para um Contencioso Administrativo dos Particulares*. Coimbra: Edições Almedina.

Silva, M. L. P. (2002). Autonomia da Pessoa e Determinismo Genético. In R. Nunes, H. Melo, & C. Nunes (Eds.), *Genoma e Dignidade Humana*. Coimbra: Gráfica de Coimbra.

Sobrino, J. M. (2012). Património é Uma Ideia (...) Património é Algo que é Necessário Conservar no Interesse de Todos. *Jornal Quercus,* 50(Jan-Fev), 4–5. Retrieved from http://www.quercus.pt/images/PDF/QA/QA50.pdf

SOER (2015). *The European Environment – State and Outlook (2015)*. Retrieved from: http://www.eea.europa.eu/soer

Soromenho-Marques, V. (2006). *O Património Incorpóreo como Meta-Património. Algumas Notas de Reflexão, Actas dos XII Cursos Internacionais de Verão de Cascais*, coordenação José Tengarrinha (pp. 57–62). Cascais: Câmara Municipal de Cascais e Instituto de Ciências e Estudos Socais.

Sousa, M. T. (1998). *A Protecção Jurisdicional dos Interesses Difusos, Temas actuais do Direito Processual Ibero-Americano/ Compêndio de relatórios e conferências apresentadas nas XVI Jornadas Ibero-Americanas de Direito Processual* (p. 383). Rio de Janeiro.

Steffen, W., Sanderson, A., Tyson, P. D., et al. (2004). *Global Change and the Earth System: A Planet under Pressure*. Berlin, Heidelberg, New York: Springer-Verlag.

Steffen, W., Richardson, K., Rockström, J., et al. (2015a). Planetary Boundaries: Guiding Human Development on a Changing Planet. *Science, 347*(6223). doi: 10.1126/science.1259855.

Taylor, P. & Stroud, L. (2012). *Common Heritage of Mankind: A Bibliography of Legal Writing*. Malta: Fondation de Malte.

Tolba, M. (1991). The Implications of the "Common Concern of Mankind" Concept in Global Environmental Issues. *Revista IIDH, 13*, 237–246. Retrieved from: http://www.juridicas.unam.mx/publica/librev/rev/iidh/cont/13/doc/doc 27.pdf

UNEP Secretariat (1991). II Meeting of the Group of Legal Experts to Examine the Concept of the "Common Concern of Mankind" in Relation to Global Environmental Issues. Geneva, March 20–22. *Revista IIDH. Vol. 13*, 253–258. Retrieved from: http://www.juridicas.unam.mx/publica/librev/rev/iidh/cont/13/doc/doc 29.pdf

UNESCO (1997). *Universal Declaration on the Human Genome and Human Rights.* Retrieved from http://www.unesco.org/new/en/social-and-human-sciences/themes/bioethics/human-genome-and-human-rights/

—. (2003). *Convention for the Safeguarding of the Intangible Cultural Heritage.* Retrieved from http://www.unesco.org/culture/ich/index.php?lg=en&pg=00006

UNITED NATIONS(1992). *Convention on Biological Diversity.* Retrieved from: https://www.cbd.int/doc/legal/cbd-en.pdf

—. (1988). *Protection of Global Climate for Present and Future Generations of Mankind.* Retrieved from: http://www.un.org/documents/ga/res/43/a43r053.htm

—. (2013). System Task Team on the Post-2015 UN Development Agenda *Global Governance and Governance of the Global Commons in the Global Partnership for Development beyond 2015.*

CHAPTER EIGHT

UNESCO HERITAGE:
TWELVE LEGAL ARGUMENTS IN FAVOUR
OF CONSIDERING THE EARTH SYSTEM
AS NATURAL INTANGIBLE ENDANGERED
HERITAGE

ALEXANDRA ARAGÃO[1]

1. Can the UNESCO Convention be used to protect the Earth System in its present status?

Yes. The status of the Earth System is of vital importance for humankind. The so-called Holocene is being jeopardized by pollution, degradation and over-extraction, threatening the ecosystem's capacity to perform vital functions not only for humankind but for all the other species that share the same ecological needs.

We argue that UNESCO's legal regime of *natural world heritage* is perfectly suited to protect the Earth System.

2. What are the consequences of declaring the Earth System as world heritage?

The Earth System (in a Holocene status) as a world natural intangible heritage does not change the existing regimes of full or limited sovereignty over some natural resources. For instance, the rights of the states over territorial waters and contiguous zones will continue. The same

---

[1] Faculty of Law, Universidade de Coimbra.

goes for the freedom of the seas. Sovereignty over the airspace remains untouched; so does the freedom of overflight.

What is compressed and conditioned is the right to use and abuse of these assets beyond the limits of what is tolerable and sustainable.

3. Does the UNESCO Convention already recognize the world natural heritage?

Yes. It has been applied in three situations:
- **Natural features** consisting of physical and biological formations or groups of such formations that are of outstanding universal value from the aesthetic or scientific point of view;
- **Geological and physiographical formations** and precisely delineated areas that constitute the habitat of threatened species of animals and plants of outstanding universal value from the point of view of science or conservation;
- **Natural sites** or precisely delineated natural areas of outstanding universal value from the point of view of science, conservation or natural beauty.

4. Does the Earth System fit into any of these three categories: features, formations or sites?

Apparently not. Formally, the Earth System (in a Holocene status) is not a geographical or physiographical formation or even a site. This does not mean that it cannot be recognized by UNESCO, even without amending the UNESCO Convention. It can be considered as world natural heritage considering its exceptional universal value.

5. What are the criteria necessary to obtain a declaration of a certain asset as Endangered World Heritage?

First criterion: the heritage to be protected should be threatened. According to the UNESCO Convention, "the cultural heritage and the natural heritage are increasingly threatened with destruction not only by the traditional causes of decay but also by changing social and economic conditions, which aggravate the situation with even more formidable phenomena of damage or destruction".[2]

Clearly, the Earth System is threatened by human drivers that are disrupting the Earth System and pushing it out of the Holocene status due to overexploitation and misuse resulting from legal and illegal activities.

Second criterion: powerlessness of states to protect the heritage acting alone. Also, according to the UNESCO Convention, "protection of this heritage at the national level often remains incomplete because of the scale of the resources which it requires and of the insufficient economic, scientific, and technological resources of the country where the property to be protected is situated".[3]

Therefore, the Earth System can only be protected effectively through a supranational and concerted action. In the expressive words of the UNESCO Convention, "In view of the magnitude and gravity of the new dangers threatening them, it is incumbent on the international community as a whole to participate in the protection of the cultural and natural heritage of outstanding universal value, by the granting of collective assistance which, although not taking the place of action by the state concerned, will serve as an efficient complement thereto".[4]

6. How can the Earth System be protected when the Convention does not expressly mention global systems?

Dating back to 1972, the UNESCO Convention requires an up-to-date interpretation. In fact, the purpose of modernizing the existing system of assets considered as common heritage follows from the reference to "modern scientific methods"[5] in the UNESCO Convention.

---

[2] Paragraph 1 of the preamble. According to the *Technical Guidelines for the Application of the World Heritage*, the threats are natural calamities, the degradation of construction materials and structures, the destruction and replacement of historic urban fabric, the threatening effects of planning, road and irrigation systems, environmental impacts and climate change, negligence or abandonment and lack of a conservation policy.

[3] Paragraph 3 of the preamble.

[4] Paragraph 7 of the preamble.

[5] "*Considering* that it is essential for this purpose to adopt new provisions in the form of a convention establishing an effective system of collective protection of the cultural and natural heritage of outstanding universal value, organized on a permanent basis and in accordance with modern scientific methods" (paragraph 8 of the preamble).

If the ultimate goal is that the system of protection established matches the reality of the world heritage in need of protection then the UNESCO Convention must be subject to an actualistic and teleological interpretation.

7. Is it possible to submit the 1972 Convention to an actualistic and teleological interpretation?

Yes, it was the recognition of the compelling need to undertake a dynamic, actualistic and teleological interpretation of the Convention that led the Intergovernmental Committee for the Protection of the World Cultural and Natural Heritage to update — more than 20 times over the past 35 years — the *Technical Guidelines for the Implementation of the World Heritage Convention*.[6]

This is the explanation of the fact that the concept of heritage, originally designed for the classification of very specific goods or strictly delineated natural areas, can now cover, according to the actualistic and authentic interpretation given by the Technical Guidelines, "serial properties". The need for this evolution of the concept of heritage emerged, for the first time, eight years after the adoption of the Convention, in the 1980 edition of *Technical Guidelines for Implementation of the Convention*.[7]

---

[6] The first version dates back to 1977 and the last one to 2012 (all the versions are available at http://whc.unesco.org/en/guidelines/).

[7] The reasoning of the Intergovernmental Committee for the protection of the world natural and cultural heritage was the following: "It should be realized that individual sites may not possess the most spectacular or outstanding single example of the above, but when the sites are viewed in a broader perspective with a complex of many surrounding features of significance, the entire area may qualify to demonstrate an array of features of global significance". In 1983, quite naturally, the "serial properties" emerge.

8. Is the extension of the concept of world heritage in conformity with the Statute of UNESCO?

Yes. According to its statute, UNESCO was created to promote peace but the intended peace is not founded on mere political and economic arrangements of governments. The aim is to achieve a peace founded on the "intellectual and moral solidarity of humankind".[8] Is there a better example to reflect the "intellectual and moral solidarity of humankind" than the Earth System?[9]

Furthermore, protection of the Earth System as a world heritage complies with the functions of UNESCO as a "laboratory of ideas, standard-setter, clearing house, capacity-builder in Member States in UNESCO's fields of competence, and catalyst for international cooperation".[10]

9. Why is the protection through already existing international instruments not enough (Convention on the Law of the Sea and Framework Convention on Climate Change)?

Experience has shown that given the immense challenges faced by the Earth System, existing international instruments have been insufficient to ensure the planetary mobilization required to change recent development trends. This vision finds support in the post-2015 Development Agenda of the United Nations and within the sustainable development goals (SDG). This United Nations strategy emphasises "the need for a coherent global

---

[8] The expression is used in paragraph 5 of the preamble of UNESCO's Constitution: "That a peace based exclusively upon the political and economic arrangements of governments would not be a peace which could secure the unanimous, lasting and sincere support of the peoples of the world, and that the peace must therefore be founded, if it is not to fail, upon the intellectual and moral solidarity of mankind".

[9] The recognition of the strong relation between peace and environment was sealed in 2007 with the granting of the Nobel Peace Prize to the Intergovernmental Panel for Climate Change.

[10] These functions are mentioned in the "Medium-term strategy 2008–2013" (34 C/4), unanimously approved in the 34th session of the General Conference of UNESCO, gathered in Paris between 16 October and 2 November 2007: "Laboratory of ideas, standard-setter, clearing house, capacity-builder in Member States in UNESCO's fields of competence, and catalyst for international cooperation".

framework to integrate existing laws covering these international areas"[11]; while, in fact, international treaties and conventions relative to the global common goods do exist, the United Nations recognizes that "the frameworks are fractured, and not comprehensive enough to include modern conservation principles or assessments".[12]

Undisputed recognition of the global importance and vital nature of the Earth System may have the potential to generate the necessary "trigger effect".

10. Is the recognition of the Earth System as world heritage only symbolic?

No. Although recognition as a world heritage is the assignment of a label that is in itself symbolic, it is not just a symbolic act. The recognition:

a) is adopted in the context of a political statement and therefore can change wills and behaviours;
b) requires states to submit periodic reports on the status of the heritage and adopt additional measures if necessary;
c) can be the legal basis to organize an ecological accountability based on the damages and benefits preformed in the common heritage; and
d) allows UNESCO to examine and give an opinion on the maintenance and management of a heritage considered of high value to humanity, on actions to prevent harm and to assist in its maintenance.

[11] UN System Task Team on the Post-2015 UN Development Agenda – Global governance and governance of the global commons in the global partnership for development beyond 2015. Thematic Think Piece – OHCHR, OHRLLS, UNDESA, UNEP, UNFPA, January 2013.
http://www.un.org/en/development/desa/policy/untaskteam_undf/thinkpieces/24_t hinkpiece_global_governance.pdf
[12] idem

11. Is this extension of the concept of heritage to the Earth System a trivialization of the world heritage as a tool to protect very high values?

No. First, because there aren't other planetary systems which can be said to be as global and as vital as the Earth System itself.

Second, because the trivialization may stem more from instrumentalizing the concept of world heritage to geostrategic interests (especially economic and touristic) rather than from the recognition of new examples of heritage with exceptional and universal value, such as the Earth System itself.

12. As part of the world natural heritage, how can the Earth System be characterised?

The Earth System is a natural, material and overall system which can and should be regarded as an example of *sui generis* natural world heritage, with features common to the "serial properties"[13] and to the "transnational properties."

This is the meaning of the words of the Intergovernmental Committee for the Protection of the World Cultural and Natural Heritage in the *Technical Guidelines for Implementation of the Convention* when it explains the need to recognize the serial properties: "We must be aware that individual sites may not, by themselves, be the most spectacular examples [of world heritage assets] but when viewed in a broader perspective, as a complex of numerous surrounding high importance

---

[13] Still according to the technical guidelines for the application of the Convention (2012 version), serial properties will include two or more component parts related by clearly defined links:
a) Component parts should reflect cultural, social or functional links over time that provide, where relevant, landscape, ecological, evolutionary, or habitat connectivity.
b) Each component part should contribute to the outstanding universal value of the property as a whole in a substantial, scientific, readily defined and discernible way, and may include, inter alia, intangible attributes. The resulting outstanding universal value should be easily understood and communicated.
c) Consistently, and in order to avoid an excessive fragmentation of component parts, the process of nomination of the property, including the selection of the component parts, should take fully into account the overall manageability and coherence of the property.

features, the whole area can be classified as a demonstration of a set of features of global importance".

It is also a complex natural global system which can and should be regarded as an example of the combined natural world heritage, material and immaterial, in a similar way to mixed cultural heritage (material and immaterial cultural heritage).

However, the vastness and complexity of the Earth System does not mean that it is not worthy of autonomous legal protection. Rather, precaution requires that legal mechanisms of protection of the Earth System as a whole are established and not just the punctual protection offered by a few isolated conventions protecting the climate or the ocean.

Finally, the recognition of the Earth System as world heritage (natural and mixed) confirms the soundness of the progress made and the coherence of the system of protection established by the United Nations in a new stage of the global protection of our planet.

CHAPTER NINE

EARTH CONDOMINIUM:
A LEGAL MODEL FOR THE ANTHROPOCENE

PAULO MAGALHÃES[1]

"It seems that the human mind has first to construct forms independently before we can find them in things."

—Albert Einstein

1. Political Impossibility?

In a seminar organized by the Academy of Environmental Law (IUCN), Simone Borg (2001) presented a paper with the title "Climate Change as a Common Concern of Humankind." In it he posed two fundamental questions:

1) Is it necessary to identify the legal status of climate?
2) Will we gain anything from doing so?

We have accepted that the good to be put under the protection of the law is not only the climate but a well-defined state of the Earth System, as Oldfield and Steffen (2004) have already demonstrated. Now, it seems to us that any satisfactory attempt to answer these questions can only be made if we first answer another question asked by Alexander Kiss (1982) on the definition of *res communis*: "Of course, one may question the exact meaning of this concept: is it a common sovereignty, a co-ownership, a condominium? We must recognize that this question has never been solved in a completely satisfactory manner – that is precisely one of the major arguments of the advocates of the conception *res nullius.*"

---

[1] Interdisciplinary Centre of Social Sciences CICS.NOVA - Faculdade de Ciências Sociais e Humanas - Universidade Nova de Lisboa

This statement redirects the point from the eventual need to recognize a *legal status* for the climate or the Earth System to the real crux of the issue: whether there is a legal framework able to receive and integrate a new *legal status* with respect to a good that is simultaneously inside and outside of all sovereignties. The problem is establishing the type of *res communis* of this new legal good, and this will be decisive in its new legal status being, or not, compatible and integrated in the existing legal framework. It is in the absence of a clear definition of what a "global common good" is exactly, that is, what is the *res communis omnium* "which is not restricted to the global commons but spans also across areas subject to national jurisdiction" (Borg 2007), that creates the breeding ground in which all uncertainties can germinate. This absence is the epicentre of our legal nebula, our confusion, our *legal black hole* through which the most vital factors for our future disappear. Awareness has been growing that the term *common concern* can only express our embarrassment, our incapacity to define in a simple manner, to name in a clear way, or capture with words a vague terrain of ideas.

Stating that the *common concern* was the fallback solution because there was no real political will to build a new legal object is only partially correct. In fact, without first identifying the legal regime of *res communis* needed to reconcile the intrinsic characteristics of the new legal object with the existing international legal framework, even if there had been political will to recognize the existence of a new legal good, the result would probably not have been very different from the existent incompatibilities that continue to relegate CHM to the ever-smaller remaining parts of jurisdictions, and the CCH for a future always postponed.

A desirable conservation of the Earth System cannot be regulated effectively if it is based only on international laws sustained purely on interstate consent and reciprocity. A new legal framework must be built that ensures also the protection and promotion of common interests by representing the interests of all humankind. Without this, vital factors will continue to be perceived as concerns, or will conflict with *ecological nonsense*[2] approaches. The question "How can we admit that a good that belongs to no one may be governed by a specific law?" (Kiss 1982) implies understanding which theoretical legal framework is more able to explain and receive this new object of law. If the basic statement that the absence of ownership is synonymous with not being governed and therefore being a *res nullius* is correct, how is it possible that a new global

---

[2] See Chapter 6 of this book, written by Prue Taylor.

legal object, called here the *favourable state of the Earth System*, can come into being and be ruled in a context of fragmented territorial sovereignty without any legal representation of a global *res communis*?

The remaining ecological space (Rockström 2014), scientifically represented by the safe operating space for humankind of planetary boundaries and the living space as the non-territorial space of the CCH, "can be considered as a fine-tuned version of the res communis status of global natural resources in light of the contemporary developments" (Borg 2009). This view could also correspond with the problem of the definition of *res communis*, as reported by Kiss. But perhaps the main response to Borg's original question is the need for the good to belong to someone in order to be ruled and not be a *res nullius*.

2. Two Different Levels of the Earth System

Two Different Levels of Human Relations

If we are to change our relationship with our life-supporting system from exploitation to stewardship, humanity has to self-organize within this remaining living space and ensure its maintenance in a well-functioning condition. This means that the main task is the internal organization between all the users of the same resource on a global scale. This fact puts humanity in the unavoidable position of relating internally in two different scales. This means that it will be in the way the Earth System is used that the relationships between all communities and individuals will be established.

Like all complex systems, the Earth System has two levels of integration, a lower level of component parts and processes and a higher level that constitutes the whole system with its emergent properties that cannot be understood or described by simply aggregating the component parts up the global level. The first level is related to the geographical area, that is, the heterogeneous physical planet with 510 million km^2 on which different state sovereignties operate, and also the *locus, the hardware* of the Earth System. The higher level (the Earth System itself) is intangible as it arises from the global interconnections and emerging phenomena through which global human relations are mediated. This higher level developed in an evolutionary fashion throughout Earth's history and it is through this evolutionary process involving the living part of the planet as well as the geophysical that, for example, the relative concentrations of gases remain relatively constant through time. A key process of the Earth System is self-regulation, which consists of feedback loops formed by component parts of the system (both inside and outside of all sovereignty and incapable of any legal abstraction of division) that work synergistically to keep the system in well-defined states.

In essence, it is the integration of the geophysical properties of the planet with the living biosphere that forms the intangible Earth System, a single global system incapable of any legal abstraction of division. In this sense, the intangible Earth System is an authentic law of nature, already described by science and recognized as the "principles" that govern the natural phenomena of the system. Humanity, as an integral component of the Earth System, is also dependent on those principles and, as such, humanity is related to the Earth System on two distinct levels on equal terms.

On a lower level, humanity is organized as independent political communities around a defined territory. On the higher level, the relationships are established and mediated through the use of a single common system, the Earth System, which does not exist legally and, as a consequence, is unmanaged.

So the main answer to Borg's initial question has to do with the reconfiguration of inter-subjective relations between all users of the same *resource*. As stated by Filipe et al. (2007), "It is from the relationships established when carrying out the use of the resource that arise concepts as the right to common property or private property".

3. A Heritage to Organize Relations

Since the use of the common resource, called here the favourable state of the Earth System, is extensive temporally and its effects intergenerational, it is also through this *resource* that relationships are established between generations past, present and unborn. Theory has defined *property* not only by the individual's relationship with the inherent characteristics of the object but also to include the underlying relationship between the owner and all other individuals. According to Hang (2003), the most relevant is the relationship between individuals: "Property rights are a relationship between individuals in relation to a resource, not a relationship between an individual and the resource". Once the use of this limited resource is not exclusive to any "user" and no user can exclude any other access, in global terms we are facing a situation of common ownership extended to the scale of all humankind *(Res communis omnium)*. From the moment it is discovered that a resource considered inexhaustible is, after all, exhaustible, internal relations are equally reconfigured among all users of that *resource*. "Property rights represent a set of ordered relationships among people which define their opportunities, their exposure to the acts of others, their privileges and their responsibilities for resource utilization" (Schmid 1995). When the resource in question is a *res incorporales* relative to a specific favourable state of the Earth System that everyone depends on, all users share the consequences of the acts of others.

Constructing a system that organizes each actor's privileges and responsibilities regarding the use of a resource that belongs to everyone, born and unborn, becomes a matter of survival.

To that extent, the legal recognition of a *favourable state of the Earth System* as a common heritage of mankind should primarily result in a regulatory instrument of relationships between individuals, states and communities. That is, if everyone has access to the good and its benefits, and no one can be excluded, we will have to answer questions like: Who is responsible for maintaining it? What are the rules for using it (rights and duties)?

The legal absence of the good also corresponds to a social failure, to the *res nullius*, that is, the absence of rules between individuals or states on the use of the good. The perceived relevance of the underlying relations of property ownership will be the most decisive factor in justifying the need to recognize legally the existence of the Earth System, and to give it a patrimonial dimension.

When we structure global and inter-subjective relations based on the relationships established through the use of a common good to which a value is assigned *per se*, we are simultaneously building a system to ensure its maintenance and allowing the construction of a larger global justice as they are intrinsically related.

As a result, the preservation of the new legal good should result from a collective action internally organized between the users rather than by a legal obligation. Thereby, the new heritage shall be the mediator of a dialectical relationship developed on a global scale between social internal relations and the object (Earth System). To that extent, planetary boundaries should not be perceived as new prohibitions but as limits that underlie and justify self-organization. We can even say that the ultimate goal of acknowledging this common natural intangible heritage of humankind is the construction of a globally organized society around a common heritage, an intangible *locus* around which humankind organizes itself.

If nothing can exist in pure disorder, the survival of the human species as a whole depends on its ability to self-organize. So, it's at the level of consequences for subjective relationships in the internal organization between users of the common resource that the greatest justification for the legal consecration of a well-defined state of the Earth System lies.

If one accepts that the legal recognition of a favourable state of the Earth System is a basic structural factor for the organization/regulation of the internal relations of humanity, a key question remains unanswered: Will it be possible to conciliate in a symbiotic way the existence of one global legal support (the legal status of the Earth System) with the fragmented territorial sovereignty? Taking as a starting point the two levels of the existing relations, we will try to understand which model of *res communis* is better able to accurately portray the facts: "the common sovereignty, co-ownership, the condominium?" (Kiss 1982).

4. Divide to Organize

Taking as a starting point the unique characteristics of the climate and the Earth System as a whole, and the alternatives presented by Kiss (1982), it seems that the hypotheses of both common sovereignty and co-ownership imply the maintenance of the idea that there is a separation between what is within the borders and the *res communis,* which corresponds with the leftover areas of the division. In this sense, none of these models seem to have the necessary characteristics to be able to deal satisfactorily with the problem of "activities affecting negatively an intangible natural resource, which spans across and beyond the national territories of States" (Borg 2009). This overlap between the private interests of states and the interests of all humanity has an inherent condition of interdependence: it is mutually beneficial or mutually destructive. The problem of reconciling seemingly opposing interests in a situation of symbiotic interdependence is not new to legal sciences, and it was structured through a private law figure that defines the situation where a materially indivisible thing, or a thing with a unitary structure, belongs to various co-owners, each of whom has private or exclusive rights of ownership over determined fractions and, at the same time, is a co-owner of the parts of the building that constitutes its common structure. This juridical figure is known as a condominium.

In order for this model to transform a theoretical impossibility into a solution, it was necessary to innovate and not be limited by the application of pre-existing forms of *dominium*. Once neither private property nor co-ownership could deal with the relationships established through the ownership and use of a materially indivisible building, the condominium was invented. First it accepted the unitary and indivisible nature of a building and then built a system that would adapt to this seemingly unsurpassable circumstance. It argued against what was previously considered to be irrefutable and created a model of ownership that cannot be associated with any other form of ownership. As magistrate Luís Hernanz Cano (1998) says, Spanish jurisprudence has perceived horizontal property as "special property" or "complex property". Its accurate designations are clearly a sign of its complexity: "house by storeys", "condominium of storeys", "*pro indivisio* communities", autonomous fraction", and "community with rights in rem" (Cano 1998). The motive for such complexity is the coexistence of apparently contradictory and antagonistic elements, which, if considered superficially, may create the supposition that the presence of one implies the absence of the other and is hardly translatable in the reductive language of definitions.

The urgent need for a solution led to one capable of combining within the same materially indivisible building a separation that allows several individuals to use the same floor as housing. Additionally, it envisages: a) that each individual has a unique right to ownership of a fraction of the building, making possible the legal trade of these properties; and b) the existence of a system of contributions to ensure the maintenance of systems of common use (water, electricity, elevators) and the parts that are legally and materially impossible to divide (stairs, roof, structure, etc.), which must all be maintained in a dependable state.

The model of the condominium, or complex property, is not a community or an arithmetic sum of individual properties. It is something complex that elevates the law to the art of reconciling extremes, of making symbiotically dependent what was apparently incompatible (Magalhães 2007).

Although with some nuances, this theoretical model has been used recurrently throughout history in international law, in situations of shared rivers, small islands, territorial enclaves, territories under dispute, and in undefined political situations; even at the level of small communities wishing to establish access to certain resources related to rural activities. Even the Antarctica Treaty System of 1959 is considered by some a *de facto* condominium (Glennon 1991) since it is not a sovereign territory (although various nations claim parts of its territory as their own) and provides voting authority for 28 nations to jointly govern the area. In all, 50 countries are part of the "condominium" although some consider it a "quasi-condominium" (Hemmings 2014).

The use of civil juridical institutes originating from national laws is not new in international law. For some authors it is even recommended. Weeramantry (2000) points out that:

> In view of the speed of progress and of technology, the national laws and international law should follow the movement and increase their productive and adaptive ability. New concepts and procedures should

rapidly be sought to confront the new situations, which are a result of technology's progress. For this effect, international law should firstly be aware of all the essential traditions of the different civilizations and adopt a multicultural attitude. Numerous principles of international law, which will be adopted in the future, may be released from the traditional juridical systems existent in the world and through which international law may receive its strength and inspiration.

The change from the soft law to the hard law should be accelerated, thus making international law more fit to adapt itself to the needs of our time. National laws will take advantage of the norms and of the universal patterns, which will equally improve the internal systems.

In the classical approach, commons management is doomed to the fate of the "tragedy of the commons". Hardin's work transformed a growing pessimism around the "commons" into a global scale pessimism, also called by some doctrines the "tragedy of the common heritage of mankind" (Shackelford 2008). "Communal sovereignty may be seen as a temporary placeholder that exists until technology enables occupation of property making it worthwhile for States to assert national sovereignty in the oldest traditions of the Westphalian system". In this view, "establishing property rights has been commonly seen in the Western world as the solution to commons management; once occupation of a territory is possible, then property rights become necessary to catalyze development" (Shackelford 2008). This leads to the still-dominant doctrine that points out as a unique solution the division and privatization of the good. However, ecological interdependence has shown that it is necessary to develop a new theory to explain phenomena that do not fit in a dichotomous world divided between individual/state interests and collective/humanity interests.

In his analysis of the strategy of conflict, Schelling (1960), winner of the Nobel Prize for Economics and one of the fathers of the theory of games, showed that many social interactions can be seen as non-cooperative games that involve both common and conflicting interests. In fact, Schelling sought to consolidate the idea that almost any problem involving the decisions of more than one person simultaneously contains elements of conflict and common interest. It is in the apparent contradiction of the symbiotic relationship between individual and collective interests (masterfully defined by Kant, "Only in the pursuit of common interests can we guarantee our individual rights)"[3] that we will try to reinterpret the analyses already carried out on the structural paradox of these interrelationships, which are exercised in a mutually advantageous form or "a failed coordination would give rise to high costs for all parties" (Filipe et al. 2007). The condominium transforms dichotomous dogma into accidental truth and achieves, without denying the classic solution of division, the integration and symbiotic unification with the common property.

The big news is that although the condominium divides in order to organize the different tasks and responsibilities, these are carried out not only to define distinct private properties but also to distinguish all private properties from parts and systems that are in a regime of common ownership. It is precisely through the distinction between different types of ownership over the same materially undivided good that this form of "complex property" can harmonise the different private and common interests, making this overlap of properties perfectly symbiotic.

Separation is managed through a legal abstraction, allowing the existence, within each individual fraction, of elements that appear to be private but are actually common (e.g., main walls, structure, exterior walls, roofs, water distribution system, and electricity). The operation is not just a mere division of spaces but a division with qualitative and functional criteria regarding the intrinsic nature of the different elements in a building.

The criterion on which this approach is based is that all those constituent and functional elements whose lack of maintenance implies damage for all owners of individual properties within the building should be integrated into the co-ownership regime. That is, common parts are all parts of a building that cannot be materially assigned to only one owner, as

---

[3] In his philosophical project entitled "Perpetual Peace" - (1795/96), Kant clearly perceives the interdependence of private and collective interests. Our global interdependence (which the environmental crisis has rendered evident) was already perceived by Kant on a social level which led him to publicly proclaim the creation of a *cosmopolitan law*. He was convinced that through the mechanism of selfish tendencies, which oppose each other in a natural manner, a space for the juridical regulation between states could be created. According to his way of thinking, the *commercial spirit* which could not coexist with war would make the states promote noble peace and drive out war. Thus, mankind's own nature, through the mechanisms of human tendencies, would guarantee permanent peace. *"Providing this guarantee is nothing but the great artist, Nature itself (natura daedala rerum), whose mechanical course evidently manifests a purpose with the strife of man, making harmony emerge even if it is against his will."*

well as all elements and systems that are decisive for the operation and security of the entire building, obliging all to participate in their maintenance.

Only through a clear identification of what those elements are and what is under common ownership is it possible to establish a system that ensures the maintenance of the common parts together with the systems and services that are of common interest. In other words, only the precise definition of all the elements that are in co-ownership will make assigning responsibility for the management and maintenance of such property and creating a contribution system among all the owners in pursuit of common interests possible.

The process of this theoretical construction was not a conceptual process that was then applied to the good, dividing it arbitrarily. On the contrary, it departed from the unitary character of the property, identified the elements that by their nature are essential to maintaining the structure and operation of the building, and considered as private all those spaces and goods whose individual ownership does not pose a problem to the unitary and functional characteristics of the common good.

This overlap between private interests and communal interests assumes that every homeowner simultaneously pursues private property rights on their fraction and co-ownership of common elements, having the right and obligation to participate in decisions concerning the management of common interests. "This duality of rights – private ownership and co-ownership of common elements – will definitely mark the unique and original character of this legal model. As in all situations where the antitheses touch and complement each other, there is a fertile field for searching for appropriate definitions and explanations of a reality that is complex" (Magalhães 2007).

Spanish jurisprudence considered it to be an authentic masterpiece of juridical creation after 1960:

> The ownership of homes by storeys is an institution of a complex nature, whose type is the right to ownership, but within it, it constitutes a class detached from the traditional ones, and it is useless to search for similarities or partial identity since there is no community because of the private elements belonging to various owners; nor does servitude help to explain the situation of all the common things, but merely determines relations which only exist between the owners of two or more storeys, but which affect everyone.

As Hang (2003) understands, the most relevant is the relationship between individuals. More important than any similarity regarding the type of the good or its scale is the structure of relationships that arise around the ownership or use of a particular materially indivisible good. In this regard, also in terms of the scale of the Earth System as a whole, the most important point to understand is the structure of relationships established through the common use of the same global and unitary system, the Earth System, so that a legal abstraction cannot divide it.

Assuming that the ecological problem is not a malfunction of the Earth System but rather a poor adaptation of human society to its functioning, it seems to us that the path to a possible solution, rather than ideological or techno/scientific choice, should be a technical answer in the social sciences with special resort to law. Here we mean law not as a system of sanctions and prohibitions but rather in its prior function of organization and regulation of human relations widened to a global scale.

5. Divide to Unite

All spaces that have become accessible to humans throughout history have been subject to their legal definition. The possibility of humanity as a whole becoming a geological force capable of changing the state of the Earth System requires that the intangible non-territorial space, the *living space*, represented through the core drivers of the state of the Earth System, becomes a safe space where its use is subject to order.

The problem arises because this new space has a new character, not geographical and territorial, distinguishable and therefore completely distinct from all other spaces previously discovered, even when compared to space exploration where the existence of intangible natural resources is already recognized today. This non-spatial space is not external to the planet but part of the Earth System, and is present inside and outside of all sovereignty, creating an "inextricable link between the activities of states within national territory and its effects on climate (...) an unprecedented situation in international law" (Borg 2007). It is from this overlap that the need for "International Law Innovation" (Prieur 2012) comes, regarding the still-dominant view that represents reality only under an optic that what is common to all humankind are the remaining areas of territorial political divisions. A clear distinction between this new intangible space and the territorial geographical space is only possible through the use of the latest scientific knowledge on the functioning of the Earth System as a whole. The possible legal definition of this new space and the resulting regulatory order of its use constitute *per se* a change in the conceptual paradigm of the international legal system. This innovation, because it is structural, implies a theoretical framework that allows an overlap of legal regimes between the *res corporales* concerning the sovereign territorial spaces of states and the natural *res incorporales* concerning the global *living space,* that is, the qualitative dimension of the structure of biogeophysical flows which are global and impossible to divide by any legal abstraction.

It is this overlap between the territorial space of sovereignty and the global intangible space of the living space that requires clarification of the type of *res communis* better able to portray the reality where tangible and intangible spaces overlap and affect human relations. That the system is common and indivisible, that all people have equal access to it and no one is able to exclude any other from using it, evident to all by virtue of sharing globally the damages, which, in turn, result in very different uses, require us to look at this deep interdependence from a legal perspective. Everything becomes even more complex when, for the same reasons, the benefits realized by the ecological infrastructure in the state of Earth System are equally shared by all on a global scale.

The distinction made by the Roman legal system between *source* and *resource* can be extremely useful in clarifying the structure of the relationships resulting from different uses of the common system. As we have already stated, "*res communis* differs from *res nullius* in that the *source* of resources cannot be appropriated but the *resources* themselves are amenable to appropriation" (Oosterlinck 1996).

The *favourable state of the Earth System* resulted from an evolutionary process throughout Earth's history involving the interactions between the living biosphere of the planet and the geophysical part, that is, the ecological infrastructures are the *sources* of this favourable state, and that allowed the development of human civilization. The *resource* is the favourable intangible structure of biogeophysical flows on the Earth System. In other words, the *resource* emerged from the interactions of the *sources*.

Conversely, in this situation, by its very nature, the *source* is appropriable (the ecological infrastructures are under the territorial jurisdiction of states) but not the *resource*, that is, the resource is dispersed all over the planet and its appropriation is physically impossible, as is any legal abstraction of division. In this regard, although the *sources* are under state jurisdiction, with territorial jurisdiction over the areas where the ecological structures exist, the benefits realized by these structures in the state of the Earth System (*resource*) are inevitably common.

On the other hand, if all states use the system, all of them have sources that contribute to the maintenance of that favourable state. However, the disparity between areas and the performance of different ecosystems on

qualitative and quantitative levels generate large differences between
states with regard to positive contributions to the maintenance of that
favourable state. If we add to this discrepancy the differences between
different uses, we fall into a chasm of inequality.

This really is a truly new situation in the history of international law,
and neither a state-centred sovereignty nor communal sovereignty (in an
isolated way) can read the relationships established through the use of the
same indivisible common system.

The tension generated by the interdependence of benefits and harms
shared on a global scale in a juxtaposition of interests is a complex
equation that requires a complex solution, which does not sit well with the
simplified concept of geographic territorial division.

In terms of buildings, the success of the condominium model was due
largely to the dual approach of the internal differentiation. It not only used
a spatial criterion to internally distinguish the private spaces of the
common spaces but also functional criteria, even within the private spaces,
that identified certain elements which, due to their characteristics and
functions, impacted the safety and functional units of the building. These
would have to be regarded as common since, if maintenance was not
provided by the private owner, the damages would be collective. By
overlapping different legal regimes (private and co-ownership) and
simultaneous use of spatial and functional criteria, it is possible to ensure
the autonomy of private property symbiotically with the functional unit of
the building. This dualistic approach to the internal differentiation of
complex property in respect to buildings can be summarized as follows:

Buildings

a) *Space division* – Division of the spaces between each private
   fraction and division between the sum of all the private fractions
   and the remaining parts that are materially indivisible (we refer
   here to the stairs, common corridors, roof, entrance, etc.).
b) *Functional division* – Non-spatial division, whose criteria is the
   functional character of the building components regardless of their
   location being within or outside the private fractions. Technically,
   these components are materially indivisible, and it is not even
   possible to carry out a legal abstraction for division. In these
   situations, these components with common functions are mixed
   within the private spaces, creating an overlap of legal regimes. Any
   attempt to materially or legally divide these components would
   result in the loss of their functionality (we refer here to the building

support structure, supporting walls, water supply systems, drainage, electricity system, communications, etc.).

If the approach to the legal organization of buildings had stayed purely spatial, all components essential to the proper functioning of the building within private fractions would be private. That means that the cost of its maintenance would be private but the benefits would inevitably be collective. As a result, there would be no maintenance of common functional components, which could lead to a collective tragedy. Without adequate legal solutions to the factual circumstances of buildings, the towns we know today, although technically possible, would be a political impossibility.

The legal framework of the condominium is a kind of hybrid property; without denying the classic solution of division, it allows the integration of separate and independent fractions with the functional unit of the entire building in a symbiotic way. Its legitimacy was based on its ability to reflect the facts of a complex reality, and to shape the need of property, use and maintenance of the good through an equally complex model of overlap of the two property regimes.

It seems to us that the great innovation was the starting point for the analysis: firstly, the functional unit of the building was taken into account through an identification of the structural elements ensuring safety and operation, and only after this task had been carried out was the space division considered, which enabled goods that are under a regime of common ownership to exist within the private spaces. It was through this internal differentiation that defining and delimiting different responsibilities, duties and equitable contributions to the maintenance and prosecution of common interests were possible. This overlap and coordination of the operations of division allowed symbiotically what was once a theoretical impossibility.

The inadequacy of sovereignty to reflect the real situation in the world is apparent in its inability to reflect the intrinsic factual features of the Earth System as a whole, treating different realities equally.

If we adapt scales and perform the same operation on the common home of humanity, the planet Earth, we find an almost perfect similarity regarding the type of interdependencies established by relations between neighbours who inhabit a materially indivisible building with a functional unit.

The growing disjunction between the functional domain of biogeophysical interconnections and the territorial scope of sovereignty has transformed the classic Westphalian approach into an *ecological nonsense.*[2] The necessary evolution for the concept of sovereignty lies in its ability to integrate the reality of the existence of a *borderless global common* that is not limited to the remaining areas of sovereignty. And "from this integration, in turn, must emerge a concept of sovereignty that reflects rather than defies environmental reality" (Brunnée 1998). If it is true that international commons are threatened due to technological progress and increased resource competition, and to reach the point where "the international commons must thus evolve to survive" (Shackelford 2008), it is equally true that all sovereignties are also threatened by the "global commons" still being subject to a legal uncertainty and unregulated use, as is the case with the Earth System (which includes the climate).

The solution will inevitably be a legal construction, and therefore the technical choices for operationalizing a global response are not different. These choices can result in either a global conflict, as a war of all against all, or the creation of a platform of solidarity, a forerunner of a globally organized society.

A new organization of global neighbourly relations requires an approach with the ability to reflect the overlap of these two realities. For this, a dualistic approach on a global scale becomes necessary as it takes into account not only the existing territorial division (where global commons are only the remaining areas of sovereignty) but, in an overlapped manner, identifies the functional elements responsible for the state of the Earth System.

Accordingly, the corresponding bio-geochemistry structure of the favourable state of the Holocene period should be identified as the most important common *resource*, which should be the subject of a legal definition and covered by a legal system regulating its use.

The Earth Condominium would then be the legal representation of a reality in which there is a clear overlap and mix between the tangible and intangible dimensions of the Earth System. Legally it would be a juxtaposition between the tangible territorial areas of the Earth System under the sovereign jurisdiction of states, and the entire intangible structure that circulates through the atmosphere and oceans and moves through the biogeophysical flows that, together, determine the movement of energy and materials through the Earth System, and on which it is impossible to carry out any type of ownership or legal abstraction for division, and therefore is truly a common good.

Lacking a physical existence but globally dispersed, the intangible elements of the Earth System are, albeit on a temporary basis due to their permanent movement, within the sovereign space and should be under the regime of an intangible natural common heritage of all humankind / or world heritage.

In this juxtaposition between space, sovereign jurisdiction and the common system should be a model in which the common intangible natural heritage/world heritage represents the functional unit of the Earth System that blends into the airspace and ocean spaces of sovereignty but, by referring to a particular favourable structure of biogeophysical flows, a different plan of sovereign powers arises, and may be summarized as follows.

Planet

a) *Spatial division* – Territorial division between autonomous sovereignty and its delimitation in regard to all the remaining parts of sovereign jurisdictions (high sea, seabed, Antarctica). This is the type of classic territorial division in relation to the physical planet of 510 million km^2, resulting from the existing geopolitical map. This operation of dividing the *res corporales* includes also all airspace of the sovereign states, the water column of the territorial seas and exclusive economic zones.

b) *Functional division* – Refers to the distinction between tangible components of the Earth System (*res corporales*), where the territorial division between states is performed, and the intangible higher level (*res incorporales*) of the Earth System, which refers to the elements that compose the biogeophysical structure of the system, both working synergistically to keep the system in well-defined states. The higher level is an emerging phenomenon resulting from the interaction and integration of the geophysical properties of the planet with the living biosphere, which forms the intangible Earth System. It is a single global system incapable of any legal abstraction of division, simultaneously inside and outside of all states, and therefore common to all humanity.

Within each state there exist ecological infrastructures of the living biosphere and geophysical elements, which, through the Earth's history, were (and still are) the *source* of the favourable state of the higher level. In this regard, ecosystems located within the jurisdiction of states provide global ecological services that are functionally common because they are dispersed globally.

Consequently, the benefits provided by ecological infrastructures inside sovereign territories that contribute to the maintenance of this ecological safety space of humanity are earth system services of global common interest. That is, as a result of the overlap of the common intangible heritage and territorial sovereign spaces on a global scale, it would be possible to include in the intangible heritage the benefits that ecosystems perform in the state of the common system.

It is in this overlap between the intangible elements of the Earth System and the sovereign rights exercised on the territories where the *sources* that contribute to the maintenance of the *living space* are located as well as the human infrastructures that use this living space that will definitively mark the character of this globa*l res communis*, which mixes sovereign territories with a common system, with benefits and damage shared globally.

In this context of interdependence between the interests of all humankind and state interests, the proclaimed necessary evolutions of the concepts of CHM, CCH, world heritage global commons, sovereignty and international law will only be viable if carried out in a theoretical context that recognizes, reconciles and synthesizes through a *res communis* the representation of this overlap of interests and the respective legal regimes.

Among the existing models, the only model able to describe this integration and overlap of two possible different legal regimes is the condominium. With the already proposed legal separation between the territorial dimension of the planet and the intangible elements of the Earth System, and through an accounting system to assess the inputs and withdrawing of the common intangible heritage, it's possible to bring ecological reality and sovereignty rights closer together, building a global condominium where the common interests of humankind are organized in symbiosis with state interests.

The application of this model on a global scale results in the recognition that the international society is neither a community nor an arithmetic sum of sovereignties. It is something complex that should elevate the law to the art of reconciling the extremes, of making symbiotically dependent what was apparently incompatible.

Accordingly, we can say that the functional unit could be ensured through the internal differentiation of legal regimes between the *res corporales* and the *res incorporales* of the Earth System. However, despite a globally organized society having dealt with ethical, philosophical and legal arguments, and whose cooperation today is already extended to scientific knowledge, for this to be more than an idea it will have to be institutionalized and an accounting system found that matches the internal unity of the system to an internal equity of human relations established through the common use of the Earth System.

6. Symbiotic Sovereignty

The concept of sovereignty has its origins in a matrix incompatibility with the unity and interactive character of the Earth System. After discovering the conceptual disintegration of sovereignty regarding where the concept is applied, old paradigms were transformed into paradoxical uncertainties. Its existence is exercised in a contra-natura tension, ranging from the reaffirmation of political authority and the dilemma of the effective impossibility of sovereignty being free of the ecological interdependencies that drive all states to almost the same level of interdependence, regardless of their technological or economic development. The language of mutual and binding interdependencies is hardly explained by international law. When a reality does not fit into our abstractions, the solution is often the simple nomination of the impossibility of understanding the problem. This strategy has a double purpose: it not only serves as a way of explaining the inexplicable but also creates the illusion that the designation of the "complex" is a synonym of its clarification.

Constructing legal abstractions (boundaries) in the lower level of integration of the Earth System can lead one to believe that those mental abstractions are reality itself. Although we see clouds, rivers and ocean currents crossing all borders, the lack of knowledge about Earth System functioning, with all its interconnections and emerging phenomena (which give it a characteristic of indivisible unity), was a key factor in the construction of this process of mental divisibility.

The confusion between social abstractions and the systemic reality of the planet soon made evident how difficult and serious the consequences of failing to harmonise social representations with natural reality are. Making non-existent, for practical matters, all reality that does not fit in the divisions that organize our perception of the world created a structural difficulty in clearly explaining the contradictions, paradoxes, dilemmas, interdependencies, and improbabilities that are the origin of life.

These are strange and difficult realities not only for law to clarify in all of their dimensions but also for natural sciences, which had to find new words and concepts for the apparent intrinsic contradictions of relationships that apparently revealed opposites or the opportunistic. These relationships of mutual benefit and dependence were called symbiotic. In some cases, these relationships of interdependency imply such an intimate interrelation among the organisms involved that it becomes mandatory, meaning that both symbionts entirely depend on each other for survival.

Non-acceptance and non-harmonisation of these dependencies correspond to mutual self-destruction.

In fact, the main feature of the interdependence is the inability to pursue any of the interests in conflict without simultaneously pursuing, or at least serving partially, the apparently opposite interest. Paradoxically, the consequence of the *failure of coordination* is the deepening of the dependence. The global ecological relationships are obligate, meaning that the inter-relationships between individual and collective interests on any scale, even the global one, are profoundly intimate and become materially mandatory; that is, they become non-derogably interdependent and humanly unavailable. When this "law of nature" does not match a socially structured organization, it becomes a real political impossibility. At the level of interstate relations, this phenomenon manifests itself through the "sovereignty paradox" (Kaul 2013), which demonstrates that states lose sovereignty through non-cooperation.

In this field of contradictions and complexities, it is essential to analyse the different elements of sovereignty and their interrelationships. Considering that territory is a crucial anchor for global and local analysis (Albert 2007), we also need to understand that this is not its only dimension. We need to ask:

a) Which elements of this collective identity lead to the perspective of sacred (absolute) sovereignty?

b) To what extent does this absolute, almost sacred character that underlies the pursuit of individual interests of the state to the detriment of global collective interest actually depend on the present and future interest of humankind as a whole?

For Eduardo Lourenço (1999), "Each people just *is,* by conceiving and living itself as destiny. Symbolically, it means as if it always existed, carrying with itself a promise of eternal existence. It is this conviction that delivers to each people and culture (both being inseparable) what we call identity".

This interesting and profound definition completely ignores the territorial dimension of this identity, and without wishing to diminish its importance, it is certain that some people exist without territories, and territories without people. Equally interesting is the importance of the temporal dimension in the formation of this "conviction" that is transformed into identity. The perception of ever having existed and a destiny or promise of eternal existence put the projection of the past towards an unlimited future into the centre of collective sentiment, offering people that which is called identity.

In this sense, territory is much more than a merely physical connotation. It is a consequence of life in society so that social relations are essentially projected towards a concrete territory and unlimited time. It follows from the above that the sacred character of physical territory of a nation-state comes from the operation in a specific space of this symbolic dimension projected towards an eternal future.

If this symbolic projection of an eternal future is only possible in the context of interdependence between all people and the mutual dependence of all people upon a specific state of the Earth System, then the possibility of a people's sovereignty will require the creation of a *common intangible living space* where everybody can develop this "long-term" unlimited temporal projection. Without it, no sovereignty would make sense.

Consequently, there will be two structural requirements for the emergence of any kind of community:

- the need for a *locus* as the stability element for building a political organization;
- the need for a temporally unlimited projection of each people in a subjective dimension.

Therefore, the subjective dimension of identity includes, in its genesis and substance, the conviction of an existential possibility temporally extended to the successive chain of generations yet unborn. So, we can say that *the future healthiness* of a certain territorial space where the social formation is located is included in the preconditions of sovereignty. The global nature of the "environmental good" transforms the scale of the future *state territory healthiness* into the *healthiness of the Earth System*. Each social formation designed in a particular territory is inevitably integrated into the whole human family, current and future, and therefore has a mutual and global interdependence. This fact transforms the absolute contraposition between the autonomous collective interests of humanity and the individual subjective interests of each state into a new context: the benefit of each state lies primarily in the implementation of the common interest or, to put it into a narrower context, at least while the benefit of each state does not jeopardize the complex balance that sustains what we call the common interest. And this relationship between the territorial sovereignty and the healthiness of the global *living space* is symbiotically necessary.

7. From Complex to Symbiotic

Although inextricably linked, sovereignty is not in essence only territory. It simultaneously contains elements that open sovereignty to the global, to future generations and to the *common interest of all humankind*.

The proof of this is that since the 1648 Treaty of Westphalia, the first exception to the principle that in international law there is no autonomous existence beyond state-centred international relations was the Common Heritage of Mankind.

> The primary exception to this principle is the international commons. In these areas, which include the deep international seabed, the Arctic, Antarctica, and outer space, concerns over free passage outweighed the great Western powers' territorial ambitions and Grotius's *mare liberum* triumphed. As a result, these regions were gradually regulated to a greater or lesser extent by the Common Heritage of Mankind (CHM) principle, in which theoretically all of humanity became the sovereign over the international commons. (Shackelford 2008)

This exception to the principle of territorial division had its origin in a historical cultural process based on the ethical perception that there is a common heritage of all humanity corresponding to the fundamentals of life and to the renewal cycles of nature, which also includes the temporally unlimited projection of each sovereign identity. We can state that the CHM has always existed latently on a higher level than the plan put into effect. That is, the foundation, the initial booster reason, has always been broader than simply looking for a legal framework for the remaining parts of the territorial divisions. However, because the scientific tools to define and delimit its implementation were absent, it was carried out in an amputated form and in an adverse context. But it is not because it is not recognized in its true dimension that it ceased to exist and the interdependencies allowed themselves to manifest.

Not to recognize and accept these dependencies is to make them paradoxical, complex and deeper.

Humanity, as an integral component of the Earth System, is immersed in a necessary symbiotic relationship with the Earth System. The sovereignty is the human manifestation of the political organization of people exercised within the Earth System. The symbiotic relationships include those associations in which one organism lives on another (ectosymbiosis) and where one partner lives inside the other (endosymbiosis).

The exercise of a symbiotic relationship requires a coordination of actions mutually beneficial for the relationship, but because they are mandatory, no coordination gives rise to mutual destruction. Regardless of the system of internal self-organization with which humanity regulates, organizes and coordinates the use and maintenance of the system in which it operates, it is necessary to find a source of political legitimacy to build this process. This can only be found in the existing political organization, within states' political authority.

> The figure of the 'international' represents sovereignty as inextricably linked to a given territory. Yet 'international relations' must not be understood as the area of politics among States, assuming that within States political authority rests on their sovereignty. Rather, seen from the vantage point of political theory, the figure of international relations is more: it does offer a powerful solution for a central problem of the political, namely the problem to provide a place in which political authority *ultimately* rests, yet *at the* same *time* it hides the fact that this 'ultimate' place is in reality highly contingent. It is in this sense that the figure of international relations allows to combine the political system's *inside program* of producing the legitimacy of political authority with the political system's *outside program* which insinuates that this political authority in need of permanent production and reproduction is fixed against its environment (of other loci of political authority). (Albert 2007)

This proposed evolution of sovereignty is therefore a natural consequence of an attempt to achieve the CCH through the de-territorialisation of CHM/world heritage. Symbiotic sovereignty is the evolution that recognizes, reconciles and synthesizes the overlap of the territorial and non-territorial elements of sovereignty that exist symbiotically inside all states in a single overarching governance condominium.

In this sense, the evolution of the theoretical concept of sovereignty turns out to be just a reconstruction because the issues on which it could potentially be considered a retreat in sovereignty had actually never been in the states' sovereign jurisdiction, because no state alone can address this issue. Sovereignty is transformed without losing its essence. On the contrary, only by harmonising the interdependent relationship between all sovereignties and the Earth System will it be possible to perform the non-territorial element of each sovereignty. We can argue that this *common intangible living space* is the summation of all the unlimited temporal projections of all the sovereignties in which theoretically all humanity became sovereign over the intangible components of the Earth System as the common natural intangible heritage of humankind.

The absence of the temporally infinite projection confines sovereignty to the territorial element, and it would be emptiness and the absence of any sense.
We could briefly review some features of symbiotic sovereignty thus:

1. Symbiotic sovereignty, as opposed to the absolute sovereignty [which incidentally has never been more than an ideal] of Westphalia, integrates knowledge, which absolute sovereignty did not have, about the territory as a "live" system of relations, of flows of energy and matter (including biologically organized matter).
2. Symbiotic sovereignty does not abolish territorial sovereignty but changes its nature and its mode of exercise because it includes in its formula the non-territorial element, temporally unlimited, common to all states, which will be the legal basis for building an equivalence platform through the accounting of compensations and penalties.
3. Territorial sovereignty is maintained as part of the symbiotic sovereignty but under two principles of conditioning that should be the subject of a binding international regime: a) territory uses may not harm the global common Earth System software or, through it, cause damage to the territories of the other symbiotic sovereign states; and b) uses of the territory may not limit the choices of future generations [intergenerational justice].
4. Territorial sovereignty, enriched with this restriction of use, is not a minor harm but a good to be stimulated. It corresponds to a demonstration of the classical principle of subsidiarity. In this light, the territorial sovereignty must be understood as the best way for humanity to be able to inhabit the planet sustainably, making it a co-sovereignty. Only through many sovereign "properties" (and not a mega-state that would eventually be totalitarian) can we care for the Earth, moving from a predatory to a synergistic relationship.
5. In fact, only in the context of this new territorial sovereignty, symbiotically transformed, will it be possible to find a basis in law for the construction of a system of compensations and penalties, which is an incentive for states to produce positive externalities (receiving rewards) and reduce the negative externalities (avoiding fines).
6. The institutional problem of public international law and constitutional law that remains open is that of conferring to the United Nations not a part of world government but a political, legal, scientific, and financial status to allow it to be the entity that

coordinates and administers this compensation system, that sets and installs policies that stimulate the correction and redefinition of the self-regulatory mechanisms.

8. Earth System Stewardship

The structural evolution of the recognition by international law of this legal global object would have cascading consequences, of which for the moment we highlight only two:

1) The common interests of all present and future humanity (which is coincident with the trans-temporal dimension of sovereignty) would exist via their representation in a common natural intangible heritage;

2) From the moment the intangible Earth System belongs to someone (in this case it belongs to all humankind as a *res communis omnium*) its use should be governed as a trust by a *specific law*.

In other words, it would be possible to discern one of the possible objects of the so-called global governance. The use of the word *governance* assumes that the object of the act of managing/governing is identified and defined. This definition can either have a territorial or a functional scope. In the absence of a defined object and a clear separation of powers among the matters that must necessarily be governed globally and the articulation/coordination with traditional powers of states, we need to admit the unavoidable emergence of modalities of uncoordinated and unregulated use and the impossibility of collective action.

Taking into account the relationship between appropriable *sources* and inappropriable *resources* dispersed globally, and the fact of the *living space* being an emerging result of the integration of the geophysical properties of the planet with the living biosphere, we can state that the intangible favourable state of the Earth System is a space of biogeophysical flows whose maintenance of a certain structure of concentrations within the limits corresponding to the stability period of the Holocene is vital for humanity. Recognizing this safe space for humanity as a common natural intangible heritage of humankind would allow the capturing and accounting of intangible flows (positive or negative for the state of the common heritage) that all human actors emit in different amounts.

According to Carl Folke (2011), "A significant part of this challenge is to make the work of the biosphere visible in society, in human actions and in financial and economic transactions".

Since most of the benefits provided by *sources* (ecosystems) are legally non-existent due to their global dispersion, only comprehensive legal support can give visibility to these positive flows. That is, due to the fact of these benefits being global, in order to stop them being "externalities" for the economy and instead become visible to society, it is necessary to first recognize their legal existence; only then may they be subject to valuation. Since all people on a global scale enjoy these benefits, and many of them are provided by *sources* (ecosystems) located in territories under sovereign jurisdiction, the state in which the *source of positive flows* is located should be financially compensated.

A structural condition for achieving the civilized journey from explorers and exploiters to guardians and managers is that the benefits achieved in the state of the Earth System do not constitute losses for the societies that perform them. According to the primitive accounting/economic methods still prevailing, the value of a forest only enters into the Gross Domestic Product (GDP) and becomes visible in the financial and economic transactions of society the day that forest is destroyed and turned into "raw material".

Changing this formula and assigning an economic/financial value to the ecosystem service requires a legal solution that recognizes the social existence (legal) of the benefit. Only non-territorial legal support can uphold global benefits and, as a consequence, financial and economic visibility may be possible. The economy cannot consider as a credit a benefit that legally does not exist.

It is no longer about simply controlling polluting emissions; it is necessary to build an economy that is able to recover the natural capital that has been destroyed and create a permanent system of *sources renewal* that assures the maintenance of the common intangible space within the limits that humanity should not surpass. This system can only be achieved on the scale required if the maintenance and reconstruction of the sources do not constitute a cost or loss to the state exercising sovereignty over the territory where that source is mainly located. Without an international ecological accounting system, where individual contributions and obligations towards the maintenance of the intangible common heritage are clearly defined, there will be no recovery and preservation. No one would undertake such tasks when the cost of doing so is private but the benefits collective.

The shift from an economy of exploration of resources and sources to an economy of production of common resources implies not only the existence of a common intangible heritage on a global scale but also an accounting system of global biogeophysical flows in a wider system of international compensation.

The introduction of benefits in the system of accountancy of ecological flows could have a trigger effect in the sense that for the first time the production of common benefits could have some individual (state) compensation.

When communities, regardless of their size, share the use of the same vital goods, they are faced with the need to create a system of shared management. As such, it is essential to compare the different benefits and the consumption by each of that common resource. The common heritage is this intangible space where accountability should be kept by an international institution (the UN) with functions of coordination; that is, if we have a system of compensation between the different performances of each state on the state of the Earth System, each state will try to have the best balance (difference between positive and negative inputs) mainly through self-regulation. To achieve that goal, and according to the key guiding principles provided in Chapter 10 and the four principles to avoid the MAECC (Mutual Assured Environmental and Climate Collapse) of Chapter 13, the condominium governance model, as a universal model optimized to manage global flows in a system of international compensation, should be guided by the following principles:

No Winners, No Losers Principle

In a condominium governance model, the one who deserves to receive compensation for the benefits provided to the common heritage is not profiting from it. It is just being reimbursed for the improvements in the common good enjoyed by everyone. Those who contribute to that compensation (through the condominium bodies) are ensuring the healthiness of their own territory and protecting the core element of a temporally unlimited projection of their own sovereignty. We live in a symbiotic mandatory condition where we are all either winners or losers.

Common Intangible Living Space

We could not protect the emergence phenomena of a favourable state but we could protect the biogeophysical conditions that assure the maintenance of the favourable state of the Earth System.

The *remaining ecological space,* scientifically represented by the *safe operating space for humankind of planetary boundaries*, which coincides with the *living space* of the CCH concept and also with the non-territorial dimension of the CHM, is the fine-tuned version of the *res communis* well-defined favourable state of the Earth System in light of contemporary developments.

Global Condominium

Global neighbourhood relations are not relationships of power and domination but ones resulting from the use of the same indivisible resources. In the Earth Condominium, all humanity, present and future, becomes co-sovereign over a well-defined favourable state of the Earth System: it is a non-spatial CHM. The condominium is the only type of *res communis* with the ability to represent the overlap of autonomous sovereignties over a global common good; it is not restricted to the traditional global commons but spans across areas subject to national jurisdiction. In a condominium model, the existence of (i) an equity criteria to ensure the fair contributions of each co-sovereign and (ii) an institutional arrangement with coordination functions for maintaining the functionality of the common home of humanity are necessary.

Sources and Resources

The favourable conditions of the Holocene arose in an evolutionary fashion throughout Earth's history and it is through this evolutionary process involving the living part of the planet as well as the geophysical hardware that, for example, the relative concentrations of gases remain relatively constant throughout time. In essence, it is the integration of the geophysical properties of the planet with the living biosphere that forms the intangible Earth System. Thereby the *source* of this favourable state is appropriable (the ecological infrastructures are under the territorial jurisdiction of states) and the *resource* (the favourable state) is inappropriable; that is, the resource disperses all over the planet and its appropriation is physically impossible, as is any legal abstraction of division.

Occupation of the Common Intangible Living Space

The over-use of the favourable state of the Earth System, although not corresponding to a physical appropriation, can lead to the exhaustion of the intangible living space. With climate change comes the discovery that a stable climate is not an inexhaustible factor, that is, the incorporeal biogeophysical conditions that determine the state of the Earth System have upper and lower limits and, therefore, are exhaustible. The occupation of this resource is not realized through a physical appropriation but rather through a change in the qualitative state of the incorporeal characteristics of the Earth System. This occupation of the remaining living space is the result of a chemical change in the qualitative state of the intangible space and affects its common use.

Enlargement of the Common Intangible Living Space

The ecosystem services of global common interest are all the biogeophysical processes performed by the ecosystems that contribute to the regulation of the stability of the Earth System within the safe operating space. These services, although they originated in ecosystems located in territories under the jurisdiction of sovereignty states, are spread diffusely in the Earth System and enlarge the remaining *living space* where all nations and citizens of the world operate.

Credits over the Common Intangible Heritage

The contribution of ecosystem services of global interest to the maintenance of the favourable state of the Earth System should generate credit on behalf of the state that exercises the sovereignty or sovereign rights over the *source* of this benefit, that is, the ecosystem infrastructure that provided those ecosystem services.

Debits over the Common Intangible Heritage

The more chemical, biological and physical processes, resulting from human activity, push the Earth System out of the safe operating space, the "less resource" (considering the favourable and stable state of the Earth System as a resource) will be available to all agents.

Because these processes contribute to the depreciation of the state of Earth System and correspond to an occupation of the intangible *living space*, they should generate a debit on behalf of the state that exercises the sovereignty or sovereign rights over the place where this activity occurs.

Standardize to Compare

It is necessary to build a common standard pattern that represents the positive and negative flows of each country on the structure of the Earth System. Conceptually, this new metric should be an aggregation of indicators that represent core processes that regulate the stability and resilience of the Earth System. Only by placing the various benefits in a common metric compatible with its consumption can we express, to their full extent, the relations to be harmonised. This new metric should be based on the best available scientific knowledge.

Life-Support Unit

The common standard pattern could be named LSU (Life-Support Unit) and should be an aggregation of PB indicators ("control variables"): stratosphere ozone depletion, aerosol loading, climate change, ocean acidification, biogeochemical flows (e.g., nitrogen, phosphorus), novel entities, biosphere integrity, "land-system change", and "freshwater use".

Ecobalance

The difference between the production of positive biogeochemical flows and the emission of negative flows of each state and the impact of it on the maintenance of the safe operating space of humanity should be the basic equity criteria of contributions for the Earth Condominium. The balance between the generation and consumption of LSUs is the ecobalance. It allows us to realize the status of the relationship of each state with the common heritage, and a structural condition for confidence building.

Legal Foundations of Contributions and Compensations

The legal basis of the obligation to contribute to the maintenance of the Earth System's state is the fact that all states use within their sovereign territorial space a good that is under a co-sovereignty legal regime.

The legal foundation of the right to be compensated for having contributed to maintaining the intangible living space is that this favourable state of the Earth System is under a co-sovereignty legal regime, and is also inside sovereign territorial spaces. All the sovereignties will benefit from the enlargement and maintenance of the remaining living space.

Agreed Value for each LSU

Using all the best available economic information about the cost of environmental damage and the benefits of ecosystem services, we must construct a monetary value for the production and consumption of each LSU. This value must be sufficient to stimulate the activity of producing positive flows for the common system and not constitute a financial loss for societies that develop those activities. It will be defined through a convention.

Equivalence Platform

Only by building a global system capable of crossing, in a comparable manner, the positive and negative flows can we build an equivalence platform of fairness and reciprocity where all actors can see their interests safeguarded. In the current attempts to organize the collective use of Earth System, positive flows to a favourable Earth System are not yet part of the accounts.

It will be an intermediate space between state parties, where each one could understand the contributions from all the others and define its own performance strategy in relation to the common heritage, taking into account the prediction of other states' behaviour.

Coordination Functions

With the definition of a new object of law and governance, a new or a reconverted international organization (UN) should form. It should have the capacity to address the Earth System as a whole, tackle the sort of challenges we are facing and assure coordination tasks. Such functions should consist of receiving and redistributing the contributions of each State party and gather the different interests then negotiate and adopt the necessary resolutions. Failed coordination would result in high costs for all parties.

The Positive Competition

All parties, depending on internal policies, might improve their balance relative to the common heritage through the encouragement of environmental efficiency and the preservation or restoration of ecosystems.

Ecological Trust Principle

The concept that best translates the idea of sustainable use of this common intangible heritage by present generations with preservation for future generations in mind is the concept of ecological trust. This trust is the juridical figure with the best capacity to fit the virtual tri-polar relation established between different generations as an object encumbered with the duty to keep within the limits of the favourable state of the Holocene. The elements of trust are:

- Past generations (Trustors);
- Present generations (Trustees) – but we need a governance mechanism here. For example, states acting within tight constraints via a revived trusteeship council; also using own sovereign territory in a way that is consistent with trustee obligations/responsibilities;
- Present and future generations (Beneficiaries) – current use rights and inheritors, etc.

9. Final Remarks

As Vandana Shiva (1999) explains, "The 'global' in the dominant discourse is the political space in which a particular dominant local seeks global control, and frees itself of local, national and international restraints". Therefore, Shiva continues, "the global does not represent the universal human interest; (instead) it represents a particular local and parochial interest which has been globalised through the scope of its reach". Although humans live in a global political space, they are fundamentally local beings. However, they are also creatures who can create a new type of political space that is not global or local but SHARED as an intangible locus, where humanity as a whole, present and future, harmonises their different contributions to the common good and ensures the necessity of each sovereignty for the unlimited timescale identity. The recognition of one global legal support and an accountability of biogeophisical global flows in a system of international compensation is a pre-structural condition for a dialogue between present living humans and the unborn.

Now we have the access to the central computer of Spaceship Earth, the condominium seems to be the conceptual legal framework for the Anthropocene, where we can get inspired to organize our global neighbourhood. And the ecological neighbourhood is not a relation of power dominance. It's a relationship of symbiotic interdependence where the military and economic powers are not the only factors in the game. I believe that the common natural intangible heritage of humankind is also the political space of the Spaceship Earth Condo where we can decide how to conduct our own collective action as neighbours.

I would like to thank to Will Steffen, Viriato Soromenho-Marques, Prue Taylor, Adília Alarcão and Pedro Magalhães for the revisions, comments, discussions and suggestions that made this chapter possible.

References

Albert, M. (2007). Restructuring World Society: The Contribution of Modern Systems Theory. In L. W. Pauly & E. Grande (Ed.), *Complex Sovereignty: Reconstituting Political Authority in the Twenty-first Century* (pp. 48-67).Toronto: University of Toronto Press.

Borg, S. (2007) *Climate Change as a Common Concern of Humankind, Twenty Years Later...From UNGA to UNSC*. IUCN Academy of Environmental Law "Towards an Integrated Climate Change and Energy Policy in the European Union". University of Malta. Retrieved from: http://www.iucnael.org

—. (2009). *Key Note Speech* at the unveiling ceremony of the Climate Change Initiative Monument, University of Malta, 21 April. Retrieved from: https://www.um.edu.mt/newsoncampus/features/?a=62770

Brunnée, J. (1998). The Challenge to International Law: Water Defying Sovereignty or Sovereignty Defying Reality? Nação e Defesa – O desafio das águas. *Segurança Internacional e desenvolvimento Duradouro*. N° 865, verão 98. 2ª Série. Lisboa: Instituto de Defesa Nacional.

Cano, L. H. (1998). *Las Comunidades de Propriedad Urbana*. Madrid: Editorial Colex.

Filipe, J. F., Coelho, M. F., Ferreira, M. A. M. (2007). *O Drama dos Recursos Comuns – À procura de soluções para os ecossistemas em perigo*. Lisboa: Edições Sílabo.

Folke, C., et al. (2011). Reconnecting to the Biosphere. *Ambio 40*(7), 719–738. doi:10.1007/s13280-011-0184-y.

Glennon, J. P. (Ed.) (1991). *United Nations and General International Matters, Volume II, Foreign Relations of the United States, 1958-1960*. Washington: United States Government Printing Office.

Hang, P. (2003). *Essays on Game Theory and Natural Resource Management*. PhD thesis, Tilburg University.

Hemmings, A. (2014). Time to Revisit the Antarctic Treaty, Maritime. Retrieved from http://www.maritime-executive.com/features/time-to-revisit-the-antarctic-treaty

Kaul, I. (2013). *Global Public Goods, A Concept for Framing the Post-2015 Agenda?* Bonn: Discussion Paper, Deutsches Institut für Entwicklungspolitik. Retrieved from http://www.die-gdi.de/uploads/media/DP_2.2013.pdf

Kiss, A. (1982). La notion de Patrimonie Commun de L'Humanité. *Acedémie de Droit International, Recuil de Cours, Vol.175* (TomoII).

Magalhães, P. (2007*). Earth Condominium – From the Climate Change to a New Juridic Conception of the Planet.* Coimbra: Edições Almedina.

Oldfield, F. & Steffen, (2004). W. Box 1.1 *The Earth System.* In Steffen, W., Sanderson, A., Tyson, P.D. et al. (Eds.), *Global Change and the Earth System: A Planet under Pressure* (pp.7). Berlin, Heidelberg, New York: Springer-Verlag, The IGBP Book Series.

Oosterlinck, R. (1996). Tangible and Intangible Property in Outer Space. In *Proceedings of the 39th colloquium of the Law of Outer Space,* 271-284.

Rockström, J. (2014). *Planetary Boundaries and Human Opportunities: The Quest for Safe and Just Development on a Resilient Planet.* Open Online Course offered by the SRC in partnership with SDSN. Edu. November 17, 2014 - February 3, 2015.

Schelling, T.C. (1960). *The Strategy of Conflict.* Cambridge, Mass: Harvard University Press.

Schmid, A. (1995). The Environment and Property Rights Issues. In Bromley, (Ed.), *The Handbook of Environmental Economics.* Blackwell Publishers Inc.

Shackelford, S. J. (2008). The Tragedy of the Common Heritage of Mankind. *Stanford Environmental Law Journal, 27,* 101–120. Retrieved from: http://www.iew.unibe.ch/unibe/rechtswissenschaft/dwr/iew/content/e3870/e3985/e4139/e6410/sel-topic_5-shackleford_ger.pdf

Shiva,V. (1999). *Biopiracy: The Plunder of Nature and Knowledge.* New York: South End Press.

Weeramantry, C. G. (2000). Sustainable Development. In BEURIER, J. P. et al. (Eds), *New Technologies and Law of the Marine Environment* (p.195). London: Kluwer Law International (International Environmental Law and Policy Series).

CHAPTER TEN

THE NEED FOR AN INTEGRATED ASSESSMENT FRAMEWORK TO ACCOUNT FOR HUMANITY'S PRESSURE ON THE EARTH SYSTEM

FEDERICO MARIA PULSELLI,[1] SARA MORENO PIRES[2] AND ALESSANDRO GALLI[3]

1. Introduction

Over the last five decades, countries around the world have experienced noticeable changes. The size of the global economy has grown (Bolt & van Zanden 2013) and socioeconomic conditions have improved in many countries, especially in the form of poverty reduction and better welfare provisions (UNDP 2013; UNEP 2012). These improvements have been coupled with fundamental changes in the society–nature relationship as human-induced pressures on ecosystems have increased and the state of ecosystems worsened (Tittensor et al. 2014). Moreover, the world's population has doubled, potentially bringing the Earth System closer to a planetary-scale critical transition (Barnosky et al. 2012) in which humans – with their technologies – have been causing ecological changes within a time period (a couple of centuries) shorter than the one (millions of years) the Earth needed for the evolution of life (Haberl et al. 2007; Steffen, Crutzen & McNeill 2007; Tiezzi 2003; Wackernagel et al. 2002).

Several HANPP (Human Appropriation of Net Primary Production) studies have found that humans appropriate most of the Earth's net

---

[1] University of Siena, Ecodynamics Group.
[2] GOVCOPP – University of Aveiro.
[3] Global Footprint Network.

primary productivity (Imhoff et al. 2004; Vitousek, Ehrlich, Ehrlich, & Matson 1986) and that such appropriation has increased two-fold over the last century (Krausmann et al. 2013). Forests, especially in tropical zones, are declining as they are cut faster than they can re-grow (130,000 km^2 yr^{-1} of forest have been destroyed during the last 15 years) and similar trends are experienced by seagrass mangroves and coral reefs (SCBD 2014). Exploitation of fish stocks has increased by approximately 30% during the last three decades and the world's fisheries are being depleted faster than they can restock (Butchart et al. 2010; UNEP 2007). Per capita food and services consumption has grown during the last four decades throughout the globe (Turner 2008), and so has the extraction of resources such as biomass, fossil fuels, metal ores, construction and other minerals (Krausmann et al. 2009). Many countries in arid and semi-arid regions of the world (e.g., Central and West Asia, North Africa) are already close to or below the threshold for water scarcity of 1000 m^3 capita^{-1} yr^{-1} (Falkenmark 1989), and greenhouse gas (GHG) emissions are accumulating in the atmosphere (IPCC 2013), causing climatic changes and potential negative feedback on the Earth System's health (Butchart et al. 2010; Haberl 2006; Tittensor et al. 2014; UNEP 2007).

Such growing human pressures – and their negative consequences upon the natural ecosystems, the biosphere and the many species that inhabit it – suggest that mankind is likely not managing the Earth System sustainably (Butchart et al. 2010; DeFries, Foley & Asner 2004; Ellis, Goldewijk, Siebert, Lightman & Ramankutty 2010; Goudie 1981; Haberl 2006; Nelson et al. 2006; Rockström et al. 2009a,b).

As decision-makers are increasingly faced with information on worsening global environmental trends (IPCC 2013; SCBD 2014; Steffen et al. 2015a; UNEP 2012; WWF, ZSL, GFN & WFN 2014), realization of the global sustainability challenge has increased in the last three decades (UNCSD 2012). Sustainably managing the planet's natural capital has become a central issue for decision-makers around the world (e.g., CBD 2010; UN et al. 2014) and this has motivated an intensive social and scientific search for concepts, policies, regulations, indicators, and accounting techniques. A broad range of empirical measurements has thus emerged that can be used to track several independent aspects of the increasing impact of humanity on the biosphere.

Leaders and decision-makers have to handle information from a wide variety of sources to inform policy choices and investment decisions. They often rely on selected indicators that are easy to understand and communicate, which, however, tend to over-simplify reality and disregard the complex nature of the Earth System. Nonetheless, setting sustainability targets requires the identification of minimum thresholds – above which human impact on the Earth System is unsustainable – and the adoption of a systemic approach reflecting the complex interactions that characterise the Earth and human systems. Research on the Millennium Development Goals (UN 2014a) and Sustainable Development Goals (SDGs) (UN 2014b), for instance, has identified many parameters to be monitored; but how can we reconcile all this information to assess whether the whole system is sustainable or not? What are the key parameters decision-makers should pay attention to? And, most importantly, could it be – as Galli (2015) put it – that many of the parameters decision-makers are currently looking at are not relevant to measuring and monitoring the "sustainable/unsustainable" state of a system (see also Costanza, McGlade, Lovins & Kubiszewski 2014a; Pulselli, Bastianoni, Marchettini & Tiezzi 2008; Tiezzi & Bastianoni 2008; Wackernagel 2013)?

The wealth of information systems and knowledge as well as the many legal protections and international environmental agreements have so far failed to "protect the critical Earth systems that allow for sustainable and thriving human societies and well-being" (Planetary Boundaries Initiative 2015): recent research (Steffen et al. 2015a) has found that a critical acceleration in human activities is in place, as of the 1950s, to the extent that the current geological epoch can be defined as "Anthropocene" (Crutzen 2002).

We argue that the failure to protect the Earth System is due to the fact that while the above trends are indicative of growing pressure on the Earth System, we are yet to shift the way we approach the sustainability challenge. We are still focusing on addressing the symptoms rather than the causes of the problem, and there are no adequate tools that allow us to measure the combined effects of key trends from a systemic point of view.

Conceiving and developing an integrated assessment framework require monitoring the complexity of the Earth System as well as the relationships among the system's compartments. Given the absence (and potential impossibility) of such an omni-comprehensive metric (Bossel 1999; Galli et al. 2012; Singh, Murty, Gupta & Dikshit 2012), attempts have been made to identify minimum preconditions for sustainability and human development, the safe operating space for human activities (Rockström et al. 2009a – see also Chapter 2 of this book), as well as critical planetary thresholds whose transgression could lead to a planetary-scale 'tipping point' (Barnosky et al. 2012).

One of such attempts is represented by Ecological Footprint Accounting, which aims to set a specific ecological budget – the biocapacity – and the extent to which human demands on renewable resources and services approach or exceed this budget – the ecological footprint (Wackernagel et al. 2002). This accounting tool indicates that the planet is no longer able to support the various human demands competing for the available ecological budget and that significant biocapacity deficits exist in many economies and at the global level (Galli 2014; WWF, ZSL, GFN & WFN 2014).

Although it attempts to embrace a systemic approach, Ecological Footprint Accounting is unable to track all competing human demands on the Earth System (Bastianoni et al. 2013; Galli 2015; Galli et al. 2012). Recent work has highlighted the presence of other key planetary thresholds that are not tracked by Ecological Footprint Accounting but are fundamental and should not be overstepped. Steffen et al. (2015b) recently found that four out of nine critical planetary thresholds have already been passed. This planetary boundaries approach, introduced by Rockström et al. (2009b), however, currently remains theoretical (not all of the nine boundaries have well-defined thresholds) and hard to implement at the sub-global level[4] (see also Rockström & Klum 2015).

In sum, shedding light on the multidimensional aspects of the relationship between man and nature remains of key importance, alongside the need for representing the role of the environment and ecosystem functions for any human activity. In this sense, we propose a wider representation, rather than a further definition, of the concept of sustainability to acknowledge the urgent need of an Earth System view through appropriate tools.

Sustainability is the opportunity to talk about humankind. In particular, the study of sustainability is the study of the relations between humankind – its individual and collective expressions – and its context. The context can be different: physical, environmental, social, economic, political, urban, juridical, etc. Three key points must be highlighted: a) the shared (holistic) picture of the reality (i.e., what should be sustainable?) demands a transdisciplinary approach in order to encompass the many dimensions of the context in which we live; b) the purpose (i.e., why should we be sustainable?) is to create and maintain the conditions for durably living better and in harmony with nature and the other individuals; and 3) the critical assessment of how we can reach these conditions (i.e., how can we be sustainable?) requires new frameworks to evaluate progress towards the desired change.

---

[4] See Cole, Bailey and New (2014) and Nykvist et al. (2013) for an attempt at applying the PB approach on the national scale in South Africa and Sweden, respectively.

The aim of this chapter is to disentangle key aspects of an Earth System's assessment framework and arrive at the identification of key guiding principles (which will imply *paradigm shifts*) needed to then create a holistic framework. As such, section 2 deals with the spreading of indicators and examines various rationales that frame the development of indicators. Section 3 provides an overview of current national and international sustainable development indicators' initiatives. Section 4 investigates and discusses conflicting views on indicators and attempts to identify an ideal win-win situation. Section 5 concludes by presenting guiding principles that will be necessary for the development of an integrated assessment framework for the Earth System.

2. Spreading Indicator Culture

The genesis of the current 'indicator era' goes back to the 1920s when the United States started to develop economic indicators to guide economic decision making (Hardi & Zdan 1997). A particular difficult economic crisis pushed back for the need for quantitative data and the Kuznets' (1934) report *National Income, 1929–1932* provided the basis for one of the most powerful indicators of the 20th century: Gross Domestic Product (GDP). Warnings about the "uses and abuses of national income measures" were presented in that same very moment (USASC 1934, 5–6):

> The valuable capacity of the human mind to simplify a complex situation in a compact characterisation becomes dangerous when not controlled in terms of definitely stated criteria. With quantitative measurements especially, the definiteness of the result suggests, often misleadingly, a precision and simplicity in the outlines of the object measured. Measurements of national income are subject to this type of illusion and resulting abuse (…).

However, such warnings were not sufficient to alert decision-makers all over the world that "the welfare of a nation can, therefore, scarcely be inferred from a measurement of national income as defined above"; that is, the GDP (USASC 1934,7). Since post-World War II, this trend has gained momentum in many supranational agencies, such as the Organization for Economic Cooperation and Development (OECD), the World Bank and the United Nations Development Programme (UNDP), which started to gather and track the performance of economic and social phenomena across countries and regions (Moreno Pires 2014). Supported by the emergence of new technologies and information systems, an indicator culture began to spread over all areas of private and public administration.

Nevertheless, traditional indicator development was applied to assess trends of specific policy areas separately, and there was no intention of aggregating or connecting views on the design of the indicators (silos thinking). Some of the critical references on environmental indicators date from the 1970s, for example, Nordhaus & Tobin (1972), Inhaber (1976) and Ott (1978). In the beginning of the 1990s, the integrative conceptual model of sustainable development (systemic thinking) changed this monodisciplinary approach to indicators (see section 4.2. for a further explanation), particularly after the United Nations Conference on Environment and Development's call for an indicator agenda "to provide solid bases for decision making at all levels and to contribute to a self-regulating sustainability of integrated environment and development systems" (cited in Chapter 40 of *Agenda 21* – UNCED 1992).

Since then, the 'indicator industry' has elicited extremely rich political, academic, scientific, and community debates on the best way to operationalize and assess sustainable development in a systemic way and at different territorial scales (Hezri & Hasan 2004). Indicator design and use have served multiple purposes, taking on multiple objectives and roles toward sustainable development, and have been interpreted from different angles (Moreno Pires 2014). Three distinctive rationales have been proposed and followed to structure the creation, presentation and communication of indicators (see Table 1).

The first more dominant and traditional rationale is the *technical or expert-oriented approach* to indicators (e.g., Bossel 1999; Gallopín 1997; Giovannini & Linster 2005; Hammond, Adriaanse, Rodenburg, Bryant & Woodward 1995; Jesinghaus 1999; Schlossberg & Zimmerman 2003; Singh, Murty, Gupta & Dikshit 2012 among many others). Numerous mathematicians, statisticians, economists, ecologists, and other scientists have proposed specific criteria to design scientifically sound sustainable development indicators and indices (see next section). They have tried designing robust methodologies to frame "ideal" indicators able to challenge the uncertainty and complexity of sustainable development. This approach generally envisages a linear input-driven policy process (Holman 2009) where indicators directly impact decision making.

The second rationale, the *participative* approach to indicators, emerged at the local level with the *community indicators movement* (Innes & Booher 2000) and was boosted by Agenda 21 (Fidélis & Moreno Pires 2009). This approach is particularly concerned with who participates in the indicator design and selection, who decides and uses the indicators and how these indicators help promote value shifts and lifestyles changes (e.g., Coelho, Mascarenhas, Vaz, Dores & Ramos 2010; Holden 2009, 2011;

Innes & Booher 2000; Kline 2000; Mascarenhas, Coelho, Subtil & Ramos 2010; Rydin 2007). This approach emerged as a criticism of the technical one, emphasising that indicators do not readily and effectively change policies just because of their scientific virtues. Because projects on sustainability indicators tend to become "myopically focused on technical issues" (Bell & Morse 2003), they have been incapable of producing concrete policy changes. With its roots at the local level, this approach is also present at regional and national levels or even at the global level with the recent UN public discussion on the indicators for the post-2015 SDGs.

The third and more recent *governance approach* considers indicators as powerful processes that can change and steer governance contexts towards sustainable development within certain conditions (Astleithner, Hamedinger, Holman & Rydin 2004; Gudmundsson 2003; Hezri & Dovers 2006; Moreno Pires & Fidélis 2014; PASTILLE 2002; Rosenström 2006; Yli-Viikari 2009 among others). Indicators have the critical potential to bring new stakeholders to sustainability debates. They favour diverse multi-stakeholder gatherings, promote new institutional arrangements and new networks as well as new communication channels that facilitate learning, and steer policy integration horizontally and vertically (Galli 2015; Moreno Pires & Fidélis 2014). This approach tries to integrate both technical and participative concerns together with governance conditions (e.g., government coordination with multiple actors, integration of policies, communication strategies, funding) and understand how this can affect the number of possible users and the different types of uses that result from indicators. Several studies (e.g., Hezri & Dovers 2006; Lyytimäki, Gudmundsson & Sørensen 2014; POINT 2011) were dedicated to assessing the diverse uses of sustainability indicators such as instrumental (concrete changes), conceptual (learning, enlightenment) or symbolic (political, tactical or ritualistic). It therefore recognizes the importance of the other two approaches, arguing for the need to rethink indicators within new ethical, conceptual, methodological, and governance challenges.

Several examples of integrated governance frameworks to develop sustainability indicators can be mentioned. The triple helix (university-industry-government relationships) system, initiated in the 1990s by Etzkowitz (1993, 2003), highlights a governance approach inspired by innovation and knowledge. The REGES Project in the Province of Siena (Italy) (Bastianoni, Marchi, Caro, Casprini & Pulselli 2014) proposes the estimation of GHGs emission and absorption for the territorial system, the connected Siena Carbon Free target, and the ISO 14064 certification of the monitoring system. Moreover, the ecological footprint has been used to inform multi-stakeholder sustainability dialogues and decision-making processes in the United Arab Emirates (Abdullatif & Alam 2011) and as an umbrella indicator in the European Common Indicators (ECI) project (Ambiente Italia 2003).

Table 1 clarifies the relationship between the type of indicators and the intended audience, which influences the potential uses of those indicators.

	Technical	Participative	Governance
Roles	Objective setting and comparison; Technical and managerial	Public communication and participation	Objective setting and comparison; Technical and managerial; Public communication and participation
Who develops the indicators	Limited range of technical actors	Broad range of non-technical actors	Broad range of technical and non-technical actors
Development process	Intended purpose + desired audience + appropriate design + relevant consultation	Contextual collaborative process; Enabling learning opportunities for different stakeholders	Wider collaborative process with governmental and non-governmental stakeholders; Strong communication strategies within networks
Criteria	Availability of data; Easy to collect; Scientific validity and reliability; Limited in number; Applicable at multiple spatial and temporal levels; Capable of aggregation; Transparent and accountable	Participation; Local knowledge; Historical weight; Adaptability and flexibility; Institutionalizing knowledge production	Political commitment; Collaborative process; Institutionalizing knowledge production; Meta-evaluation; Scientific validity and reliability; Different types of knowledge
Who is responsible for data collection	Experts	Community	Networks

Intended audience	Experts; Decision-makers	The public; Decision- makers	Experts; The public; Decision- makers
Frameworks	Conceptual (economic, capital, pressure-state and response and its variations, human and ecosystem well-being and theme-based) as well as statistical and accounting frameworks	Theme-based conceptual frameworks (e.g., triple bottom line); Process-related frameworks	Process-related frameworks
Type of indicators	Index; Headline indicators; Lists of indicators; Raw data	Index; Headline indicators	Index; Headline indicators; Lists of indicators; Raw data
Intended uses	Instrumental	Conceptual; Instrumental ultimately	Instrumental; Conceptual; Symbolic

Table 1. Rationales behind Sustainable Development Indicators

The pyramid of Hammond, Adriaanse, Rodenburg, Bryant and Woodward (1995) (left pyramid of Figure 1) is composed of different levels of data, with raw data at the bottom and an index at the top. If indicators are to be effective, meaning that they are used by their target groups and serve their intended purposes, it is critical to connect both figures. The pyramid of Braat (1991) argues that indexes are preferable for the general public as they convey unambiguous messages, free of redundancy and in a single piece of information. As for other users, Braat considers that policy-makers prefer less aggregated data that can be related with policy objectives, evaluation criteria, control variables, and targets. Finally, professional analysts and scientists prefer raw data that can be analysed statistically.

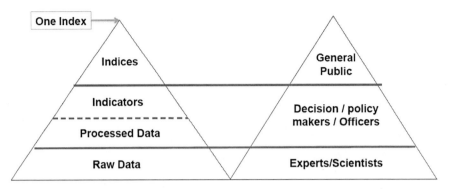

Figure 1. 'The Information Pyramid' and its potential users. Source: Adapted from Hammond et al. (1995) and Braat (1991).

3. Overview of National and International Sustainable Development Indicators' Initiatives

Already a decade ago, several authors (e.g., Lawn 2006; Pintér, Hardi & Bartelmus 2005; UNECE/OECD/Eurostat 2008) recognized the growth in sustainability indicator systems and frameworks,[5] and adverted to the growing inefficiencies in our ability to monitor progress towards sustainability goals due to the lack of cooperative actions and broad consensus.

From the global international perspective, the United Nations Commission on Sustainable Development (UNCSD) had an initial critical supportive role with the publication of *Indicators for Sustainable Development: Frameworks and Methodologies* in 1996. Since then, a number of very different institutions (governments, non-governmental organizations, research institutes and universities) have been working to define sustainability indicators for given regions, countries and the world.

At the national level, many countries established their own sustainable development indicators after the Rio 1992 Summit, often working closely with international organizations such as the UN, OECD, the World Bank,

---

[5] For further discussion on the development and progress of sustainable development indicators at different territorial levels, see, for example, Coelho, Mascarenhas, Vaz, Dores and Ramos (2010), Galli (2015), Hass, Brunvoll and Høie (2002), Pintér, Hardi and Bartelmus (2005), and Singh, Murty, Gupta and Dikshit (2012).

the EU, and other organizations. Canada, the United States, the Netherlands, Switzerland, the United Kingdom, and Sweden are examples of such countries, with the UK probably the country with the longest experience (UNECE/OECD/Eurostat 2008). The 2002 Summit on Sustainable Development in Johannesburg gave a new push for many countries to develop their sustainable development strategies and related indicator sets. General features of these initiatives have been studied and compared (e.g., Coelho, Mascarenhas, Vaz, Dores & Ramos 2010; Hass, Brunvoll & Høie 2002; UNECE/OECD/Eurostat 2008).

Evidence shows that: (i) most indicator sets adopt a list of indicators (between 30 and 60 on average) and headline indicators instead of developing a single index; (ii) indicators are strongly dependent on the output of national statistical offices, with few considerations for international comparison; (iii) they use causality-chain indicator frameworks but also other types of frameworks (triple bottom line or associated with policy goals considered in sustainability strategies); (iv) national-regional-local scale interaction among indicators is a concern, with several challenges to address (Coelho, Mascarenhas, Vaz, Dores & Ramos 2010); (v) main stakeholders are involved in the participation process, from the public administration to universities, private groups (business and industry) and the general public (communities and non-governmental organizations); (vi) sophistication in communication is also a new national feature since recent sustainable development reports have fewer pages, fewer indicators and more images (Dahl 2012).

At the local level, hundreds of indicator sets have been developed to assess local sustainability through a participative and bottom-up process. Sustainable Seattle's Indicators of Sustainable Community in the United States remains one of the best known practices at the international level to value and measure local quality of life and sustainability (Holden 2006). Many of these indicator sets, generated from community experiences, are based on their particular needs and circumstances, considering the available resources and the perspectives of the people involved (Moreno Pires 2014), but disregard national and international comparability. At the same time, a parallel movement characterised by the proliferation of open and standardized data in cities all over the world is demanding a serious debate on the risks, uses and abuses of harmonised indicators (Holden & Moreno Pires 2015; Moreno Pires, Fidélis & Ramos 2014) and their relationships with the global sustainability challenge.

Sustainability Metric	Authors	Year
Stressing the ecological dimension		
Ecological Footprint Accounting (EFA)	Wackernagel and Rees	1996
Environmental Space	Friends of the Earth, Wuppertal Institute	1994
Environmental Performance Index (EPI)	Yale and Columbia Universities	2006
Environmental Vulnerability Index (EVI)	Jonathan Mitchell (SOPAC)	2004
Emergy Accounting	Odum	1996
Human Appropriation of Net Primary Production (HANPP)	Vitousek et al.	1986
The Living Planet Index (LPI)	World Wildlife Fund (WWF)	1998
Sustainable Process Index (SPI)	Institute of Chemical Engineering, Graz University	1996
Stressing the economic dimension		
Eco-efficiency (EE)	World Business Council on Sustainable Develop.	1992
Index of Sustainable Economic Welfare (ISEW)	Daly and Cobb	1989
Measure of Economic Welfare (MEW)	Nordhaus and Tobin	1972
Genuine Progress Indicator (GPI)	Cobb et al.	1994
Sustainability Performance Index (SPI)	Krotscheck and Narodoslawsky	1994
Genuine Savings	Pearce and Atkinson	1993
Dow Jones Sustainability Index	Dow Jones & Company	1999

Stressing the social dimension

Human Development Index (HDI)	UNDP	1990
Capability Poverty Measure (CPM)	UNDP	1995
Index of Social Progress (ISP)	Richard Estes	1974
Social Progress Index	Social Progress Imperative	2013
Inclusive Wealth Index	UNU-IHDP and UNEP	2012

Integrative approaches

Barometer of Sustainability (BS)	IUCN - Prescott - Allen	1995
Environmental Sustainability Index (ESI)	World Economic Forum, Yale Univ., Columbia Univ.	1999
Well-being of Nations Index	Prescott - Allen	2001
Dashboard of Sustainability (DS)	International Institute for Sustainable Development	2000
Compass of Sustainability	AtKisson Group	1992
Better Life Index	OECD	2011
Happy Planet Index	New Economics Foundation	2006

Table 2. Examples of Sustainability Indexes and Accounting Frameworks

Finally, endeavours have also been directed towards developing sustainability indicators that assess particular policy sector performance (such as agriculture, forestry, energy, biodiversity, water, transport, industry among others) or towards assessing the sustainability performance of private institutions, companies or organizations. Several examples can be drawn from the OECD's Guidelines for Multinational Enterprises, the International Organization for Standardization indicators, and the Global Reporting Initiative (GRI) framework.

Table 2 presents an overview of some of the most well-known projects on sustainability metrics (including indexes and accounting tools).

4. The Need for Appropriate Indicators: Is There a Win-Win Solution?

Preserving both information and the systemic viewpoint

Ideally, our decision-making processes should be oriented by a set of indicators reflecting the different contexts in which human society connects. This does not necessarily mean that the number of indicators should increase but that they should be qualitatively different and variegated to depict the complex multidimensional characteristics of the Earth System, of which humankind is just one component.

In 1884, the English theologian and pedagogue Edwin Abbott wrote a romance called *Flatland* in which he described a two-dimensional world. The rigid and hierarchically organized society of Flatland develops in the large plane in which it lives, and flat authorities ensure that no flat citizen (the inhabitants are all flat geometric figures) escapes from the two-dimension reality. The novel's example can be used to argue that despite the proliferation of metrics, our decision-making process tends to be guided by the quasi-imposed limited set of information tools – mainly economic – that we use every day. In other words, concepts like Earth System, planetary boundaries or biophysical limits, environmental sustainability, social welfare and other important elements of our life on this planet are not satisfactorily incorporated on our knowledge horizon.

The ecological economist Herman Daly (1996) successfully represented the evolution of the human-environment integrated system as the transition from empty- to full-world economy. The growing economic system is occupying larger and larger portions of land, progressively using the capacity of the finite biosphere to produce resources and absorb waste. Particular attention is paid to welfare as a psychic category: according to Daly, in the empty world, welfare was mainly fed by ecosystem services;

in the full-world economy, welfare depends on economic and market services, and this causes the progressive loss of ecological awareness (see also Daly & Farley 2004 for a complete description of the model).

Prioritizing economic growth measures tends to dominate other important aspects (energy, mass, entropy, wastes, heat, sunlight, sources, sinks, ecological processes and so on) that represent the physical relationship between man and nature and our own material essence. This risks skewing decision making toward greater consideration of economic factors at the expense of biophysical ones (Ewing et al. 2012). The symbiosis between the economy and the environment must be taken into account in our information system and the investigation must refer to this integrated system as a whole, rather than single parts in isolation from each other. That is the practical essence of the Earth System view.

A characteristic adage of systems science can be used here to explain the essence of systemic thinking: "The whole is greater than the sum of the parts". It means that every system whose components interact with each other in mutual cooperation presents emerging properties that are different from the properties of the individual components, and the whole system has a specific identity. In other words, systemic thinking implies that the essential properties of an organism or living system are properties of the entire system, which no single component has per se. These properties emerge from the interactions and relations among the parts of the system (see Capra 1996). As indicated by Jørgensen (2012, 4),

> All systems with emerging properties cannot be described by listing the components and their properties, but it is necessary to capture, understand and describe the emerging system properties.

A few disciplines (or branches) are characterised by a systemic approach, such as systems chemistry (Nitschke 2009), ecology (Jørgensen 2012) and adaptive management (Newman & Jennings 2008). However, a systemic-thinking view seems to be missing the tools we use today to guide most of our decision-making processes. Too often silos thinking is used, which impedes cross-cutting assessments of the multiple diverse components that form the system in which we live. This, in turn, impedes the understanding and management of both the essence and the emerging properties of the Earth System.

In our search for the guiding principles necessary to define an integrated assessment framework for managing the Earth System, we can refer to the definition of ecological indicators given by Müller and Burkhard (2012, 26) and extend it to a larger set of tools and disciplines.

Ecological indicators are communication tools that facilitate a simplification of the high complexity in human-environmental systems. Indicators generally are variables that provide aggregated information on certain phenomena. They are selected to support specific management purposes, with an integrating, synoptic value, functioning as depictions of qualities, quantities, states or interactions that are not directly accessible.

While measuring the sustainability of human pressure on the Earth System requires multiple interacting processes to be jointly addressed (Steffen et al. 2015b), the policy-making process operates at sub-global levels: national and local governments are ultimately responsible for taking action. As highlighted by Knight (2015), sustainability requires full knowledge of the workings of Earth's multiple physical systems but the management tools used by societal actors have a low adaptive capacity to address ongoing changes to the physical environment. An integrated assessment framework accounting for humanity's pressure on the Earth System must thus be able to bridge the gap between the "scientific need" for a global systemic thinking and the "governance need" for local action and policy implementation.

Pros and cons of juxtaposition and aggregation of information

As described in section 2, the number of assessment tools has been increasing since the 1970s, to the extent that we now have more and more details that describe the peculiarities of our system(s); however, we are lacking a way to synthesize this large set of information so that it can refer to the entire Earth System. As Costanza et al. (2014b) put it, the articulation and measurement of an overarching sustainability goal – which they define as "a prosperous, high quality of life that is equitably shared and sustainable" – is currently missing in our societal attempt to identify and measure sustainability.

An indicator is thus an integration of information, mainly extracted from direct measures, that helps represent a trend, behaviour or threshold. An indicator is different from the details that compose it because, though it is a synthetic "low definition" measure, it provides a picture of the whole system that is not visible if we observe only the parts. This means that the indicator is not a punctual measure: it does not measure, it indicates.

In the production of indicators aimed at investigating the complexity of the human-environment relationship, we tend to move between two extremes: a) the increase of punctual measures that describe the many smaller portions of the system or particular isolated phenomena; and b) the aggregation of details into one single omni-comprehensive metric.

The first tendency can be defined as a juxtaposition of information on different fields/phenomena. It consists of the production of several punctual measures placed next to each other. The recipient for this information is usually a dashboard that divides measures into themes/chapters (e.g., economic, social, environmental, etc.), providing a detailed and informative picture for policy-makers to operate (see Figure 1). Section 3 pointed to this trend at local and national levels.

The second tendency, namely aggregation, consists of concentrating a lot of information into a single number on the basis of a certain methodology. It often results in a synthesis of various data and, for this reason, it is useful to orient policy-makers and inform the general public. For instance, composite indicators are "indices that aggregate multidimensional processes into simplified concepts".[1] These indicators (see Table 2) can help us visualize the big picture of the global sustainability challenge, which is essential (see Clapp & Dauvergne 2005) for macro-level guidance in the formulation of recommendations and policies.

Given the above, the distinction between environmental and sustainability indicators can be mentioned here. Environmental indicators (e.g., those following a DPSIR approach) are punctual experimental measures on the status of the environment (e.g., the concentration of a given pollutant in a water body). They are very precise, often obtained through the use of sophisticated instruments, but specifically determined in space and time depending on the location and duration of the monitoring system. At most, they can represent a set of necessary conditions: if the system exceeds the legal limits for air and water pollution, it is unlikely to be sustainable; at the same time, the fact that these environmental indicators give positive results is not reassuring about the degree of sustainability of the area in which they are obtained. Conversely, sustainability indicators aim to represent something relative to the entire system: sustainability is not a natural phenomenon but it depends on the capacity of the system to obtain results and maintain certain conditions within limits; together with the details (measures), we need to know how a certain state is reached and the history of the processes necessary to reach it. This type of analysis also enables an understanding of the mechanisms leading to unsustainability and what improvements can be undertaken. Knowledge of the system properties rather than of the microscopic parts is needed (see Pulselli, Bastianoni, Marchettini & Tiezzi 2008).

---

[1] See OECD and JRC (2008), and JRC Composite Indicators WebPages at https://ec.europa.eu/jrc/en/research-topic/composite-indicators)

Nonetheless, attention must be paid to problems that may arise when using either of these tools. For example:

- juxtaposing information may lead to a reductionist vision of the systems, which is represented by a huge (often growing) number of disaggregated data. The construction of a dashboard is often affected by a certain level of arbitrariness, especially in the selection of weighting parameters;
- aggregating information may lead to a loss of information: if we use a ratio between two entities, or relative rather than absolute parameters, the same results can be obtained in infinite ways without adding information (see Figure 2).

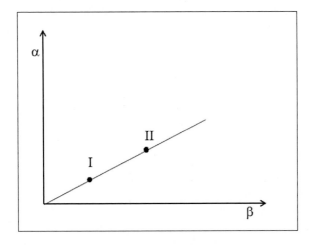

Figure 2. The ratio between α and β is the same in points I and II. These results must be broken down to gain further information.

- a synthetic number obtained from a multiple set of data may facilitate *substitutability* or *compensation* among its components: for example, if we had an omni-comprehensive metric for sustainability, composed of environmental, social and economic parts, we might always accept a reduction of the environmental quality so as to have better economic conditions without knowing the real importance of what we are losing;
- the use of *intensive indices* may sometimes be misleading: for instance, a decreasing carbon intensity (i.e., the ratio of GHG emission to the GDP of a nation, expressed in $tCO_{2-eq}/\$$) can be

coupled to an increase – rather than a decrease – of the absolute quantity of emissions in a country for the well-known "rebound effect";

- interpretation and communication of results should be clear, transparent and unequivocal.[2]

5. The Form of System Indicators: Guiding Principles for a New Assessment Order

To conclude, some key guiding principles are needed, which can then conceive and develop an assessment framework for monitoring human pressure on the Earth System. They are summarized as follows:

1) **From relative to absolute measures:** The Earth System is a thermodynamically closed system, which exchanges energy but not matter with the external space. Self-organization enables this system and its subsystems, fed by sunlight, to produce a continuous flow of resources, including the provision of matter and energy and the absorption of pollutants and residues. However, the capacity of the biosphere to provide these services is limited (i.e., not infinite), and overcoming biophysical limits means threatening the capacity of the planetary vital mechanisms to provide environmental goods and services in the future. The Earth System is therefore a finite unit, with well-defined absolute geographical and physical boundaries, that obeys natural laws. Being part of this biophysical infrastructure implies adapting to the limited space with constrained properties, which must be measured in absolute terms as well. Relative measures (e.g., intensity, efficiency, rates, percentages, per capita values) are important to "ensure sensitivity" (see Nykvist et al. 2013) and measure changes in relative entities such as growth and equity; however, the role played by humans in an absolute sense must be carefully acknowledged. For instance, let us consider the information extracted from two complementary (and not substitutable) measures like the energy intensity calculated for an economic system (the ratio of energy consumption to GDP, expressed in Joules/currency) and the absolute consumption of

---

[2] See the examples of the Happy Planet Index or the Better Life Index that allow users to choose how to weight variables, helping them to understand how different weights can lead to different results (Constanza et al. 2014b).

energy (in Joules per year) within the same system: the former is a relative projection useful to evaluate changes, technological advancements, efficiency and so on; the latter is the physical "footprint" that can be considered within the planetary platform, a more suitable tool with which to gain information on the limits of the Earth System. In other words, improvements on the energy intensity measure do not impede the overall increase of energy demand. Only looking at relative measures does not ensure human metabolism stays within the Earth's biophysical limits.

2) **From silos to systemic thinking:** As stated in this chapter, a systemic approach is needed to widen our view and see the system "as a whole". Details are important but the emerging properties of the complex system of interaction and retroactions among the elements of reality must be considered in order to take into account the evolutionary implications of our behaviour. Unpredictable, unexpected, unavoidable consequences deriving from myopic and punctual action must be avoided as well. The Earth System view, in this case, suggests a multidimensional and cross-cutting approach able to encompass the different aspects and implications of a sustainable decision-making process.

3) **From short terminism to long terminism**: A shift in mindset is needed to bridge the gap between the geological time of the Earth System (long term) and the human time of the governance process (short term). As recent research indicates (Steffen et al. 2015b), it might take a million years before an Earth System process is destabilised. However, once the safe operating space is passed and a critical threshold approached, abrupt and sudden changes are likely to take place, seriously (and likely irreversibly) affecting human well-being. Such a shift in mindset from short- to long-term thinking is therefore not only needed but urgent. In practical terms, this implies progressive acknowledgement of the differences between the economic, political and environmental cycles; progressive awareness of the influence of the fast anthropogenic changes on the slow dynamics of the biogeosphere; and progressive knowledge of ecosystem functions as they support economic and social processes.

4) **From addressing symptoms to addressing causes:** The lack of a systemic approach in most of our societal processes (see also principle 2), our inability to look at the inherent and emerging characteristics of the Earth System and to articulate and measure an overarching sustainability goal has led us to focus on a myriad of

details, a multitude of punctual measures. In most cases, these punctual measures focus on societal outcomes (namely, *symptoms*), which have become the end-objectives of most of our actions. Perhaps the most striking example of this tendency is our "attachment" to economic growth and its maximization (primarily measured through GDP) to the extent that growth is no longer seen as a strategy to reach a final goal (well-being) but rather as a goal in itself. The parameters whose calculation we are most comfortable with have become our goals. This tendency needs to be inverted by focusing on a new assessment framework of the underlying causes of human pressure on the Earth System.

5) **Production and consumption:** Consumption, as a statistical aggregate, is an important component of GDP. Its level influences the national income and, in times of crisis, some operators and agents claim, first of all, the recovery of consumption level as a prerequisite for positive economic growth rates. A huge number of implications must, however, be considered behind the idea of consumption, such as the type of production processes, the workers involved, the investments made, the energy spent, the quantity of raw materials that are extracted and processed, and the destiny of products after their use. In brief, a lot of things must be known to assess the sustainability of a production/consumption system for a given product. Systematically taking into account such a wide scheme is called "life cycle thinking", and a number of more or less analytical approaches able to identify and evaluate the steps that characterise the story of goods and services already exist. Life cycle assessment, emergy evaluation, ecological (as well as carbon and water) footprint analysis and environmentally extended input-output analyses are some of the methods used to extract crucial information about the material essence of the products we consume, their supply chain and the processes designed for their production. A systemic production/consumption monitoring system would also inform on why resources, energy and emission flows are generated, help understand how to optimize (or avoid) these flows and, ultimately, assign the individual or collective responsibility for their consequences (see, for example, the debate on the producer- vs consumer-based accounting principles for greenhouse gas emission; among others, see Bastianoni, Pulselli & Tiezzi 2004; Caro, Bastianoni, Borghesi & Pulselli 2014; Peters & Hertwich 2008; Weber & Peters 2009).

6) **Ethical judgements on the distribution of burdens:** Human impacts on the Earth System have been historically disproportionate among countries, and for the past decades, the fewer rich ones have been responsible for the great majority of pressure on the Earth System. Lack of trust among countries in international cooperation agreements is based on these unequal (ecological) burdens and (economic) benefits for each region or country. Furthermore, the Earth System in itself is unequal since its components cannot be distributed geographically in equal form. The inequalities of biophysical conditions tend to emphasise further the clash between rich and poor countries: some of the most important conditions for the functioning of the Earth System, such as tropical forests or water reservoirs, are located in developing countries. Therefore, any assessment framework aiming to orient the maintenance of a relatively stable state of the Earth System as a whole, our "common intangible heritage", must recognize these geographic, social, economic, biophysical, and temporal inequalities. This is not a new proposition in the scientific community but the lack of frameworks to efficiently relate these inequalities within the management of the global and common sustainability remains. This is why an assessment framework must consider two inseparable aspects mediated by different possible tools (e.g., Nykvist et al. 2013): 1) the incorporation of factors that relate historical and geographical trends with future risk analysis to understand the potential real (ecological, economic, and social) costs and benefits for rich and poor countries, and the planet as a whole, and how to cope with uncertainty; and (2) the incorporation of an incentive structure associated with the assessment framework for transforming our common inhabitation of the planet based on the balance of credits and debits over the "common intangible heritage" and on global funding schemes associated with this balance.

7) **"Scientific need" for systemic thinking and "governance need" for local actions:** Citing a traditional adage of systemic thinkers, we have argued in this chapter that "the whole is greater than the sum of the parts". Tracking and addressing sustainability thus requires understanding the way in which the Earth's multiple physical systems function and interact. At the same time, the policy-making process – as well as the management tools used to inform it – operates at national and local levels (with the exception of a few international agreements). Policy-makers at these levels

are ultimately responsible for taking action. Accounting for humanity's pressure on the Earth System thus necessitates an integrated assessment framework able to bridge the gap between the "scientific need" for a global systemic thinking and the "governance need" for local actions and policy implementation.

These seven principles – among the many possible – can be seen as a contribution for identifying a holistic system/framework of status indicators to be used in building a legal representation of the Earth System. If the final objective is to find solutions capable of provoking change, a new assessment framework needs to be carefully linked to a legal recognition of the Earth System.

References

Abdullatif, L., & Alam, T. (2011). *The UAE Ecological Footprint Initiative*. Retrieved from http://awsassets.panda.org/downloads/en_final_report_ecological_foot print.pdf

Ambiente Italia (2003). European Common Indicators: Towards a Local Sustainability Profile. Final Project Report Development, Refinement, Management and Evaluation of European Common Indicators Project. Retrieved from http://ec.europa.eu/environment/urban/pdf/eci_final_report.pdf

Astleithner, A., Hamedinger, A., Holman, N., & Rydin, Y. (2004). Institutions and Indicators – The Discourse about Indicators in the Context of Sustainability. *Journal of Housing and the Built Environment*, 19, 7-24. doi: 10.1023/B:JOHO.0000017704.49593.00.

Barnosky, A.D., Hadly, E.A., Bascompte, J., Berlow, E.L., Brown, J.H., (…), & Smith, A.B. (2012). Approaching a State Shift in Earth's Biosphere. *Nature*, 486 (7401), 52–58. doi: 10.1038/nature11018.

Bastianoni, S., Pulselli, F.M., & Tiezzi, E. (2004). The Problem of Assigning Responsibility for Greenhouse Gas Emissions. *Ecological Economics*, 49 (3), 253-257. doi: 10.1016/j.ecolecon.2004.01.018.

Bastianoni, S., Niccolucci, V., Neri, E., Cranston, G., Galli, A., & Wackernagel, M. (2013). Ecological Footprint as Accounting Tool for Sustainable Development. In: *Encyclopedia of Environmental Management*. Taylor and Francis, NY, USA, 2467–2481, doi: 10.1081/E-EEM-120047347.

Bastianoni, S., Marchi, M., Caro, D., Casprini, P., & Pulselli, F.M. (2014). The Connection between 2006 IPCC GHG Inventory Methodology and

ISO 14064-1 Certification Standard – A Reference Point for the
Environmental Policies at Sub-national Scale. *Environmental Science
& Policy*, 44, 97-107. doi: 10.1016/j.envsci.2014.07.015.

Bell, S., & Morse, S. (2003). *Measuring Sustainability: Learning from
Doing*. London: Earthscan.

Bolt, J., & van Zanden, J.L. (2013). *The First Update of the Maddison
Project – Re-Estimating Growth before 1820*. Maddison Project
Working Paper 4. Retrieved from
http://www.ggdc.net/maddison/maddison-project/home.htm

Bossel, H. (1999). *Indicators for Sustainable Development: Theory,
Methods, Applications*. Manitoba: IISD.

Braat, L. (1991). The Predictive Meaning of Sustainability Indicators. In
O. Kuik & H. Verbruggen (Eds), *In Search of Indicators of Sustainable
Development* (pp.71–88). Dordrecht: Kluwer Academic Publishers.

Butchart, S.H.M., Walpole, M., Collen, B., van Strien, A., Scharlemann,
J.P.W., (…) & Watson, R. (2010). Global Biodiversity: Indicators of
Recent Declines. *Science*, 328 (5982), 1164–1168. doi:
10.1126/science.1187512.

Capra, F. (1996). *The Web of Life: A New Scientific Understanding of
Living Systems*. New York, USA: Anchor Books.

Caro, D., Bastianoni, S., Borghesi, S., & Pulselli, F.M. (2014). On the
Feasibility of a Consumer-based Allocation Method in National GHG
Inventories. *Ecological Indicators*, 36, 640–643. doi:
10.1016/j.ecolind.2013.09.021.

CBD (Convention on Biological Diversity) (2010). Decision X/2, The
Strategic Plan for Biodiversity 2011–2020 and the Aichi Biodiversity
Targets. Nagoya, Japan, 18 to 29 October, 2010.

Clapp, J., & Dauvergne, P. (2005). *Paths to a Green World: The Political
Economy of the Global Environment*. Cambridge, Massachusetts
02142, USA: The MIT Press.

Coelho, P., Mascarenhas, A., Vaz, P., Dores, A., & Ramos, T.B. (2010). A
Framework for Regional Sustainability Assessment: Developing
Indicators for a Portuguese Region. *Sustainable Development*, 18(4),
211–219. doi: 10.1002/sd.488.

Cole, M.J., Bailey, R.M., & New, M.G. (2014). Tracking Sustainable
Development with a National Barometer for South Africa using a
Downscaled "Safe and Just Space" Framework. PNAS 111(42),
E4399-E4408. doi: 10.1073/pnas.1400985111.

Costanza, R., McGlade, J., Lovins, H., & Kubiszewski, I. (2014a). An
Overarching Goal for the UN Sustainable Development Goals.
Solutions, 5(4), 13–16. Retrieved from

http://www.thesolutionsjournal.com/node/237220
Costanza, R., Kubiszewski, I., Giovannini, E., Lovins, H., McGlade, J. Pickett, K., Ragnarsdóttir, K. Roberts, D., Vogli, R. & Wilkinson, R. (2014b). Development: Time to Leave GDP Behind. *Nature* 505, 283–285. doi:10.1038/505283a.
Crutzen, P.J. (2002). Geology of Mankind – The Anthropocene. *Nature*, 415, 23. doi: 10.1038/415023a
Dahl, A.L. (2012). Achievements and Gaps in Indicators for Sustainability. *Ecological Indicators,* 17, 14–19. doi:10.1016/j.ecolind.2011.04.032.
Daly, H.E. (1996). *Beyond Growth. The Economics of Sustainable Development*. Boston, USA: Beacon Press.
Daly, H.E., & Farley, J. (2004). *Ecological Economics. Principles and Applications*. Washington DC, USA: Island Press.
DeFries, R.S., Foley, J.A., & Asner, G.P. (2004). Land-use Choices: Balancing Human Needs and Ecosystem Function. *Frontiers in Ecology and the Environment*, 2 (5) 249–257. Retrieved from http://water.columbia.edu/files/2011/11/DeFries2004LandUse.pdf
Ellis, E.C., Goldewijk, K.K., Siebert, S., Lightman, D., & Ramankutty, N. (2010). Anthropogenic Transformation of the Biomes, 1700 to 2000. *Global Ecology and Biogeography,* 19, 589–606. doi: 10.1111/j.1466-8238.2010.00540.x.
Etzkowitz, H. (1993). Technology Transfer: The Second Academic Revolution. Technology Access Report, No 6, 7–9.
—. (2003). Innovation in Innovation: the Triple Helix of University-Industry-Government Relations. *Social Science Information*, 42, 293–338. doi: 10.1177/05390184030423002.
Ewing, B.R., Hawkins, T.R., Wiedmann, T.O., Galli, A., Ercin, A.E., Weinzettel, J., & Steen-Olsen, K. (2012). Integrating Ecological and Water Footprint Accounting in a Multi-regional Input-Output Framework. *Ecological Indicators*, 23, 1–8. doi: 10.1016/j.ecolind.2012.02.025.
Falkenmark, M. (1989). The Massive Water Scarcity now Threatening Africa: Why Isn't It Being Addressed? *Ambio: A Journal of the Human Environment*, 18 (2), 112–118.
Fidélis, T. & Moreno Pires, S. (2009). Surrender or Resistance to the Implementation of Local Agenda 21 in Portugal: The Challenges of Local Governance for Sustainable Development. *Journal of Environmental Planning & Management*, 52(4), 497–518. doi: 10.1080/09640560902868363.

Galli, A. (2015). On the Rational and Policy Usefulness of Ecological Footprint Accounting: The Case of Morocco. *Environmental Science & Policy*, 48, 210–224. doi: 10.1016/j.envsci.2015.01.008.

Galli, A., Wiedmann, T., Ercin, E., Knoblauch, D., Ewing, B., & Giljum, S. (2012). Integrating Ecological, Carbon and Water Footprint into a 'Footprint Family' of Indicators: Definition and Role in Tracking Human Pressure on the Planet. *Ecological Indicators*, 16, 100–112. doi:10.1016/j.ecolind.2011.06.017.

Galli, A., Wackernagel, M., Iha, K., & Lazarus, E. (2014). Ecological Footprint: Implications for Biodiversity. *Biological Conservation*, 173, 121–132. doi:10.1016/j.biocon.2013.10.019.

Gallopín, G.C. (1997). Indicators and Their Use: Information for Decision-Making. In Moldan, B., Billharz, S. (Eds). *Sustainability Indicators – Report on the Project on Indicators of Sustainable Development. Scientific Committee on Problems of the Environment (SCOPE), 58,* 13–27. Chichester: Wiley

Giovannini, E., & Linster, M. (2005). *Measuring Sustainable Development: Achievements and Challenges.* Paper presented at the Expert Group Meeting on Indicators of Sustainable Development, United Nations Division for Sustainable Development, New York. Retrieved from http://www.un.org/esa/sustdev/natlinfo/indicators/egmIndicators/crp5.pdf

Goudie, A. (1981). *The Human Impact on the Natural Environment: Past, Present and Future.* USA: Blackwell Publishing.

GRI (Global Reporting Initiative). (2013). Report or Explain – A Smart Policy Approach for Non-Financial Information Disclosure, GRI non-paper 5 March, 2013. Retrieved from https://www.globalreporting.org/resourcelibrary/GRI-non-paper-Report-or-Explain.pdf

Gudmundsson, H. (2003). The Policy Use of Environmental Indicators – Learning from Evaluation Research. *Journal of Transdisciplinary Environmental Studies*, 2(2).

Haberl, H. (2006). The Global Socioeconomic Energetic Metabolism as a Sustainability Problem. *Energy,* 31, 87–99. doi:10.1016/j.energy.2004.04.045.

Haberl, H., Erb, K.H., Krausmann, F., Gaube, V., Bondeau, A., Plutzar, C., Gingrich, S., Lucht, W., Fischer-& Kowalski, M. (2007). Quantifying and Mapping the Human Appropriation of Net Primary Production in Earth's Terrestrial Ecosystems. *Proceedings of the National Academy of Sciences of the United States of America*, 104, 12942–12947.

Hammond, A., Adriaanse, A., Rodenburg, E., Bryant, D., & Woodward, R. (1995). *Environmental Indicators: A Systematic Approach to Measuring and Reporting on Environmental Policy Performance in the Context of Sustainable Development*. Washington DC: World Resources Institute.

Hardi, P., & Zdan, T. (Eds) (1997). *Assessing Sustainable Development: Principles in Practice*. Winnipeg, Canada: IISD.

Hass, J. L., Brunvoll, F., & Høie, H. (2002). *Overview of Sustainable Development Indicators used by National and International Agencies*. OECD Statistics Working Paper 2002/1, OECD, Paris.

Hezri, A., & Hasan, N. (2004). Management Framework for Sustainable Development Indicators in the State of Selangor, Malaysia. *Ecological Indicators*, 4, 287–304. doi:10.1016/j.ecolind.2004.08.002.

Hezri, A., & Dovers, S. (2006). Sustainability Indicators, Policy and Governance: Issues for Ecological Economics. *Ecological Indicators*, 60, 86–99. doi:10.1016/j.ecolecon.2005.11.019.

Holden, M. (2006). Revisiting the Local Impact of Community Indicators Projects: Sustainable Seattle as Prophet in its Own Land. *Applied Research in Quality of Life*, 1, 253–277. doi: 10.1007/s11482-007-9020-8.

—. (2009). Community Interests and Indicator System Success. *Social Indicators Research*, 92, 429–448. doi: 10.1007/s11205-008-9304-x.

—. (2011). Public Participation and Local Sustainability: Questioning a Common Agenda in Urban Governance. *International Journal of Urban and Regional Research*, 35(2), 312–329. doi: 10.1111/j.1468-2427.2010.00957.x.

Holden, M., & Moreno Pires, S. (2015). The Minority Report: Social Hope in Next Generation Urban Indicators Work – Commentary on Rob Kitchin et al.'s Knowing and Governing Cities through Urban Indicators, City Benchmarking, and Real-Time Dashboards. *Regional Studies, Regional Science*, 2 (1), 33–38. doi: 10.1080/21681376.2014.987541.

Holman, N. (2009). Incorporating Local Sustainability Indicators into Structures of Local Governance: A Review of the Literature. *Local Environment*, 14(4), 365–375. ISSN 1354-9839.

Imhoff, M.L., Bounoua, L., Ricketts, T., Loucks, C., Harriss, R. & Lawrence, W.T. (2004). Global Patterns in Human Consumption of Net Primary Production. *Nature* 429(6994), 870–873. doi: 10.1038/nature02619.

Inhaber, H. (1976). *Environmental Indices*. New York: John Wiley & Sons.

Innes, J.E. & Booher, D. (2000). Indicators for Sustainable Communities: A Strategy Building on Complexity Theory and Distributed Intelligence. *Planning Theory and Practice*, 1(2), 173–186. doi: 10.1080/14649350020008378.

IPCC (Intergovernmental Panel on Climate Change) (2013). *Climate Change 2013: The Physical Science Basis. Contribution of Working Group I to the Fifth Assessment Report of the Intergovernmental Panel on Climate Change* [T. F. Stocker, D. Qin, G.-K. Plattner, M. Tignor, S. K. Allen, J. Boschung, A. Nauels, Y. Xia, V. Bex and P. M. Midgley (Eds.)]. Cambridge, United Kingdom and New York, USA: Cambridge University Press, 1535 pp.

Jesinghaus, J. (1999). *Indicators for Decision Making, European Commission*. JRC/ISIS/MIA, TP361, 1-21020 Ispra (VA), Italy.

Jørgensen, S.E. (2012). *Introduction to Systems Ecology*. CRC Press, Taylor & Francis Group, Boca Raton, USA.

Kline, E. (2000). Planning and Creating Eco-cities: Indicators as a Tool for Shaping Development and Measuring Progress. *Local Environment*, 5(3), 343–350. doi: 10.1080/13549830050134275.

Knight, J. (2015). Anthropocene Futures: People, Resources and Sustainability. *The Anthropocene Review*, 26. doi: 10.1177/2053019615569318.

Krausmann, F., Gingrich, S., Eisenmenger, N., Erb, K.H., Haberl, H. & Fischer-Kowalski, M. (2009). Growth in Global Materials use GDP and Population during the 20th Century. *Ecological Economics,* 68, 2696–2705. doi:10.1016/j.ecolecon.2009.05.007.

Krausmann, F., Erb, K.H., Gingrich, S., Haberl, H., Bondeau, A., Gaube, V., Lauk, C., Plutzar, C. & Searchinger, T.D. (2013). Global Human Appropriation of Net Primary Production Doubled in the 20th Century. *PNAS,* 110(25), 10324–10329. doi: 10.1073/pnas.1211349110.

Kuznets, S. (1934). *New York: National Bureau of Economic Research*. Retrieved from http://www.nber.org/chapters/c2258.pdf

Lawn, P. (Ed.) (2006). *Sustainable Development Indicators in Ecological Economics*. Cheltenham, UK: Edward Elgar.

Lyytimäki, J., Gudmundsson, H., & Sørensen, C.H. (2014). Russian Dolls and Chinese Whispers: Two Perspectives on the Unintended Effects of Sustainability Indicator Communication. *Sustainable Development,* 22, 84–94. doi: 10.1002/sd.530.

Mascarenhas, A., Coelho, P., Subtil, E., Ramos, T.B. (2010). The Role of Common Local Indicators in Regional Sustainability Assessment. *Ecological Indicators,* 10(3), 646–656. doi:10.1016/j.ecolind.2009.11.003.

Moreno Pires, S. (2014). Indicators of Sustainability. In: A.C. Michalos (Ed.). *Encyclopedia of Quality of Life and Well-Being Research* (pp. 3209–3214). Dordrecht, Netherlands: Springer. ISBN 978-94-007-0752-8.

Moreno Pires, S. & Fidélis, T. (2014). Local Sustainability Indicators in Portugal: Assessing Implementation and Use in Governance Contexts. *Journal of Cleaner Production.* doi: 10.1016/j.jclepro.2014.08.002.

Moreno Pires, S., Fidélis, T. & Ramos, T.B. (2014). Measuring and Comparing Local Sustainable Development through Common Indicators: Constraints and Achievements in Practice. *Cities*, 39, 1–9. doi: 10.1016/j.cities.2014.02.003.

Müller, F. & Burkhard, B. (2012). The Indicator Side of Ecosystem Services. *Ecosystem Services*, 1, 26–30. doi:10.1016/j.ecoser.2012.06.001.

Nelson, G.C., Bennett, E., Berhe, A.A., Cassman, K., DeFries, R. ... & Zurek, M. (2006). Anthropogenic Drivers of Ecosystem Change: An Overview. *Ecology and Society,* 11(2), 29. Retrieved from http://www.ecologyandsociety.org/vol11/iss2/art29/.

Newman, P. & Jennings, I. (2008). *Cities as Sustainable Ecosystems.* Washington: Island Press.

Nitschke, J.R. (2009). Systems Chemistry: Molecular Networks Come of Age. *Nature*, 462, 736–738. doi: 10.1038/462736a.

Nordhaus, W. D. & Tobin, J. (1972). Is Growth Obsolete? In Nordhaus and Tobin (Ed.), *Economic Research: Retrospect and Prospect Vol 5: Economic Growth.* New York: National Bureau of Economic Research. Retrieved from http://www.nber.org/chapters/c7620.pdf

Nykvist, B., Persson, Å., Moberg, F., Persson, L., Cornell, S., & Rockström, J. (2013). *National Environmental Performance on Planetary Boundaries – A Study for the Swedish Environmental Protection Agency. Stockholm: Swedish Environmental Protection Agency.* Retrieved from http://www.naturvardsverket.se/Documents/publikationer6400/978-91-620-6576-8.pdf

OECD & JRC (2008). *Handbook on Constructing Composite Indicators: Methodology and User Guide, OECD.* Retrieved from http://www.oecd.org/std/42495745.pdf

Ott, W.R. (1978). *Environmental Indices – Theory and Practice.* Michigan: Ann Harbor Science.

PASTILLE (2002) *Indicators into Action – Local Sustainability Indicator Sets in their Context.* PASTILLE Consortium, London: LSE.

Peters, G.P. & Hertwich, E.G. (2008). CO_2 Embodied in International Trade with Implications for Global Climate Policy. *Environ Science and Technology*, 42, 1401–1407. doi: 10.1021/es072023k.

Pintér, L., Hardi, P. & Bartelmus, P. (2005). *Sustainable Development Indicators: Proposals for a Way Forward.* Winnipeg: IISD. Retrieved from http://www.iisd.org/pdf/2005/measure_indicators_sd_way_forward.pdf

Planetary Boundaries Initiative (2015). Retrieved from http://planetaryboundariesinitiative.org/about-2/aboutpbs/

POINT (2011). A Synthesis of the Findings of the POINT Project. No. 15. POINT Policy Use and Influence of Indicators – Current Use of and Emerging Needs for Indicators in Policy. The Bayswater Institute.

Pulselli, F., Bastianoni, S., Marchettini N., & Tiezzi, E. (2008). *The Road to Sustainability. GDP and Future Generations.* Southampton, UK: WIT Press.

Rockström, J., Steffen, W., Noone, K., Persson, Å., Chapin III, F. S. ... & Foley, J. (2009a). Planetary Boundaries: Exploring the Safe Operating Space for Humanity. *Ecology and Society*, 14 (2), 32. Retrieved from http://www.ecologyandsociety.org/vol14/iss2/art32/.

Rockström, J., Steffen, W., Noone, K., Persson, Å., Chapin III, F. S. ... & Foley, J. (2009b). A Safe Operating Space for Humanity. *Nature*, 461, 472–475. doi:10.1038/461472a.

Rockström, J., & Klum, M. (2015). *Big World, Small Planet: Abundance within Planetary Boundaries.* Stockholm, Sweden: Max Ström.

Rosenström, U. (2006). Exploring the Policy Use of Sustainable Development Indicators: Interviews with Finnish Politicians. *Journal of Transdiscip Environmental Studies,* 5(1–2).

Rydin, Y. (2007). Indicators as a Governmental Technology? The Lessons of Community-based Sustainability Indicator Projects. *Environment and Planning D: Soc Sp*, 25(4), 610–624. doi:10.1068/d72j.

Schlossberg, M., & Zimmerman, A. (2003). Developing Statewide Indices of Environmental, Economic and Social Sustainability: A Look at Oregon and the Oregon Benchmarks. *Local Environment*, 8(6), 641–660. doi: 10.1080/1354983032000152743.

SCBD (Secretariat of the Convention on Biological Diversity) (2014). *Global Biodiversity Outlook 4.* Montréal, Canada, 155 pages. ISBN-92-9225-540-1.

Singh, R.K., Murty, H.R., Gupta, S.K., & Dikshit, A.K. (2012). An Overview of Sustainability Assessment Methodologies. *Ecological Indicators*, 15, 281–299. doi:10.1016/j.ecolind.2011.01.007.

Steffen, W., Crutzen, P.J., & McNeill, J.R. (2007). The Anthropocene: Are Humans Now Overwhelming the Great Forces of Nature? *Ambio: A Journal of the Human Environment,* 36 (8), 614–621. doi: 10.1579/0044-7447(2007)36[614:TAAHNO]2.0.CO;2.

Steffen, W., Broadgate, W., Deutsch, L., Gaffney, O., & Ludwig, C. (2015a). The Trajectory of the Anthropocene: The Great Acceleration. *The Anthropocene Review,* 1–18. doi: 10.1177/2053019614564785.

Steffen, W., Richardson, K., Rockström, J., Cornell, S.E., Fetzer, I., Bennett, E.M., Biggs, R., Carpenter, S.R., de Vries, W., de Wit, C.A., Folke, C., Gerten, D., Heinke, J., Mace, G.M., Persson, L.M., Ramanathan, V., Reyers, B., & Sörlin, S. (2015b). Planetary Boundaries: Guiding Human Development on a Changing Planet. *Science.* doi: 10.1126/science.1259855.

Tiezzi, E. (2003). *The End of Time.* Southampton, UK: Wit Press.

Tiezzi, E., & Bastianoni, S. (2008). Sustainability of the Siena Province through Ecodynamic Indicators. *Journal of Environmental Management,* 86 (2), 329–331. doi: 10.1016/j.jenvman.2006.04.015.

Tittensor, D.P., Walpole, M., Hill, S.L.L., Boyce, D.G., Britten, G.L. ... & Ye, Y. (2014). A Mid-Term Analysis of Progress toward International Biodiversity Targets. *Science,* 346, 241–244. doi: 10.1126/science.1257484.

Turner, G.H. (2008). A Comparison of the Limits to Growth with 30 Years of Reality. *Global Environmental Change,* 18(3), 397–411. doi: 10.1016/j.gloenvcha.2008.05.001.

USASC (United States Acting Secretary of Commerce) (1934). *National Income, 1929–1932: Letter from the Acting Secretary of Commerce Transmitting in Response to Senate Resolution No. 220 (72nd Cong.) A Report on National Income, 1929-32.* New York: National Bureau of Economic Research. Retrieved from https://fraser.stlouisfed.org/scribd/?title_id=971&filepath=/docs/public ations/natincome_1934/19340104_nationalinc.pdf

UN (United Nations) (2014a). *Millennium Development Goals Report 2014.* New York, USA: United Nations.

—. (2014b). *Open Working Group Proposal for Sustainable Development Goals.* New York, USA: United Nations.

UNCED (United Nations Conference on Environment and Development) (1992). *Agenda 21.* Retrieved from http://www.un.org/esa/sustdev/documents/agenda21/english/Agenda21 .pdf

UNCSD (United Nations Commission on Sustainable Development) (1996). *Indicators of Sustainable Development: Frameworks and Methodologies*, New York, USA: United Nations.

—. (2012). *The Future We Want: Outcome Document Adopted at Rio+20.* Retrieved from http://www.uncsd2012.org/content/documents/727The%20Future%20 We%20Want%2019%20June%201230pm.pdf

UNDP (United Nations Development Programme) (2013). *Human Development Report 2013. The Rise of the South: Human Progress in a Diverse World.* New York, USA: UNDEP. ISBN 978-92-1-126340-4

UNECE/OECD/Eurostat (2008). Report on Measuring Sustainable Development: Statistics for Sustainable Development, Commonalities between Current Practice and Theory. Working Paper ECE/CES2008/29, Paris.

UNEP (United Nations Environment Programme) (2007). *GEO4 Global Environment Outlook: Environment for Development.* Malta: Progress Press Ltd.

—. (2012). *Global Environmental Outlook 5 (GEO5).* ISBN: 978-92-807-3177-4.

United Nations, European Union, Food and Agriculture Organization of the United Nations, International Monetary Fund, Organization for Economic Cooperation and Development, & The World Bank (2014). *System of Environmental-Economic Accounting 2012–Central Framework.* Document symbol: ST/ESA/STAT/Ser.F/109. ISBN: 987-92-1-161563-0.

Vitousek, P.M., Ehrlich, P.R., Ehrlich, A.H., & Matson, PA. (1986). Human Appropriation of the Products of Photosynthesis. *Bioscience.* 36 (6), 363–373.

Wackernagel, M. (2013). Letter to the Editor: Comment on Ecological Footprint Policy? Land Use as an Environmental Indicator. *Journal of Industrial Ecol*ogy, doi: 10.1111/jiec.12094.

Wackernagel, M., Schulz, B., Deumling, D., Linares, A.C., Jenkins, M., Kapos, V., Monfreda, C., Loh, J., Myers, N., Norgaard, R., & Randers, J. (2002). Tracking the Ecological Overshoot of the Human Economy. Proceedings of the National Academy of Sciences of the USA, 99 (14), 9266–9271. doi: 10.1073/pnas.142033699.

Weber, L.C., & Peters, G.P. (2009). Climate Change Policy and International Trade: Policy Consideration in the US. *Energy Policy,* 37, 432–440. doi:10.1016/j.enpol.2008.09.073.

WWF (WWF International), ZSL (Zoological Society of London), GFN (Global Footprint Network), & WFN (Water Footprint Network)

(2014). *Living Planet Report 2014*. Gland, Switzerland: WWF. ISBN 978-2-940443-87-1. Retrieved from http://wwf.panda.org/about_our_earth/all_publications/living_planet_report/

Yli-Viikari, A. (2009). Confusing Messages of Sustainability Indicators. *Local Environment*, 14(10),891–903. doi: 10.1080/13549830903255405.

CHAPTER ELEVEN

STRUCTURAL CONDITIONS TO OVERCOME THE DILEMMA OF COLLECTIVE ACTION

IVA MIRANDA PIRES[1]

1. Introduction

The "Tragedy of the Commons" by Garret Hardin (1968), published in *Nature* almost half a century ago, is among the most well-known and commented-upon articles on the management of common resources, and for a long time Hardin's ideas were used. In the following years, there were many debates regarding the metaphor employed by the author to explain the inevitability of coercive state intervention or privatization as the only ways of circumventing the irreversible degradation of ecosystems.

He used a metaphor of herdsmen with free access to common grazing grounds, acting independently in the pursuit of self-interest. In this situation, they will be motivated to maximize their individual benefits and obtain immediate gains by adding more sheep to their herds while the costs are shared by the entire group. Having no incentive to cooperate to overcome the commons dilemma, their behaviour will culminate in the overexploitation of the pastures.

This leads to a situation described as a "social dilemma" or "social trap", in which non-coordinated decisions pave the way for the pursuit of individual benefits that produce a suboptimal use of resources for everyone in the long term. The only two obvious solutions to overcoming this social trap, where no one will change their behaviour to benefit the collective, seemed to be privatization or state coercion. For a long time, these conventional approaches to the management of global vital non-renewable resources were not questioned.

---

[1] Interdisciplinary Centre of Social Sciences CICS.NOVA - Faculdade de Ciências Sociais e Humanas - Universidade Nova de Lisboa (CICS.NOVA.FCSH/UNL)

Elinor Ostrom's work, awarded with the Nobel Prize in Economics in 2009, refreshed the discussion on the management of common pool resources (CPRs) by offering innovative approaches and stating that it is possible to balance both group and individual interests. Based on her fieldwork in the groundwater West Basin, Southern California for her PhD dissertation, she realized that collective action in the management of CPRs was undermined namely by the size of the group involved, its asymmetric interests and the lack of arrangement between the "problem" and governmental units. In spite of that, she considered that some conditions for collective action were in place. A large set of actors with diversified interests organized in a polycentric system (farmers, private firms, city governments and national agencies) did find ways to discuss a common problem (the scarcity of groundwater due to overexploitation) and find acceptable solutions considering the complexity of the problem. To overcome this social dilemma, some key conditions for the construction of trust and reciprocity should be ensured, namely, that those using a CPR share a similar view of the problem, design rules to which most could contingently agree, monitor that they are respected and discipline those who do not comply (Ostrom 1999).

In her "Long Polycentric Journey", Ostrom (2010) faced an academic world dominated by men, who greatly disregarded her skills as a researcher but she kept pushing her innovative perspective based on her fieldwork and ended, unexpectedly, by being awarded with a Nobel Prize in Economics in 2009.

Her conclusions were innovative and based on intensive fieldwork, observing the real world where people lived, interacted and organized themselves to manage common resources and punish infringers. Despite the good practices that can be drawn from the already large literature on CPRs that are successfully managed at the local and regional levels, upgrading to the global scale will be the great challenge for the future.

This chapter on structural conditions to overcome the dilemma of collective action aims to contribute to a broader discussion centred on the role of Ostrom and her contribution, drawing attention to other possible solutions for the management of the commons.

2. The Tragedy of the Commons and Other Metaphors

Garrett Hardin (1968) believed that exponential population growth would lead to overpopulation and that, in turn, would generate misery because in a finite world there must be limits. Population growth belonged to a group of problems he called "no-technical-solution problems" in the sense that improving the technology to increase food production or harvest the oceans would not solve the problem. Unless something was done, exponential population growth in a finite world would lead to a tragedy of the commons. Citing a philosopher, he goes on to explain that "The essence of dramatic tragedy is not unhappiness. It resides in the solemnity of the remorseless working of things" (p. 1244).

Hardin created his metaphor based on William Forster Lloyd's *Two Lectures on the Checks to Population*, written in 1833. Lloyd was discussing the principle of mitigating the conflicts that will arise due to the different paces of food and population growth, as the first could never keep up with the second.

> If a person puts more cattle into his own field, the amount of the subsistence which they consume is all deducted from that which was at the command of his original stock, and if, before, there was no more than a sufficiency of pasture he reaps no benefit from the additional cattle, what is gained in one way being lost in another. But if he puts more cattle on a common, the food which they consume forms a deduction which is shared between all the cattle as well that of others as his own in proportion to their number and only a small part of it is taken from his own cattle. (1833,31)

In his "Tragedy of the Commons", Hardin used the metaphor of a community of herdsmen exploiting a common pasture. No problem will arise while wars, poaching and diseases "keep numbers of both man and beast well below the carrying capacity of the land" (p. 1244). However, the herdsmen will act rationally and try to maximize their income by increasing their herd. The benefits from their sale will be appropriated by each herdsman (positive component of this utility) whereas the negative component, a result of the overgrazing created by one more animal, will be shared by all, and so will be much lower than the benefits. Acting rationally, each herdsman sharing a common pasture will reach the same conclusion, that is, by increasing his herd, he can get more profits than costs, which will be shared by all, ultimately leading to the "tragedy of freedom in a commons" through the disappearance of the pasture by overgrazing.

In these so-called "no-technical-solution problems", Hardin also includes the example of pollution. In this case it is not because of taking something from the commons but about adding something. The national parks, for instance, will erode if they are open to all with no restrictions on the number of visitors.

He concludes that the solution for these and similar problems is what he calls "mutual coercion", meaning coercion mutually agreed upon by the majority of people affected. This would be the only solution, although not just, as the "alternative of the commons is too horrifying to contemplate. Injustice is preferable to total ruin" (p. 1247).

One year before Hardin's essay, Harold Demsetz, in a paper published in 1967 on the "Theory of Property Rights", also discussed privatization of land as the only solution to preventing the tragedy of the commons, recognizing that there is a close relationship between property rights and externalities, using as an example the Indians in the Labrador Peninsula and the fur market. As the fur trade grew and its commercial value increased considerably, the conflicts over the management of common hunting territories also increased. Privatization and the allotment of land was the solution adopted by the Indian community to solve the problem of over-hunting and the rapid decrease of resources. In that paper, Demsetz concludes that the only way to incentivise users to utilize resources more efficiently is privatization and the concentration of benefits and costs in the same person:

> In effect, an owner of a private right to use land acts as a broker whose wealth depends on how well he takes into account the competing claims of the present and the future. But with communal rights there is no broker, and the claims of the present generation will be given an uneconomically large weight in determining the intensity with which the land is worked. (...) Communal property means that future generations must speak for themselves. No one has yet estimated the costs of carrying on such a conversation. (1967, 355)

Therefore, Demsetz discusses privatization as a solution because it contributes to the reduction of the transaction costs of the negotiation process as well as the cost of policing an agreement. When a land is communally owned, the need to include the divergent interests that always exist in large groups will make it difficult or even impossible to find a solution, while privatization will reduce these costs by reaching a solution with only the one or two neighbours whose activities may affect the plot of land.

Later on, K. Boulding (1966) used the metaphor of Spaceship Earth. In the past, there seemed to be no borders – if anything went wrong, due to degradation of ecosystems and deterioration of the social structure, there was always spare space to start again. Gradually humans were accustomed to the image of a spherical planet with limits. But, he claimed, "Even now we are very far from having made the moral, political, and psychological adjustments which are implied in this transition from the illimitable planet to the closed sphere", in particular, the economists (p. 2). He used the image of a cowboy with unlimited stock looking at endless plains to exploit in contrast with the "spaceman economy" in which the time the trip lasts will depend on how we manage the finite stocks of natural resources and the limited reservoir for pollution. He argued that, with "modest optimism", it is possible to overcome the "obsession for production and consumption" that will lead to an environmental crisis and focus more on human welfare as the core objective.

Although different in their objectives and approaches, the solutions Hardin and Demesetz offer to avert the exhaustion of natural resources and prevent pollution, deterioration of the environment and the tragedy of the commons were either the privatization of property (enclosing farm lands and restricting pastures as well as hunting and fishing areas) or the coercive intervention of the state (imposing rules, limits of users and tax penalties).

3. Tragedy or Drama? Not Only a Semantic Question

The situations described in the previous section frame what is normally designated as a "social dilemma" or "social trap"; situations where non-coordinated decisions initiate the pursuit of individual benefits that produce a suboptimal use of resources for everyone.

Collective action problems are frequently represented by these social dilemmas, which assume that when it is not possible to exclude others from benefiting from the use of a common resource, there is a temptation for some individuals to act as "free riders", that is, they are willing to benefit from the provision of those collective benefits without paying any of the cost. These problems are based on the premise that if a person cannot be excluded from the benefits produced by others, there is little incentive to act rationally and cooperate and contribute to a common effort (Ostrom 1999, 2000). Paradoxically, an individual rational strategy based on "zero contribution" to the collective (Zero Contribution thesis, Mancur Olso) while at the same time free-riding on the benefits of the others will lead to collective irrational outcomes (Ostrom 1999).

Furthermore, individuals will be unable to escape these social traps even if their non-coordinated decisions produce suboptimal use of resources for everyone in the long term. The only two obvious solutions to overcoming this social trap were, as proposed by Hardin, either privatization or state coercion.

But something was wrong with these theories, with their interpretation or with the policy prescription, if the "only ways" to overcome the tragedy associated with the use of CPR to reduce externalities and increase efficiency were two state-established institutional arrangements – the imposition of state control or the imposition of private property (Becker and Ostrom 1995, 115). So, instead of Hardin's reductionist view, Ostrom proposed looking at the diversity of the real world.

Throughout her research career, Elinor Ostrom endeavoured to show that sometimes there is a happy ending and that individuals who share a common good are capable, in certain circumstances, of organizing themselves in order to overcome social traps and finding solutions that are beneficial to everyone. Success is not guaranteed, but nor is it with the solutions proposed by Hardin (Dietz, Ostrom & Stern 2003).

For over more than two years, Ostrom's team read over 500 case studies to extract a sample of 91 cases of fisheries and irrigation systems that explicitly recorded information about the actors, their strategies, the condition of the resource, and the rules-in-use (Ostrom 2010a, 10).

The case studies reported diversified solutions for the management of a CPR "... such as a lake or ocean, an irrigation system, a fishing ground, a forest, or the atmosphere, [that] is a natural or man-made resource from which it is difficult to exclude or limit users once the resource is provided, and one person's consumption of resource units makes those units unavailable to others" (Ostrom 1999, 497). They have several distinctive attributes: a) the difficulty of exclusion; b) the subtractability of benefits consumed by one person from those available to others (Ostrom, Gardner & Walker 1994; Becker & Ostrom 1995); and c) the degree of mobility of resource units and the presence or absence of storage (Schlager et al. 1994).

After analysing the case studies, Ostrom concluded that, despite the substantial differences among them, it was possible to outline eight design principles and threats to a self-organized resource regime. They include clearly defined boundaries, the collective-choice arrangements, the need to monitor the use of the resource, and the existence of graduated sanctions and conflict-resolution mechanisms.

Ostrom's designed principles are (1990, 90, Table 3.1):

1. Clearly defined boundaries – Individuals or households who have the right to withdraw resource units from the CPR must be clearly defined, as must the boundaries of the CPR itself.
2. Congruence between appropriation, provision rules and local conditions – Appropriation rules restricting time, place, technology, and/or quantity of resource units are related to local

conditions and to provision rules requiring labour, material and/or money.

3. Collective-choice arrangements – Most individuals affected by the operational rules can participate in modifying them.
4. Monitoring – Monitors, who actively audit CPR conditions and appropriate behaviour, are accountable to, or are, the appropriators.
5. Graduated sanctions – Appropriators who violate operational rules are likely to be assessed graduated sanctions (depending on the seriousness and the context of the offence) by other appropriators, by officials accountable to the appropriators or by both.
6. Conflict-resolution mechanisms – Appropriators and their officials have rapid access to low-cost local arenas to resolve conflicts among appropriators or between appropriators and officials.
7. Minimal recognition of rights to organize – The rights of appropriators to devise their own institutions are not challenged by external governmental authorities.
8. Nested enterprises – Appropriation, provision, monitoring, enforcement, conflict resolution, and governance activities are organized in multiple layers of nested enterprises.

These rules clearly define who can use the CPR, in what conditions, and the penalties that will be applied to those who do not respect them. These design principles explain the success and longevity of so many communities in their management of CPR, stemming from the organizational foundations that enable the emergence of trust among users and reduce the probability of free-ride behaviour.

Based on her own fieldwork and upon extensive review of several CPR systems managed at local and regional scales, Ostrom proved that a "happy end" is possible. So, instead of tragedy, Ostrom prefers the use of the word "drama" in the sense that dramas have both unhappy and happy ends.

4. From Local and Regional CPR to Global CPR

Lloyds wisely asserted that "In neither case, if individuals are prudent, do they alone reap the benefit, nor, if they are imprudent, do they alone feel the evil consequences" (1833, 33).

We are a "civilization in trouble" (Brown 2006) sharing the same planet, and cooperative action is imperative to manage the commons in a context of economic and environmental interdependencies after decades of "irresponsible growth" (Jackson 2009) that led to the transition to the Anthropocene.

The Anthropocene (Crutzen 2002, 2006; Steffen et al. 2007; Zalasiewicz et al. 2010) marks a transition in which the human species no longer had to adapt to environmental changes and became instead the driving force of the planetary system (Allegre 1990; Biermann 2014). The Anthropocene concept leads us beyond the more immediate concerns about the scarcity of resources. The main concern is no longer the ability of ecosystems to support a greedy market economy (Meadows et al. 1973; 2004) or the fact that the ecological footprints of the most developed countries already exceed the capacity of regeneration of ecosystems, jeopardizing their sustainable use (York, Rosa & Dietz 2003, Jorgenson & Clark 2011; Galli et al. 2012), but rather the consequences of human intervention on the Earth Systems that by their very nature operate on a global scale (Stern, Young & Druckman 1992). Such interventions create global-scale stresses (such as climate change) that pose new challenges because local actions might reduce exposure to the stresses but seldom decrease their magnitude (Chapin et al. 2009).

The Anthropocene comes in the context of a risk society and is embedded in the dynamics of reflexive modernity, marked by uncertainty, unpredictability, risk (Beck 1996; 1999), and complexity (Berkes 2008, editorial special issue). The complexity of the problems that our society faces is expressed in the Rittel and Webber (1973) expression "wicked problem", indicating problems that are difficult to solve because they challenge the consensus about being problems since they have unknown and untimed effects (Norton 2005). We know when they begin but we can't predict when their impact will end (Beck 1992) because there is no adequate or complete information to support a decision and because of the diversity of contemporary society. While pre-industrial society had a homogeneous culture, the industrial age expanded diversity, and post-industrial society is even more heterogeneous than the previous ones (Rittel & Webber 1973). Any model to manage common resources has to take into account these cultural diversities and needs to reconcile them in a meta-perspective (Brondizio, Ostrom & Young 2009).

The inevitability that we live in an interdependent world is not restricted to the economy, as the recent global crisis has shown; ecological interdependencies also frame the challenges currently faced by humanity.

This demands "governance for navigating change" (Armitage & Plummer 2010) as well as new and innovative perspectives (Biermann 2014) created within a collaborative scientific environment (Becker & Ostrom 1995; Hackmann & St. Clair 2012, 16; Pahl-Wostl et al. 2013) that

"(...) requires that both the physical and social sciences be included in its study. If researchers are to generate accurate analyses of environmental change, the first step, we believe, is to push beyond the present cacophony and construct a common understanding of issues related to scale" (Gibson, Ostrom & Ahan 2000). However, this collaborative environment has not been readily accepted, given that natural and social sciences have evolved towards specialisation (Fischer, Tobi & Ronteltap 2011).

Assuming that there are still knowledge and research gaps, as well as uncertainty and unpredictability regarding global changes and the evolution of socio-ecological systems, a growing body of literature is emphasising the need to change to a new integrated approach paradigm that crosses scales (from local to global) and disciplines (from natural to social sciences), and considers the interests of present and future generations (Costanza et al. 2008; Brondizio, Ostrom & Young 2009).

E. Ostrom's work on the institutional conditions for collective action and self-organizing systems for community-based management of CPR is paramount. Empirical results from several CPR systems managed at the local and regional scale are encouraging, and show that it is possible to overcome social dilemmas that prevent individuals from organizing themselves in order to jointly manage common resources for the benefit of all (Armitage 2008). Empirical studies also show that self-organizing systems are often more efficient in the long run than those in which the state sets the rules and imposes them coercively, though Ostrom does conclude, "Instead of pure pessimism or pure optimism, however, the picture requires further work to explain why some contextual variables enhance cooperation while others discourage it" (2000, 154).

Another major challenge stems from the transition from local/regional scales to the global one. Dietz, Ostrom and Stern (2003) consider that systems that are intrinsically global (such as the climate system) or are under global market pressure (like forests) pose the most important contemporary environmental challenges.

Ostrom's eighth principle, on nested enterprises, might be a starting point as it applies to CPRs that are part of large systems where "establishing rules at one level, without rules at the other levels, will produce an incomplete system that may not endure over the long run" (Ostrom 1990, 112).

But establishing rules and up-scaling governance to the planetary scale is a very difficult challenge associated with multiple problems, among them the impossibility of privatization of the Earth System and the absence of institutions with the competency to govern the use of CPR at this level. There are also problems associated with scale and time mismatches that reduce the sense of urgency in acting at the global scale, considering that human experience is felt at the local/regional levels and short to medium-time scales are more adequate than political cycles, although they are not the most adequate for the sustainable management of natural resources (Pahl-Wostl et al. 2013). Building trust relationships is also very difficult as the group of actors grows larger at a global scale, where the reciprocal altruism that can be found in small communities tends to break down (Levin 2010).

Human-induced climate change is a good example of the difficulty in reaching global consensus on when, where and how to act, on how to accommodate different and even divergent interests, on the creation of legally binding commitments to prevent the rise of global average temperatures above the threshold of 2°C, and on how to enforce and supervise their application. Therefore, climate change is frequently referred to as a "super wicked" problem as "time is running out; those who cause the problem also seek to provide a solution; the central authority needed to address it is weak or non-existent; and, partly as a result, policy responses discount the future irrationally", thus creating a tragedy because the existing institutions are unable to deal with it (Levin et al. 2012, 124). The same issue of climate change and the governing institutions, like the IPCC and its geography of expertise, was used by Hulme to synthetize several critics and the dangers of scaling-up to a global level, ignoring "the multiple ways of knowing environments, of living in places and of imagining the future which are embedded in local cultural practices and knowledge-making traditions" (2010, 560).

Effective governance of CPR is easier to achieve when a set of conditions exist, namely, when the resources and their use can be monitored, when communities maintain frequent face-to-face communication and dense social networks, outsiders can be excluded at a relatively low cost, and users support effective monitoring and rule enforcement. However, these circumstances are rarely found in the real world. So, in the absence of ideal conditions, the main challenge will be to create the conjunctures so that these conditions are met or to design governance models according to this challenge (Dietz, Ostrom & Stern 2003, 1908).

As we have discussed, Elinor Ostrom and other commons theorists developed and elaborated the concept of polycentric governance as the most adequate for the management of CPR.

Further elaborating on the idea of polycentric governance, particular attention must be given to the issue of scale as well as to horizontal and vertical linkages because local communities are just one layer in a

multilevel world involved in the efficient and sustainable management of
CPR (Berkes 2008, Marshall 2008, Armitage 2008). Other relevant bodies
of literature should include socio-ecological systems (SES) and their
characteristics and dynamics, namely resilience, transformation and
adaptation (Folke 2006), complex adaptive systems, adaptive management,
and adaptive governance of complex socio-ecological systems (Dietz et al.
2003; Norton 2005; Folk et al. 2005).

Adaptive management is a process of social learning and cooperation
that enables ongoing adjustment depending on the solution's feasibility to
reduce uncertainty in the future (Norton 2005). Dietz et al. (2003, 1910)
use the concept of adaptive governance, affirming that at least three
principles are particularly relevant for problems on larger scales: i) well-
structured dialogue involving scientists, resource users and an interested
public; ii) institutional arrangements must be complex, redundant and
nested in many payers; and iii) governance should imply mixtures of
institutional types. These principles will enable commons governance in
order to prevent large-scale tragedies.

Marshall (2008) argues that the lengthy process of learning from the
attempts to manage CPR at a local level in so many diversified cultural
and socioeconomic contexts, in addition to the lessons coming from
successful and failed experiences, should be used to design management
models for the global CPRs, guided by the principle of subsidiarity.
Decentralized decision making, where tasks should be allocated at the
lowest possible level as part of larger nested governance polycentric
systems, facilitates the flow of information, provides feedback on the
performance of each unit and contributes to the robustness of the SES
through overlapping and redundancy of governance.

Some conditions are nevertheless necessary. An integrated approach
requires information that should be highly scientific as well as useful to
the decision-makers and the other users, not only on the stocks, flows and
processes of the Earth Systems but also on the human-environment
interactions affecting them (Dietz, Ostrom & Stern 2003). It also requires
new forms of science funding, innovative methodologies and data
collection, and transdisciplinary research (Pahl-Wostl et al. 2013). It
demands new ecosystem and social indicators that are sensitive to slowly
changing causes and initial phases of degradation (Chapin et al. 2009),
"liquid" knowledge that is able to move and flow freely around the world
but at the same time is readily able to absorb new perspectives, values and
meanings (Hume 2010, 563), a learning environment that requires
leadership, changes of social norms within management organizations
(Folke et al. 2005), an emphasis on diversity, either institutional diversity

(Becker & Ostrom 1995) or a diversity of solutions (Chapin et al. 2009), and the creation of social capital (Brondizio, Ostrom & Young 2009). Also of key relevance are high indexes of participation and cooperation across the levels and social actors involved, iterative social learning to facilitate adaptation (Armitage 2008; Chapin et al. 2009) and multilevel governance systems.

At the end of her "Long Polycentric Journey" (2010, 19), Elinor Ostrom states that she is optimistic about the future namely because of the increasing research opportunities for women and minority scholars, since interdisciplinary scholarship is presently more feasible than it was and given the attention that scientists are paying to complex phenomena, responding to the challenge of unpacking their complexities in order to understand them.

We share Ostrom's optimism about the future. On the one hand, and quoting Derek Armitage (2008), "governing the commons in a multilevel world requires novelty and innovation" but creativity is a characteristic of the human species. On the other hand, "for those individuals and communities that are committed to transcending divisiveness and paralysis and engaging in cooperative action, there is a clear and optimistic road forward" (Norton 2005, xv).

Because time is running out, and due to the uncertainty and complexity of global change, it is urgent that we discuss sustainable ways to manage the global commons whether the solution is a polycentric governance, an adaptive management, an active ecosystem stewardship, or other forms of multilevel governance.

5. Final Remarks

At the end of the '60s, Garret Hardin discussed the tragedy of the unregulated commons and concluded that the only way to manage them was either through privatization or management by the state. He used the metaphor of shepherds with free access to a common grazing ground, acting independently in the pursuit of self-interest. In this and other similar metaphors, individuals were unable to escape the "social dilemma" or "social trap" in which non-coordinated decisions led to the pursuit of individual benefits that produced a suboptimal use of resources for everyone in the long term. The only two obvious solutions to overcome this social trap, where no one changes their behaviour to benefit the collective, seemed to be privatization or state coercion. For a long time these conventional approaches to the management of vital global non-renewable resources were not questioned.

On the reverse, Elinor Ostrom pointed out that there are other solutions to the tragedy of the commons, showing that it is possible to engage in collective action. It is obviously much easier to build solutions for collective action regarding small-scale problems than those related to global commons. However, it is of the utmost importance to use the acquired knowledge in the management of common property, to build a shared global solution in which everyone feels that their interests are safeguarded. According to Ostrom, the polycentric approach is the right one for managing systemic risk and change, and for successfully managing common resources in complex interconnected systems.

References

Allegre, C. (1990). *Économiser la planète*. Paris: Fayard.
Armitage, D. (2008). Governance and the Commons in a Multi-level World. *International Journal of the Commons*, 2, 7–32. Retrieved from https://www.thecommonsjournal.org/index.php/ijc/article/viewFile/28/16
Armitage, D. & Plummer, R. (2010). Adapting and Transforming: Governance for Navigating Change. In Derek Armitage and Ryan Plummer (Eds.), *Adaptive Capacity and Environmental Governance* (pp.287–302). Berlin: Springer Series on Environmental Management.
Bierman, F. (2014). The Anthropocene: A Governance Perspective. *The Anthropocene Review*, 1(1), 57–61. doi:10.1177/2053019613516289
Beck, U. (1992). *Risk Society: Towards a New Modernity*. London: Sage.
—. (1996). World Risk Society as Cosmopolitan Society?: Ecological Questions in a Framework of Manufactured Uncertainties. *Theory, Culture and Society 13*(4), 1–32. doi:10.1177/0263276496013004001
Brondizio, E. S., Ostrom, E., & Young, O.R. (2009). Connectivity and the Governance of Multilevel Social-Ecological Systems: The Role of Social Capital. *Annu. Rev. Environ. Resour. 34*, 253–278. doi:10.1146/annurev.environ.020708.100707.
Brown, L. (2006). *Plan B 2.0: Rescuing a Planet under Stress and a Civilization in Trouble.* NY: W.W. Norton & Co., Earth Policy Institute. Retrieved from http://www.earth-policy.org/books/pb2/pb2_table_of_contents.
Chapin et al. (2009). Ecosystem Stewardship: Sustainability Strategies for a Rapid Changing Planet. *Trends in Ecology and Evolution, 24*(4), 241–249. doi:http://dx.doi.org/10.1016/j.tree.2009.10.008

Crutzen, P. (2006). The Anthropocene. In Eckart Ehlers & Thomas Krafft (Eds.), *Earth System Science in the Anthropocene* (pp. 13–18). Berlin Heidelberg: Springer-Verlag.

Crutzen, P. J. (2002). Geology of Mankind: the Anthropocene. *Nature 415*, 23.

Demsetz, H. (1967). Toward a Theory of Property Rights. *The American Economic Review, 57(*2), 347–359. *Papers and Proceedings of the Seventy-ninth Annual Meeting of the American Economic Association.*

Dietz, T., Ostrom, E., & Stern, P. C. (2003). The Struggle to Govern the Commons. *Science 302*(5652), 1907–1912. *doi:*10.1126/science.1091015.

Fischer, A., Tobi, H., & Ronteltap, A. (2011). When Natural Met Social: A Review of Collaboration between the Natural and Social Sciences. *Interdisciplinary Science Reviews 36*(4), 341–58.

Folke, C. (2006). Resilience: The Emergence of a Perspective for Social-Ecological Systems Analyses. *Global Environmental* Change, 16, 253–267.

Folke, C., Hahn, T., Olsson, P., & Norberg, J. (2005). Adaptive Governance of Social-Ecological Systems. *Annu. Review Environ. Resources, 30*, 441–73.

Galli, A., Wiedmann, T., Ercin, E., Knoblauch, D., Ewing, B., & Giljum, S. (2012). Integrating Ecological, Carbon and Water Footprint into a "Footprint Family" of Indicators: Definition and Role in Tracking Human Pressure on the Planet. *Ecological Indicators 16*, 100–112.

Gibson, C., Ostrom, E., & Ahn, T. (2000). The Concept of Scale and the Human Dimensions of Global Change: A Survey. *Ecological Economics, 32*, 217–239.

Hackmann, H., & St. Clair, A.L. (2012). *Transformative Cornerstones of Social Science Research for Global Change.* Paris: International Social Science Council. Retrieved from http://www.worldsocialscience.org/documents/transformative-cornerstones.pdf

Hardin, G. (1968). The Tragedy of the Commons. *Science, 162*(3859), 1243–1248. *doi:*10.1126/science.162.3859.1243

Hardin, G. (1974). Lifeboat Ethics: the Case against Helping the Poor. *Psychology Today, September 1974.* Retrieved from http://www.garretthardinsociety.org/articles/art_lifeboat_ethics_case_against_helping_poor.html

Helbing, D. (2013). Globally Networked Risks and How to Respond. *Nature* 497. doi:10.1038/nature12047.

Hulme, M. (2010). Problems with Making and Governing Global Kinds of Knowledge. *Global Environmental Change 20*, 558–564.

Kelly Levin, K., Cashore, B., Bernstein, S., & Auld, G. (2012). Overcoming the Tragedy of Super Wicked Problems: Constraining our Future Selves to Ameliorate Global Climate Change. *Policy Science 45*, 123–152. doi:10.1007/s11077-012-9151-0.

Jackson, T. (2009). Prosperity without Growth? The Transition to a Sustainable Economy. Sustainable Development Commission. Retrieved from
http://www.sd-commission.org.uk/data/files/publications/prosperity_without_growth_report.pdf.

Krier, James E. (2009). Evolutionary Theory and the Origin of Property Rights. *Law & Economics Working Papers, Archive: 2003-2009*. Paper 98. Retrieved from
http://repository.law.umich.edu/law_econ_archive/art98.

Levin, S. (2010). Crossing Scales, Crossing Disciplines: Collective Motion and Collective Action in the Global Commons. *Phil Trans. R. Soc. B, 365*, 13–18. doi:10.1098/rstb.2009.0197.

Lloyds, W.F. (1833). *Two Lectures on the Checks to Population*. Book digitized by Google from the library of Oxford University and uploaded to the Internet Archive by user tpb. Retrieved from
https://archive.org/details/twolecturesonch00lloygoog

Marshal, G. (2008). Nesting, Subsidiarity, and Community-based Environmental Governance beyond the Local Level. *International Journal of the Commons, 2*, 75–97. Retrieved from
https://www.thecommonsjournal.org/index.php/ijc/article/viewFile/50/19.

Meadows, D. H., Meadows, D. L., Randers, J., & Behrens, W. W. (1972). *The Limits to Growth*. New York: Universe Books.

Meadows, D. H., Meadows, D. L., & Randers, J. (2004). *Limits to Growth: the 30-year Update*. Vermont: Chelsea Green.

Norton, B. (2005). *Sustainability: A Philosophy of Adaptive Ecosystem Management*. Chicago: The University of Chicago Press.

Ostrom, E. (1990). *Governing the Commons The Evolution of Institutions for Collective Action*. Political Economy of Institutions and Decisions. Cambridge: Cambridge University Press.

—. (1999). Coping With Tragedies of the Commons. *Annu. Review Political Science 2*, 493–535. doi: 10.1146/annurev.polisci.2.1.493

—. (2000). Collective Action and the Evolution of Social Norms. *Journal of Economic Perspectives, 14*(3), 137–158, Summer.

—. (2010a). Beyond Markets and States: Polycentric Governance of Complex Economic Systems. *American Economic Review 100*, 1–33.

—. (2010b). A Long Polycentric Journey. Workshop in Political Theory and Policy Analysis, Indiana University. *Annu. Rev. Polit. Sci., 13*, 1–23.

—. (2011). Background on the Institutional Analysis and Development Framework. *The Policy Studies Journal, 39*(1), 7–27.

Ostrom, E., Walker, J., & Gardner, R. (1992). Covenants With and Without a Sword: Self-Governance Is Possible. *The American Political Science Review, 86*(2), 404–417.

Ostrom, E. et al. (1999). Revisiting the Commons: Local Lessons, Global Challenges. *Science 284*(5412), 278–282. doi:10.1126/science.284.5412.278.

Pahl-Wostl, C., Giupponi, C., Richards, K., Binder, C., Sherbinin, A., Sprinz, D., Toonen, T., & van Bers, C. (2013). Transition towards a New Global Change Science: Requirements for Methodologies, Methods, Data and Knowledge. *Environmental Science & Policy, 28*, 36–47.

Rittel, H. W. J. & Webber. M. M. (1973). Dilemmas in a General Theory of Planning. *Policy Sciences* 4(2), 155–169. Amsterdam: Elsevier Scientific Publishing Company.

Rockström, J., et al. (2009). Planetary Boundaries: Exploring the Safe Operating Space for Humanity. *Ecology and Society 14*(2), 32. Retrieved from http://www.ecologyandsociety.org/vol14/iss2/art32/

Schlager W. et al. (1994). *Journal of Sedimentary Research, 64*, 270–281.

Steffen, W., Crutzen, P., & McNeill, J. (2007). The Anthropocene: Are Humans Now Overwhelming the Great Forces of Nature? *Ambio 36*(8), 614–621.

Stern, P., Young, O., Druckman, D. (Eds.) (1992). *Global Environmental Change: Understanding the Human Dimensions.* Washington, DC: The National Academies Press.

Vandenbroeck, P. (2012). *Working With Wicked Problems.* Brussels: King Baudouin Foundation.

York, R., Rosa, E., & Dietz, T. (2003). Footprints on the Earth: The Environmental Consequences of Modernity. *American Sociological Review 68*(2), 279–300.

Zalasiewicz, J., Williams, M., Steffen, W., & Crutzen, P. (2010). The New World of the Anthropocene. *Environ. Sci. Technol. 44*(7), 2228–2231. doi:10.1021/es903118j.

CHAPTER TWELVE

TRANSFORMING THE UNITED NATIONS TRUSTEESHIP COUNCIL FOR PROTECTION OF THE EARTH SYSTEM

KUL CHANDRA GAUTAM[1]

1. Introduction

Previous chapters of this book have shown how our understanding of the Earth System today is vastly ahead of our organizational capacity to properly manage it. We can see with our own eyes how climate change induced by global warming is causing natural disasters of unprecedented nature and scale. New diseases are emerging with the potential to cause massive pandemics. On the positive side, we have seen and can further imagine how our openness and willingness to manage the global and local commons in a more enlightened manner could bring about great long-term benefits for humanity, and for the Earth System on which we all depend.

Though still inadequate, our understanding of the Earth System, its planetary boundaries and how we as human beings can contribute to its better management have greatly improved, but the societal organizations that have evolved over the past millennia are still woefully inadequate to face the challenges and seize the opportunities that lie ahead.

Human institutions evolved from families of hunters and gatherers to communities of farmers and traders; from informal cooperatives to more formal local governments; from nation-states to regional block of nations, and to the United Nations.

This is a great advance for humanity. However, as previous chapters indicate, we have now reached the stage where we need to make a

---

[1] Former Assistant Secretary-General of the United Nations.

quantum jump to a whole new mode of managing our Earth System. Many new institutions and systems will need to be developed for this purpose.

Currently, the only existing institution with the most universal membership and legitimacy to help in such process is the United Nations. This chapter deals with how the legitimacy, capacity and potential of the UN might be harnessed to help bring about some modest incremental changes in our quest for a more enlightened management of the Earth System through a radically transformed Trusteeship Council of the UN, specifically designed for this purpose.

2. Evolution of the UN Trusteeship System

By way of background, when the UN was established in 1945, there were only 50 founding member states, compared to 193 members today. Most countries that were not members of the UN at that time were colonies of various imperial powers. The UN put in motion a process of decolonization and promoted the principle of self-determination that led to the eventual independence of many countries and their joining the UN as new members.

But there was also a group of about a dozen countries or territories that were not colonies as such, but were not independent states either. These "non-self-governing" territories were under the "trusteeship" or protectorate status of other states – such as Southwest Africa (Namibia) under South Africa; Somaliland under Italy; New Guinea under Australia; Nauru under New Zealand; Tangyanika and Zanzibar under Britain; New Caledonia under France; Micronesia and Palau under the USA, etc.

The UN set up a special Trusteeship Council to oversee the process of self-determination of these trust territories, most of which later became independent or joined some existing states. By the early 1990s, the UN Trusteeship Council became practically obsolete and unnecessary although it continues to exist on paper even today. It is now in need of a new mandate if it is not to be abolished altogether.

A proposal to convert this defunct Council into a UN Trusteeship of the Global Commons was first proposed in a 1994 report entitled "Our Global Neighbourhood" by the Commission on Global Governance. Co-chaired by former Swedish Prime Minister Ingvar Carlsson and former Secretary-General of the Commonwealth Sridath Ramphal of Guyana, the Commission comprised such leaders and luminaries as Ali Alatas of Indonesia, Oscar Arias Sanchez of Costa Rica, Jacques Delors of France, Enrique Iglesias of Uruguay, Wangari Mathai of Kenya, Sadako Ogata of

Japan, Maurice Strong of Canada, Yuli Vorontsov of Russia and many others.

Coming from such highly respected mainstream national and global leaders, the idea certainly deserves careful consideration. And if the idea was considered relevant two decades ago, it is even more so today as the negative as well as positive forces of globalisation have made it even more pertinent and urgent.

3. Trusteeship of the Global Commons

The Commission on Global Governance noted that by 1994, the Trusteeship Council, one of the UN's six principal organs, had already completed its major task of facilitating the post-war process of decolonization and had overseen the progress of the so-called "trust territories" to self-government or independence. Meanwhile, a new need had emerged, that of international trusteeship to be exercised over the global commons in the collective interest of humanity, including our future generations. The Commission, therefore, recommended that the UN take over this responsibility through a thoroughly redesigned Trusteeship of the Global Commons.

The global commons would include the atmosphere, outer space, the oceans beyond national jurisdiction, and the related environment and life-support systems that contribute to the support of human life. The new global trusteeship would also encompass the responsibilities that each generation must accept towards future generations.

As the Commission argued, these are all areas of vital interest to all nations. Prudent and equitable management of the global commons is crucial to the future well-being and progress, perhaps even the survival, of humanity.

The management of the commons, including the articulation of the rights and responsibilities of states and other entities for the development and use of their resources, should ideally be subject to trusteeship exercised by a body acting on behalf of all nations. The high-level and transnational nature of the responsibilities make it appropriate for this body to be a principal organ of the United Nations, like the Economic and Social Council, the Security Council and the General Assembly, hence the Commission's proposal that the Trusteeship Council, now free of its original responsibilities, be given the mandate of exercising trusteeship over the global commons, or what is referred to as the Earth System in this book.

Currently, the issue of the global commons is handled in a rather haphazard manner by several UN agencies and entities – including the General Assembly, ECOSOC, the Commission on Sustainable Development, the UN Environmental Programme (UNEP), UNCHS/Habitat, UNDP, etc. But the global commons is not on the prime agenda of any of these agencies and entities, and is always relegated to low priority.

Recognizing the great difficulty in amending the UN Charter to create a new principal organ of the UN or a brand new specialised UN agency dedicated exclusively to the cause of the global commons, there is much practical wisdom in giving a new mandate to the existing but moribund Trusteeship Council.

The new Trusteeship Council for the Global Commons would become the chief forum for dealing with global environmental issues and other transnational matters that transcend national jurisdiction and cannot be handled effectively through normal market mechanisms alone. Its functions would include administration of environmental treaties in such fields as climate change, biodiversity, outer space, and the Law of the Sea. It would refer, as appropriate, any economic or security issues arising from these matters to the UN's Economic and Social Council, the Security Council or the General Assembly.

The current UN Commission on Sustainable Development (CSD) would continue to report certain issues to ECOSOC, as at present, but it would refer matters related to the global commons or "problems without borders or passports" to the new Trusteeship Council.

The role proposed for the revamped Trusteeship Council would be in keeping with the important responsibilities originally assigned to it when it was established as a principal organ of the UN, with its own chamber at the UN in New York, but the changes in its mandate would require amendments to Chapters XII and XIII of the UN Charter.

The new Council could be composed, as the old one was, of representatives of a number of member states. The General Assembly of the UN, representing all member states, would determine the number and criteria for its membership and operational modalities.

The Commission on Global Governance in its wisdom acknowledged that the functions of the Trusteeship Council in this new role would be such that it would benefit enormously from the contributions of civil society organizations. It noted, for example, that as provided for in Article 86.2 of the UN Charter, each member of the new Trusteeship Council could designate one specially qualified person to represent it. A similar provision could leave it open to governments to nominate a public official or someone with the required qualifications from civil society.

Many administrative and substantive matters would need to be considered if this proposal were to be implemented but the most important step would be a conceptual breakthrough acknowledging that the security of our planet, and the shared responsibility for managing the global commons, requires the kind of solidarity that transcends the conventional nation-state and laissez-faire market mechanisms, and the empowerment of the UN system to take a leadership role in doing so.

Compared to the current situation, this is a bold proposal with exciting possibilities. However, it may not be ambitious or comprehensive enough to fully implement the ideas presented in various chapters of this book. Some of the authors of the present book would probably consider this proposal rather modest and minimalist. For example, it deals with some aspects of the global commons but not with the shared management of the *local commons,* about which many members of civic groups around the world feel quite passionate.

On the other hand, many governments at the UN considered even the modest initial proposal by the Commission on Global Governance as too radical. It is worth noting that despite the euphoria of the end of the Cold War and visions of openness to restructure the United Nations at the dawn of the new millennium, hardly any of the original major recommendations of the Commission on Global Governance, and several other creative proposals for the reform of the UN, were implemented.

However, we have now arrived at a juncture in human history where we have no choice but to begin to think beyond the paradigm of sovereign nation-states and conventional market mechanisms to broader planetary concerns, as issues of climate change, global warming, pandemic diseases, weapons of mass destruction and cyber security have brought home to all of us.

And beyond these phenomena, the positive possibilities brought about by the rapid pace of globalisation in every sphere of life and social intercourse also call for some out-of-the-box approaches to re-engineering global governance and global institutions like the United Nations.

4. Challenges of Reforming the UN

It should be noted that there is an inbuilt, deeply rooted conservatism in the UN system that makes it extremely difficult to bring about any radical reform that might undermine the powers of the most powerful founder-members of the UN, as well as those of small powers that jealously safeguard what they consider their sovereign rights.

Thus, we continue to have a very undemocratic and outdated composition of the Security Council – with a few countries wielding veto power – that reflects the world of 1945 rather than the current realities of the 21st century. A similar situation prevails regarding the appointment of the senior-most officials of the UN Secretariat and heads of the Bretton Woods institutions, where some archaic un-written "gentlemen's agreements" prevail over the more transparent and merit-based recruitment system.

That is why most comprehensive UN reform proposals either drag on endlessly – such as in the case of the reform of the Security Council – or are implemented in a very sporadic manner – such as the merit-based and competitive selection of UN's top officials. And some really creative proposals are adopted in a half-hearted and watered-down manner, such as the "responsibility to protect".

Sometimes, when the really significant reform proposals get nowhere, diplomats at the UN tinker with endless procedural reforms of the executive boards and other governance structures of UN funds and programmes, and inter-agency coordination at headquarters and the field-level, which do not affect the power and perks of the most powerful nations. Sometimes, to accommodate the interests of the newly emerging powers – without compromising those of the old world powers – new institutions and mechanisms are created, such as the G-7 and the G-20.

Now, while radical reforms of existing international organizations may be difficult, we must not underestimate the possibilities of incremental reforms and the many good things that can be accomplished through such reforms. Let us remember the old saying that perfection can be the enemy of the good. Over time, incremental reforms can also add up to significant change. In that spirit, today may be the opportune time to push for the transformation of the UN's currently defunct Trusteeship Council into a new and vibrant Trusteeship for the Earth System or the global commons.

While many of us would want this revamped Trusteeship Council to be as powerful as we can make it, and empower the one truly global organization we have – the United Nations – it is perhaps wise not to put all our eggs in that single basket. Accordingly, we should also develop other viable alternative or complementary mechanisms for the management of the Earth System.

The original proposal for the UN Trusteeship of the Global Commons dealt only with the management of the physical environment – the oceans beyond national jurisdiction, outer space, and the related environment and life-support systems. But today, many advocates of the commons approach would also want it to include two other important issues:

1) management of intellectual property, such as the discovery of life-saving and life-enhancing agricultural, industrial and medical inventions, and information and communication technology, including the Internet, and
2) management of the "*local* commons".

David Bollier, a prolific American writer, activist and policy strategist on the global and local commons, offers many innovative suggestions and insights on these issues in his very touching essay "The Healing Logic of the Commons".

5. Intellectual Property and Cultural Heritage

Bollier and many others make the case that the governance of the global commons, whether through the UN or other mechanisms, should include the management of some aspects of intellectual property that can be used to either vastly empower and liberate people or dominate and oppress them.

There are many proposals for the management of the commons at the global level, including charging very modest rental or transaction fees that could mobilize huge sums of money to finance multilateral development programmes and institutions. These could include carbon emissions, military spending and arms exports, foreign exchange transactions, international trade, airline tickets, maritime freight, ocean fishing, seabed mining, satellite parking spaces, use of the electromagnetic spectrum, and the Internet.

The income generated from the fees for the use of these global commons could be used to protect our planet from global warming, restore any damage to the global commons, reimburse those negatively affected by the use of these resources, provide public goods, combat poverty, and invest in transitioning to a sustainable future for all.

There is a certain urgency to do this as there is now a dangerous large-scale market-driven campaign of privatization of the global as well as local commons. The corporate sector is now furiously encroaching on and enclosing the commons space. It is not only land and oceans that are being enclosed – mathematical algorithms can also now be privately owned if they are embedded in patented software, and genetic codes of food grains can be patented for the benefit of new entrepreneurs, potentially depriving farmers who cultivated such grains for centuries, even millennia.

We hear about the great battles and multi-billion-dollar lawsuits for trademarks and copyrights among the world's corporate giants, such as

Apple versus Samsung, Coke versus Pepsi, McDonald's versus Burger King, Microsoft versus the European Union. Some of these encroach on what should really be in the public domain.

For example, the Internet and related technologies should now be subject to some rules of global governance as public goods or global commons. But they are now vulnerable to gross abuse not only by authoritarian governments like those of North Korea or Zimbabwe but, as we have seen recently in the WikiLeaks affair, even democratic countries like USA abuse them to spy against their allies and restrict their own citizens' right to information.

On the positive side, we are witnessing today a spontaneous and powerful global movement called "commons-based peer production". Wikipedia, with millions of entries in over 160 languages, is a prime example of it, as are the open-access academic journals bypassing expensive commercial journal publishers, and thousands of other nonproprietary "open source" software produced collaboratively.

How we manage these global commons can either greatly benefit or harm the whole of humanity. It is our duty to ensure enlightened stewardship of these commons we inherit or create together, such as the gifts of nature, intellectual property and our cultural heritage, and pass them on, undiminished or enhanced, to future generations.

6. Management of the Local Commons

Another important dimension of the management of the commons that deserves greater attention and action is the governance of the local commons, and how we can empower local communities to manage their own resources with minimal reliance on the market or the state.

Professor Elinor Ostrom of Indiana University, USA, won the Nobel Prize in Economics in 2009 for her pioneering work on the management of local commons such as community forests and water resources around the world, and how they support environmental sustainability and social justice. A big part of Ostrom's field research was conducted in the villages of my home country of Nepal. Her work in Nepal as well as in Africa and elsewhere showed how societies have developed diverse institutional arrangements to manage natural resources and avoid ecosystem collapse in many cases.

After many years of painstaking field research and innovative theorizing, Ostrom identified some basic design principles of successful commons management in her path-breaking 1990 book, *Governing the Commons*. Hundreds of studies by Ostrom and other scholars over the past several decades have shown that people can and do successfully manage their land and water, forests and fisheries as shared commons. Ostrom's great achievement was to debunk the established wisdom of mainstream economics that glorifies unfettered market-mechanism and private property rights.

Most economists tend to subscribe to the view popularized by biologist Garrett Hardin, who wrote a famous essay in 1968 entitled "The Tragedy of the Commons." The classic example of this "tragedy" is this – if you have a shared pasture upon which many herders can graze their cattle, no single herder will have a rational incentive to hold back and so he will put as many cattle on the commons as possible, taking as much as he can for himself. The pasture will inevitably be overexploited and ruined, thus causing a "tragedy."

This line of reasoning implied that only a regime of private property rights and markets could solve the tragedy of the commons as only people with private ownership would be motivated to protect their grazing lands. But Hardin and others misrepresent the concept of the commons as an open-access regime, operating in a free-for-all scenario where there are no boundaries to the grazing land, no rules for managing it and no community of users. However, a properly managed commons has boundaries, rules, monitoring of usage, punishments for free riders, and social norms. A commons requires that there be a community willing to act as a steward of a resource.

Elinor Ostrom's work helped dispel the portrayal of the commons as a "tragedy" and established it as a positive communal resource that can be harnessed for the public good. But the management of the local commons requires a different approach to that of the global one.

While the UN can set some normative guidelines, we should be mindful that no single government or intergovernmental mechanism at the global level can effectively tackle the complex and diverse challenges of managing the local commons. Hence careful consideration should be given to Ostrom's suggestion for a polycentric approach, where key management decisions are made as close to the scene of events and the actors involved as possible.

7. Beyond Markets and GNP

Many advocates of the commons approach strongly criticize market-centric neoliberal economics and the state-dominated international order. But to be fair, we must acknowledge that neoliberal economic policies have revved up the engines of economic growth, the Industrial Revolution, and great technological innovations that have improved living standards and lifted billions of people out of poverty.

Where these policies have failed is in giving adequate attention to issues of equity, inclusion, social justice, the neglect of the degradation of our natural environment, and non-recognition or poor management of the global and local commons. These issues are of vital concern for all of us who care deeply about leaving behind a pristine planet Earth in which our children and future generations can grow to their full human potential. As a former UNICEF official, I recall how much of the focus of our policy and programme work was inspired by advocacy of the credo – we must protect the environment for our children, and we must protect our children so they can safeguard the environment.

The single-minded pursuit of the Gross National Product, or GNP, as the principal measure of a country's prosperity and people's well-being has long been recognized as deeply flawed. Those of us who believe in and advocate for the commons approach are deeply sceptical about the trickle-down approach of economic growth and glorification of GNP.

While private income and collective GNP are, of course, important, we must not forget their limitations. American leader Robert F. Kennedy captured these limitations beautifully when he said way back in 1968 that:

> The Gross National Product does not allow for the health of our children, the quality of their education, or the joy of their play. It does not include the beauty of our poetry or the strength of our marriages; the intelligence of our public debate or the integrity of our public officials. It measures neither our wit nor our courage; neither our wisdom nor our learning; neither our compassion nor our devotion to our country; it measures everything, in short, except that which makes life worthwhile.

The commons approach too is, of course, not a magic bullet or a panacea that is somehow exempt from the frailties of human follies. Indeed, the "commoners" are often viewed by mainstream economists and politicians as naïve, idealistic fringe activists. But I believe that we are on the right side of history as some of our ideas and ideals that were once seen as naïve and unrealistic are now increasingly becoming recognized as practical and even essential.

Let us remember that a revolutionary idea of one century or a generation becomes the common sense of the next one. Three centuries ago when feudalism was the global norm, it would have been difficult to imagine that one day the world would embrace the concept of human rights – of liberty, equality and fraternity among human beings.

Two centuries ago, it would have been difficult to imagine that the very common practice of slavery would be seen as inhuman and would be abolished. Even a century ago, it would have been hard to imagine that women should and would have equal rights with men. And who would have imagined a century ago that one day great colonial empires, where the sun never set, would be dissolved and a United Nations organization created?

Let us not despair when our advocacy for a non-market-exclusive and non-sovereignty-restrained global governance of the common heritage of humanity is laughed at as impractical and idealistic by the rulers of our world today. Let us persevere for our long-term goal of a world without national borders, national armies and national sovereignty, and for humane global and local governance to promote the best interests of humanity, including our future generations.

8. Setting Up Trusteeship for the Earth System

In pursuing the proposal for setting up a UN trusteeship of the Earth System, and the broad governance agenda for the global commons, we need to capitalize on the work of the Commons Cluster of the ECOSOC-accredited NGOs at the United Nations. It has been advocating for the UN and other international organizations to adopt a long-term development strategy that recognizes and cherishes the global commons as the common heritage of humanity.

Indeed, a network of civil society organizations, including the Commons Cluster, the Institute of Planetary Synthesis, the Association of World Citizens, etc., offered a number of interesting and creative suggestions in the lead up to the 2012 Rio+20 Conference to help restore, protect and replenish natural resources, and fund the shift to a commons-based global economy. Some of these ideas are reflected in the post-2015 global development agenda that the UN is now formulating. But much more needs to be done.

As we approach the 70th anniversary of the founding of the UN, and the beginning of a new post-2015 global agenda for sustainable development, the time has come for the international community to consider setting up a new high-level international commission, similar to those that helped establish the Bretton Woods institutions and the United Nations. Such a commission could be tasked with developing a bold new vision and plan for the protection of our fragile Earth System through the creation of a worldwide commons-based economy and its global and local governance.

This task will not be easy, and some of us may not see it accomplished. But as the old Chinese saying goes, the journey of a thousand miles begins with a single step. Let us be prepared now to take those baby steps and judiciously accept incremental changes, even as we continue to push the envelope and strive for more radical but enlightened reforms of global governance, with the United Nations at its heart.

Conclusion

The current system of nation-state-based governance is inadequate to tackle such issues as climate-change-induced global warming, pandemic diseases and other threats to human security and prosperity; nor can it reap the full benefit of globalisation in an increasingly borderless world. A United Nations trusteeship system should be developed for the management of the whole Earth System and, within it, the global and local commons.

This new global trusteeship would enable people and nations to collectively govern the global commons better, including the atmosphere, outer space, the oceans beyond national jurisdiction, and the related environment and life-support systems. It would encompass the responsibilities that each generation must accept towards future generations.

CHAPTER THIRTEEN

FROM MUTUAL ASSURED DESTRUCTION
TO COMPULSORY COOPERATION

VIRIATO SOROMENHO-MARQUES[1]

1. Introduction

In 2009, not long before the dramatically announced and long-awaited
COP15 was held in Copenhagen, a fiction novel was published. The title
was *Ultimatum*; the author hidden behind the pseudonym of Matthew
Glass. The plot of what we may call an eco-thriller takes place in the years
2032 and 2033. In a dark and very realistic depiction of international
affairs, Glass offers the reader the tragedy of a nuclear war engulfing the
USA and China, with its roots precisely in the need to sign a binding
agreement able to meet the challenge of a ravaging climate change
process, which is the cause of the presence of millions of victims and
refugees in some coastal areas of the United States (Glass 2009).

My essay attempts to unfold some of the ideas and problems roughly
entangled in the fantasy Glass draws. Indeed what we need to think about
is the solution to the following riddle: will we be able, as members of the
global community, to stay at the level of the huge challenges posed by the
growing environment crisis process? Will the international system of
nations and states be in a condition to tackle the Hobbesian nightmare of
scarcity, turmoil and conflict that could trigger an endless race to the
bottom, a formidable and bloody "war of all against all" on a global scale?

---

[1] Viriato Soromenho-Marques - University of Lisbon.

2. This Time is Different: The Ontological Crisis

We are fully aware that humans have always faced environmental problems along their history. But this time the nature of the challenge, both in quantity and quality, is rather different.[2]

The first approach to the uniqueness of the current situation could be based on sheer quantitative data. The acceleration trends of the combined human impact on Earth, from demography to global GDP, not forgetting our ecological footprint, are simply breathtaking if we just consider the last 50 years. But we need to go beyond scale and volume features and focus our attention on qualitative indicators as well. In that sense, the "Anthropocene Era" proposal invites us to consider human action on Earth under a new and bold perspective (Arendt 1993; Crutzen & Stoermer 2000).[3] Since the start of the Industrial Revolution, humankind is the strongest driving force modelling the face of our planet, encompassing all the angles of the Earth, from water to land, from ice to air, including the web of life.

Long before Crutzen, some brilliant minds, like the one of Bertrand Russell, were able to see the cloudy future ahead of humankind. He wrote: "Both industry and agriculture to a continually increasing degree are carried on in ways that waste the world's capital of natural resources" (1949). Russell understood with accuracy the global nature of the environmental problem and, consequently, the need of a response at the same global level. However, almost 70 years after the great British philosopher published his thoughts, we are still far from a strong

---

[2] See Chapter 2 of this book, written by Will Steffen.

[3] "To assign a more specific date to the onset of the 'Anthropocene' seems somewhat arbitrary, but we propose the latter part of the 18th century, although we are aware that alternative proposals can be made (some may even want to include the entire Holocene). However, we choose this date because, during the past two centuries, the global effects of human activities have become clearly noticeable" (Crutzen & Stoermer 2000). A philosophical anticipation of the Anthropocene can be seen in the way Hannah Arendt identified a dangerous qualitative shift in the essence of technology/science with the irruption of Faustian technologies like those connected to the atomic military and energy complex: "The moment we started natural processes of our own – and splitting the atom is precisely such a man-made natural process – we not only increased our power over nature (…) but for the first time have taken nature into the human world as such and obliterated the defensive boundaries between natural elements and the human artifice by which all previous civilizations were hedged in" (Arendt 1993).

consensus on the diagnosis, and even more distant from the adequate
dimension and scale needed to produce an effective therapeutic answer.

It would be too simplistic and naïve to blame only the flaws of our
political systems, which are very much inclined to the influence of
powerful economic factions. We need to acknowledge that some of the
main difficulties come from the inner heart of scientific activity itself,
understood in its real essence as a complex societal process. Science is in
general a difficult activity. It demands long academic preparation and
uninterrupted training throughout one's life. Taking into account the
personal sacrifices and the degree of dedication and discipline this job
demands, it is no accident that science is said to be not just a profession
but also a call, rooted in a vocation (the German game of words between
Beruf and *Berufung* helps to visualize the semantic paradox of vicinity and
distance). The Anthropocene, as a synonym for the environmental crisis, is
overwhelmed by cross-cutting environmental challenges. Most of the
major environmental issues are by nature interdisciplinary; they demand a
combined effort from different areas of knowledge. The construction of
heuristic approaches to establishing the collection of environmental data,
as well as its analysis and interpretation, constitutes a huge
epistemological challenge, especially if we consider the vertical structure
of the different areas and the actual orientation of universities towards
specialisation, at least at a graduate level and for those immediately above.
Project leaders faced with the difficulties raised by the epistemological
complexity of environmental issues will hesitate between going ahead and
carrying out a more comfortable project within their own narrower
speciality (Soromenho-Marques 2014).

The epistemic division of scientific teaching and research contributed
to a large degree to the epistemic late arrival of the true and complex
nature of the environmental crisis. Specialisation of scientific work and
research is driven basically by pragmatic and technical goals, which are
immediately rewarded in the fiscal language of the marketplace. On the
contrary, to study long-term environmental impacts on ecosystems and
human health is far from being the best choice if you want a prominent
academic career. Many of the environmental problems have a cross-
cutting nature, implying strenuous interdisciplinary strategies very hard to
assemble and manage, and even harder to finance properly (Hansen &
Tickner 2013).[4]

---

[4] The interdisciplinary complex nature of environmental research is particularly
visible within the realm of the precautionary principle (S. F. Hansen and J. A.
Tickner 2013, 17–44).

Besides political resistance, vested economic interests and strong and sometimes savage opposition, the main obstacle to the true understanding of the core characteristics of environmental global crisis originated in the old habit of confining research to the safe areas of individual or team expertise, while the striking evidences of a growing global crisis, from the biosphere to climate, were best seen from a transboundary epistemic angle, very hard to find and above all to maintain in a sustainable manner.

Therefore I maintain two main hermeneutic proposals about the environmental crisis. The first one (see Table 1) suggests that the environmental crisis contains a series of five main predicates that combine the complex and dangerous uniqueness of its critical dimension.

➤ Planetary dimension (e.g., climate change).
➤ Irreversibility and entropy (e.g., massive biodiversity extinction).
➤ Cumulative acceleration (oceans' decline).
➤ Growing political and social unrest (decline of classical state power; risk of international conflict).
➤ Ontological debt (war between generations?).

Table 1. The uniqueness of the global environment crisis
Source: Soromenho-Marques 1994, pp.143–146

My second hermeneutic proposal (see Table 2), also very much developed by other authors in this book under different perspectives, maintains that the driving forces of the environment crisis are not solid and identifiable objects, which we may remit to geographical spaces, but basically complex and dynamic processes. So, we are not speaking about natural resources but about natural sources; not natural services already available but about productive natural cycles, located in between areas, in a kind of no-man's land both for scientific disciplines and regarding the horizon of clear and definite political borders. Therefore, we are not dealing with concrete and strictly quantifiable entities; we are speaking about the "global commons" (such as the atmosphere, the oceans, the carbon cycle among many others) view as meta-values, as the condition *sine qua non* for the good functioning of the fabric of life as a planetary whole.

➢ **Meta-values**: they are the ontological condition of "useful" things in the realm of benefit-cost analysis.
➢ They are "autonomous **and independent**", before and beyond the economic theory of value (from Locke to Marx): "Sources" are before "(Re) sources" (see Holmes Rolston III).[5]
➢ They have **creative functional powers**, contrary to the entropy prevailing in human technology (according to Spinoza's distinction between *natura naturans* and *natura naturata*) (Spinoza 1996).

Table 2. Understanding the three core meta-values of environmental global commons

3. Climax and Decay of the Strategic Rationality

A nuclear war between major powers, such as the one anticipated in Glass's novel mentioned above, on account of the disarray in a set of global commons and entangled in the dangerous climate change challenge would be a complete failure of the endeavour pursued by the authors in this book. Instead of an Earth Condominium, we would end up in a cataclysm of fire and destruction, probably sentencing human history to a long-lasting doom.[6]

However, environmental disputes have been, almost as a general rule, historically submitted to the logic of competition and conquest, the source of many conflicts and wars. If we want to help shape new models of negotiation among states, against the old habits of empire and warfare, we not only need to suggest new legal patterns but also understand deeply how war rationality works, and try to discern any intrinsic contradictions that could provide us with a glimpse of a hope of a possible peaceful outcome instead of the fatalistic acceptance of the inevitability of a global Armageddon.

Modern war coincides with the modern international system erected with the peace of Westphalia (1648), which brought an end to more than a

---

[5] "Forests and soil, sunshine and rain, rivers and sky, the cycling seasons – these are *resources*, but they are also *sources*, the perennial natural givens, that support everything else" (Rolston III, H. 1994,134).

[6] Climate change as a trigger of conflict is not just a matter of literary fiction. A solid corpus of environmental security research is already showing how and where those conflicts may occur: "If climate protection policy fails and the 2°C guard rail is not adhered to, the international community must prepare itself to deal with climate-induced conflicts" (WBGU 2008, 13; see also Rüttinger et al. 2015).

century of bloody religious wars in Europe. The main operating concept, valid for both peaceful and bellicose international relations thereafter, is the absolute centrality of state sovereignty. This was first a matter of decision for kings and respective councils, but later, with the expansion of republican and democratic ideals and institutions, that same centrality was transferred to the nation and gaining the status of "national interest". Nevertheless, the most acute conscience of the new paradigm of international relations in the sphere of military and political interconnection within the realm of warfare was reached in the master-work of a Prussian officer, Carl von Clausewitz, *Vom Kriege (On War)* in 1832. A posthumous book organized by the author's wise wife Marie von Clausewitz, it contains the essential rules that define what we may designate as "strategic rationality". In my reading, there are three basic rules, and they may be described as follows:

> 1. Only the organized violence among states can be considered as War. State is understood as an organic actor, or a living community looking for a shared destiny while united with a Nation (Clausewitz 1980, 648).

> 2. The essence of war belongs to Politics: "War has its own grammar but not its own Logic [which belongs only to the realm of Politics] (*Er hat freilich seine eigene Grammatik, aber nicht seine eigene Logik*)" (ibid, 675).

> 3. War implies a kind of vibrant "dialogue" in time and space; a skilled management of limited organized violence oriented by the final goal of a "decision by weapons" *(Waffenentscheidung)* (ibid, 48).

In the military literature, there is a large and sometimes confused dispute about Clausewitz's legacy but what is undeniable is his key contribution to a pattern of rational behaviour in warfare (according to the three rules proposed in my reading above). Although accused many times of advocating extreme violence, the truth is that Clausewitz always considered the goals of war to be entirely of a political nature and to be decided by the political authorities of a country and not by the general staff.

If the two world wars of the 20th century were predominantly waged under the influence of the Clausewitz methodology, we also saw a profound shift in the nature of warfare. New technologies and weapons increased the speed of movement of the military forces and the intensity of firepower, and, above all, increased almost to the infinite degree the capacity for construction by countries equipped with nuclear weapons after the Hiroshima and Nagasaki bombings in 1945.

Indeed, the crucial factor that transformed the strategic view of warfare directly inspired by Clausewitz was the fact that the new weapons of massive destruction (nuclear, but also biological and chemical – NBC) introduced a *hubris* dimension, an overwhelming killing capacity, that was completely absent in the Napoleonic battlefields where Clausewitz was several times personally engaged. Even before the nuclear bombs and missiles, the strategic air bomber raids launched by the allies against Germany in the Second World War destroyed the Clausewitz notion of the "front" as a specific space where enemy armies collide.

We may, therefore, speak of a progressive destruction of the hardware conditions of warfare, which eroded some of the main methodological concepts developed by Clausewitz. In very brief terms, we may identify the following sharp differences in the bloody experience of war introduced, specifically by new technological skills and tools, in the period stretching from the latter part of the 18th century to the mid-20th century, and thereafter:

1. The erosion of the concept of "front", brought into the phenomenology of war by the capacity of deploying painful destruction far away from the spot where land armies were clashing. Erosion of the concept started first with the strategic bombing in WW II and continued, after the nuclear attacks against Japan in 1945, to the current capacity of sending nuclear ballistic missiles from land silos (ICBM), aircrafts (ALBM) and submarines (SLBM).
2. The "relativity" in strategic time-space management. Before nuclear weapons, the deployment of armed forces, basically the sole providers of firepower against the enemy, was a long and strenuous process. It implied the recruitment, training and deployment of hundreds of thousands of men against enemy targets. Today, a single nuclear warhead contains more potential destruction than all the combined firepower used in WW II (around 3 megatons). Today, an all-out nuclear conflict, with the "instant mobilization" of ballistic missiles, could erase entire continents, killing billions of people in less than 35 minutes…
3. The eclipse of the "victory" concept by the shadows of "mutual assured destruction" (MAD). The relative "parity" reached in the nuclear arsenals of the USA and the USSR in the 1960s brought with it a deep commotion in the core mantra of strategic rationality.

If a war was able to bring absolute destruction to every belligerent nation involved, the solid rock upon which the institution of war's rationality was grounded – the possibility of obtaining a victory by the "decision of weapons" – was dramatically abolished. It became a contradiction in terms.

Atomic weapons introduced into warfare what we may call the "overkill paradox". War was forbidden not because of the insufficient firepower to launch it but, on the contrary, because the intensive and extensive destruction capacities amassed by rival states were so immensely huge and disproportionate that they could trigger a cataclysm of violence beyond imagination and purpose. The excess of firepower, the *hubris*, accumulated in novel weapons stripped from the heart of war its most profound rational meaning: the possibility of gaining a victory. In a MAD world, the understanding of war as "the continuation of politics through other means" (a famous motto from Clausewitz) became not only meaningless but deeply absurd.

For the first time in recorded human history, a central collision of major world powers ended without a major and definite all-out conflict. At the end of the day, Clausewitz had the final word. If war was just the grammar and politics the larger logic, the decision of abolishing a war that could bring total collapse and destruction was, indeed, a wise political decision. On the margin of the abyss, sound logic prevailed over a bellicose grammar on the verge of madness.

4. Is There an Environmental Equivalent to MAD?

As we have seen, the reasons why there was no global warfare in the mid-1980s lie more in epistemic and political considerations than in the blunt simplistic arithmetic calculation of weaponry and overall power capacity in the two opposite fields. Both the United States and the Soviet Union leadership were able to fully understand the extreme danger of trying to find a "suitable" battlefield in which even nuclear weapons of smaller sizes and superior accuracy could be released. The "Euro-missile crisis" of the 1979–1985 period was precisely the dramatic process where a consensus was about the reality of the MAD outcome in case a global central war between the two superpowers was actually fought. During those intense years, the Western and Soviet schools of thought that envisioned the possibility of victory in a nuclear war were politically, and I dare say also morally, defeated by those who anticipated not only the phenomenon of mega-death but the complete destruction of human civilization and its environmental framework (Soromenho-Marques 1985).[7]

It was not easy to overcome Clausewitz's strategic world view in international relations regarding the feasibility of warfare and its core concepts around the idea of a "decision by weapons" depicted above. A war that resulted only in a general and bloody defeat, a war without victory or victor, a war with severe and deep pain but no rewards went directly against the rationality of strategic thought based on the modern concept of national interest and state sovereignty.

In 1985, instead of nuclear warfare in Europe, we saw the arrival to power in the Soviet Union of Mr Gorbachev. The failure of the frantic attempt to reform the Soviet model of government, through *perestroika* and *glasnost*, was a cheap price to pay compared to the infinite burden resulting from the unlimited use of NBC weapons in a global conflict. For the first time in world history, a major opposition between two mighty major alliances, provided with rather different *Weltanschauungen*, ended in a political process of reform and multilateral dialogue. Atomic Armageddon was avoided for epistemological and moral reasons. A war would have been the suicidal and pointless collapse of human endeavour on Earth.

When we turn our eyes to the growing environmental crisis, from the depletion of biological diversity to climate change, what do we really see? Unfortunately, it seems to me that we are still far from adapting a similar understanding of the wisdom contained in the MAD doctrine of nuclear deterrence to environmental diplomacy and environmental international relations. The dominant pattern is still "business as usual". Countries tend to compete in a race to the bottom regarding the access and use of valuable natural resources and non-renewable energy sources. Although a great deal of lip-service has already been offered in the diplomatic arena, the truth is that concern about sustainable use, production and consumption of resources, as well as effective apprehension about the mitigation or avoidance of negative environmental impacts, are still second priorities.

However, if we want to avoid the risk of collapse contained in the overwhelming process known as the "great acceleration" of the last 65 years or so, we need to learn fast and act accordingly. The world is shifting faster than our capacity to cope with every feature of global change (Steffen, et al. 2004). Probably the most striking example of the rapid path

---

[7] By the close of the Cold War, I wrote and published a book about the danger of limited nuclear war confined to European soil: *Europa* (Soromenho-Marques 1985).

global transformation is taking may be seen in the field of climate change. Not only is the level of greenhouse gases (GHG) concentration climbing to new heights but there is also a noticeable drift from traditional major economies to emergent ones as the new dominant global emitters. In a few years, China became the major source of CO_2, surpassing the combination of US and EU emissions and going beyond the level of EU per capita emissions.

Country or Region	% of global total
China	29 (7.2 t *per capita*)
USA	15
EU	10 (6.8t *per capita*)
India	7.1
Russian Federation	5.3
Japan	3.7
Germany	2.2
Republic of Korea	1.8
Iran	1.8
Saudi Arabia	1.5

Table 3. Top CO_2 emitters in 2013
Source: Global Carbon Project

Therefore, in order to avoid a clash between nations and state alliances on the ground of disputes about scarce strategic resources or on account of unfair distributional impacts caused by the ill- management of global commons, as is the case of the atmosphere and the oceans, we need to deploy a new code of diplomatic behaviour between international actors. If we follow the analogy of nuclear MAD, we will need to go down two tracks simultaneously. The first is expanding into the general public the constant new information regarding the worrying environmental state of the planet. Access to the relevant environmental and climate indicators by the broader public needs to become an intrinsic part of general education and an issue to be discussed in the public sphere in every corner of the planet. The second track deals with the urgent task of developing a common set of values to guide diplomats and political decision-makers in the process of shaping a new international order so they are able to replace *zero-sum* games of competition without boundaries with win-win games of responsible cooperation, including the particular interest of a nation or a private entity within the realm of an international order abiding by strong rules enforced by the strength of a common deliberation.

| The principle of common but differentiated responsibilities |
| The principle of physical constraint and time scarcity |
| The principle of justice between generations |
| The principle of compulsory cooperation towards sustainability |

Table 4. Four principles to avoid MAECC (Mutual Assured Environmental and Climate Collapse)

An environmental proxy of the nuclear MAD would integrate four main principles (Table 4), which I'll describe as follows:

The principle of common but differentiated responsibilities. This principle, although not universally applauded and already enshrined in the legal wording of some international regimes, particularly in the field of climate change, still faces strong opposition in key countries like the US. The American Congress was always against the Kyoto Protocol, basically because the Washington legislators refused to accept what they considered a positive discrimination status given to countries like China and India. If we consider fairness as a sound metric, however, this principle stands on solid ground. Countries that historically first took advantage from global commons had to acknowledge that there isn't a fair relationship with newcomers (typically the North–South divide). European countries, like Britain, the pioneer of the Industrial Revolution after 1750, and the United States started the driving mechanism of climate change – the chemic shifting of our atmosphere by transferring gigantic quantities of carbon from soil to air – well before major or minor developing countries. China, if we need a critical example, started its economic transformation basically in the last quarter of the 20th century while developed countries performed their modernization over the last two and a half centuries. This principle is not solely a matter of the North–South divide; it is of universal reach as we may see in the burden-sharing negotiations among the European Union countries. Indeed, the EU more than attained its GHG reduction targets within the Kyoto, respecting, however, the inner differences among their member states. European latecomers to the industrial age, with its massive use of fossil fuels, like Portugal, were allowed to increase the overall emission of CO_2 equivalent during the 1990–2012 time frame while the EU as a whole was drastically cutting back its combined emissions.

The principle of physical constraint and time scarcity. This is the first of the three other principles that need to be integrated in the table of a new global environmental diplomacy. This principle gives visibility to the ecological limits of the Earth System. We live on a planet that has functional boundaries. Humankind works within a finite "ecological space". The absolute rule in diplomatic negotiations is not given by diplomats or heads of state but by the uncompromising evidence that the Earth System works according to natural laws we may know but cannot persuade or "buy" to act according to our wishes and desires. Therefore, we need to design our institutional arrangements and our funding mechanisms taking into consideration the "despotic character" of factual truth in the realm of nature (Arendt 1993).

The principle of justice between generations. This is a rather classical concept, developed in the last decade of the 18th century by different thinkers and men of action like Thomas Jefferson, James Madison, Edmund Burke, and Immanuel Kant (Soromenho-Marques 2010). The most extensive pioneering contribution on this topic was given to us in the correspondence between Jefferson (while US Ambassador to France) and Madison. For the future third president of the US, no generation was entitled to endanger the freedom of the coming generations. He was thinking essentially of two major obstacles to the freedom of the future inhabitants and citizens of the Earth: a) constitutional gridlock; and b) the burden of public debt. For those two evils he suggested the correct medicine: a) periodic and mandatory constitutional revisions; and b) fiscal prudence and discipline, avoiding the externalisation of the debt burden from the living to the still unborn. We may depart from Jefferson's keen remarks and expand his wisdom to environmental diplomacy. Isn't the essence of the global environmental crisis really a matter of injustice between generations? Isn't climate change truly a new type of global public debt? I mean an *ontological debt*, without haircut or restructuring alleviation devices. Climate change is indeed a debt that must be paid back until the last cent, not by those who made it but by coming generations...

The principle of compulsory cooperation towards sustainability. My fourth principle is also a synthesis of all four I am proposing in a combined and interactive manner, as a kind of new *Organon* for environmental diplomacy, as a bridge for the building of a new and long-lasting international system. This principle enhances the analogy with the nuclear MAD since each major country has the power either to undermine – if no harsh and effective GHG emission mitigation measures are taken – or to protect the atmosphere as a global commons, therefore we need to shift the focus from competition ("race to the bottom") to a global strategy of TRUST (*Towards Rapid and Responsible Universal Sustainability Transition*). This principle is critical to tackling the challenges of the environmental crisis and, urgently, climate change, also at the institutional level. As happened with nuclear weapons at the closing stage of the Cold

War, when a common understanding about the irrationality of waging a war with no victor prevailed over strategic and military habits with at least four millennia of undisputed dominance, we need today a new culture for diplomacy among nations in a world ravaged by environmental crises and climate change. Only with a strong consensus on the need for compulsory cooperation can we unfold common semantics, new accurate monitoring mechanisms and binding reduction goals or aims for both developed and developing countries in every area of our fragile environment, with an especial urgency for our endangered climate system.

Setting minimal common standards regarding other key areas: adaptation, technology, financing, marketplace mechanisms...
Creating "spill over" dynamics through large regional "functional" communities with developed and developing countries, adding shared convergence sustainability targets to previous binding ones.
Making room for multi-layer and multi-actor climate partnerships (universities, industry sectors, cities...) and increasing efficacy in GHG reduction.

Table 5. Basic requirements of the TRUST evolutionary process in the field of climate change

5. Concluding Remarks

In many ways, contemporary politics has become an exercise of escape. Instead of a candid insight into the trends and challenges that are shaping the future, political discourse, supported in many cases by strong private vested interests, refuses to go beyond a narrow time frame, depriving the search for the global common good of a truly strategic roadmap.

The two basic messages of this chapter, completely harmonised with the wisdom and knowledge mirrored in the pages of all the other chapters of this book, could be summarized as follows:

- The global *necessitas* of environmental crisis and climate change *should be* today the core issue concentrating the attention and creative capacities of public policies in every nation of the world.
- In a world that's dangerously close to the brink of ecological collapse, the international system is no longer a place for *zero-sum* games. We need a goal-oriented compact approach, guided by the

mobilizing concept of an Earth Condominium, if we want to survive as a civilized species on this wonderful and unique planet.

On the decisions of this generation, our intellectual wisdom, resilience of will, moral courage, and political determination depend not only the shaping of the future but also the rescue of our collective memory and, in short, the possibility of a sequel to the astonishing and breathtaking humankind adventure on Earth.

References

Arendt, H. [1961] (1993). Concept of History: Ancient and Modern. In *Between Past and Future: Eight Exercises in Political Thought* (p. 60). New York: Penguin Books.

Arendt, H. (1993). Truth and Politics. In *Between Past and Future. Eight Exercises in Political Thought* (227–264). New York: Penguin Books.

Clausewitz, C. v. [1832] (1980). *Vom Kriege*. Frankfurt am Main: Ullstein.

Crutzen, P. J. & Stoermer, E. F. (2000). The 'Anthropocene'. In *Global Change Newsletter* 41, 17–18.

Glass, M. (2009). *Ultimatum*. New York: The Atlantic Monthly Press.

Hansen, S. F. and J. A. Tickner (2013). The Precautionary Principles and False Alarms – Lessons Learned. In EEA Report *Late Lessons from Early Warnings: Science, Precaution, Innovation* (pp.17– 45). Copenhagen: EEA. doi: 10.2800/73322

Rolston III, H. (1994). *Conserving Natural Value*. New York: Columbia University Press.

Russell, B. (1949). Can a Scientific Society be Stable? *British Medical Journal*, December 10, 1949, 1308.

Rüttinger, L., Smith, D., Stang, G., Tänzler, D., Vivekananda, J. et al. (2015). *A New Climate for Peace: Taking Action on Climate and Fragility Risks. An Independent Report Commissioned by the G7 Members.* Adelphi, International Alert, Woodrow Wilson International Center for Scholars, European Union Institute for Security Studies.

Steffen, W. et al. (2004). *Global Change and the Earth System. A Planet under Pressure*. Berlin-Heidelberg-New York: Springer-Verlag.

Soromenho-Marques, V. (1985). *Europa: O Risco do Futuro*. Lisboa: Publicações Dom Quixote.

—. (1994). *Regressar à Terra. Consciência Ecológica e Política de Ambiente*. Lisboa: Fim-de-Século, 1994, 143–146.

—. (2010). Ontological Debt and Intergenerational Justice. The Case of Climate Change. *Intergenerational Justice Review*, 10(1), 30.

—. (2014). Towards a Ptolemaic Revolution in the Anthropocene Era. *Journal of Engineering Studies*, Beijing, 6(2), 140–144. (translated from English to Chinese by Chen Xiaoli).

Spinoza, B. (1996). *Ethics, Part I, Prop.29, Scholium*. London: Penguin Books (translated from the Latin by Edwin Curley).

WGBU (German Advisory Council on Global Change) (2008). *Climate Change as a Security Risk*. London and Sterling: Earthscan. Retrieved from
http://www.wbgu.de/fileadmin/templates/dateien/veroeffentlichungen/hauptgutachten/jg2007/wbgu_jg2007_engl.pdf

CHAPTER FOURTEEN

SAFE OPERATING SPACE OF HUMANKIND TREATY [SOS TREATY]: A PROPOSAL

PAULO MAGALHÃES[1]

Preamble

Considering that:

- All countries are exposed to environmental impacts, positive and/or negative, from other countries. Given that knowledge of this reality is still recent and the Earth System continues to be used in a non-regulated manner, humanity has now reached a point where it is destabilising its own life-support system.
- The main structural motive at the origin of this unregulated use is the fact that the Earth System does not exist from a legal perspective, and is therefore being used as a no-man's land (*res nullius*).
- The global commons were always (and continue to be) understood as the mere remaining geographical spaces of political division between states. The ecological goods that exist in and outside all sovereignties simultaneously currently find no legal autonomous existence within the current legal framework. Humanity, as a whole, both in the present and the future, corresponds in the same way to this juridical inexistence.
- The global, diffuse and intangible dimensions of a vital good such as a stable climate, which sustain effects from damage over several generations, transform this traditional approach into an ecological nonsense. Today's doctrine recognizes that international law contains a

---

[1] Interdisciplinary Centre of Social Sciences CICS.NOVA - Faculdade de Ciências Sociais e Humanas - Universidade Nova de Lisboa.

structural theoretical error in its approach towards global ecological goods and their intergenerational dimension.

- Recent developments in Earth System science, which define and describe the *Earth System* as a whole, provide us with insights into the nature and limits of the Holocene epoch (the last 11,700 years) – the only state of the Earth System that we know with certainty can support advanced human civilizations.

- It is now possible to understand the chemical, biological and physical processes of the Earth System that are conducive to maintaining a favourable state for humanity (i.e., the Holocene) and those that act to push the Earth System out of a stable, desirable state.

- A tipping point is when a system fundamentally changes structure and function, tips over and settles into a new stable state. And the prerequisite to do so is that a feedback mechanism, which keeps the system tightly in one state, changes direction.

- This favourable state, which arose in an evolutionary fashion throughout Earth's history, is an "intangible natural limited resource" on Earth. With the shift of the biogeophysical structure, the system changes fundamentally from one stable and favourable state to another stable state.

- With the growing understanding of the Earth System and the recent possibility of measuring its state through the definition of planetary boundaries (Rockström et al. 2009; Steffen et al. 2015), we now have a scientific basis upon which to define the *Safe Operating Space for Humanity* of the Earth System.

- With the ability to quantify and define the desirable state of the Earth System, we've made a giant step in solving the legal vacuum created by the indeterminate and vague concepts that have characterised national or international legal texts over the last decades. Expressions such as the *common concern of humankind, the common interest of humankind, the life-support system, intergenerational solidarity,* and *ecological integrity and sustainability* now have a set of indicators and numbers that encircle and delimitate what global sustainability is.

- This new knowledge can be instrumental in the architecture of new solutions that allow us to overcome the existing dysfunctionality between ecological reality and the current legal constructions.

- Throughout history, newly discovered spaces became objects of legal definition. The knowledge of this intangible and non-territorial *Safe Operating Space* of the Earth System obliges our social institutions to respond to the most recent scientific evolutions and build new representations capable of going beyond the reductionist legal, physical or biological approaches that represent nature merely as a geographically delimited space or as a collection of biological species that can benefit from legal protection.

- To achieve this fundamental shift, we need to be capable of representing the Earth System as a whole in international law. To do this in a legal sense, we need to identify the legal status of the Earth System. *"How can a good that belongs to no one be subject to a legal regime?"* (Kiss 1982).

- In this sense, the first step to structurally organizing this interdependence is to achieve a clear delimitation of the common good/resource to be protected (both inside and outside of all sovereignty) and upon which we all depend. Only then will we have the structural conditions necessary to organize its use in a sustainable way.

- To make this evolution real, every benefit of and/or damage made to the Earth System can no longer disappear into a "legal black hole". Economics calls those benefits and/or damages "positive and negative externalities" but they cannot be "external" to our societies.

- If we are able to identify and measure the core global drivers that define the state of the Earth System, we have the necessary conditions to start to manage its use. Once it is measured, it can be managed and operationalized.

- In the theory of the international public domain, it is possible to attribute certain goods to interests of the community without changing the rules of jurisdiction, that is, without subtracting these goods from the sovereignty of territorial states or from the property of other entities.

- Today's institutional architecture does not operate as a governance *system* capable of addressing global challenges and rising above the fragmentation, segmentation and incoherence that result in today's ineffective institutions.

- Before undertaking practical reform, we need a new approach able to close the gap between the theory that underlies the organization of international institutions and the reality of Earth System dynamics.

- If we are able to create a new legal fiction capable of addressing the intangible quality and the non-territorial dimension of the Earth System state, which has a dialectical relationship with tangible territories of states but is not confined to any state (and therefore cannot be considered a subtraction to the sovereign power of a state), we can create a legal object distinguishable from every sovereignty.

- The actual legal inexistence leads to the absence of a scheme of contributions or responsibilities to ensure both the maintenance and necessary improvements for a well-functioning Earth System, and leads to the lack of an administrator (or an institution with similar functions) in charge of ensuring its ongoing maintenance in a sustainable way.

- A legal model for the Anthropocene requires a regulation responsible for ensuring the protection and promotion of common interests through the construction of a new way that represents the interests of all humankind, both in the present and the future.

Mindful of the will of the people, set out solemnly in the Charter of the United Nations, to safeguard the values and principles enshrined in the Universal Declaration of Human Rights and all other relevant instruments of international law,

Concerned by the fate of future generations in the face of the vital challenges of this century,

Conscious that, at this point in history, the very existence of humankind and its environment are threatened,

Recalling the UNESCO Declaration on the Responsibilities of the Present Generations towards Future Generations from 21 October to 12 November 1997,

Bearing in mind that the fate of future generations depends to a great extent on decisions and actions taken today, and that present-day problems, including poverty, technological and material underdevelopment, unemployment, exclusion, discrimination, and threats to the environment must be solved in the interests of both present and future generations,

Convinced that there is a moral obligation to formulate behavioural guidelines for the present generations within a broad, future-oriented perspective,

TAKING INTO ACCOUNT the need to define and develop the provisions of international instruments in relation to the our use of the Earth System... **have agreed on the following:**

General Dispositions

Part 1 - Objective

ARTICLE 1

Objective

This Draft Covenant provides a legal framework with the aim of transforming our common inhabitation of the planet from a system of exploitation to a system of stewardship of the Earth System through a process of self-organization to manage its use.

Part 2 – Fundamental Principles

Conscious that the global and deeply interconnected functioning of the Earth System requires new organizational solutions, all parties shall cooperate in a global partnership, looking for new pathways to achieve the objective of this covenant by the following fundamental principles:

ARTICLE 2

Earth System

The Earth System consists of the interacting physical, chemical and biological processes that cycle materials and energy throughout the system at the planetary level. In essence, it is the integration of the geophysical properties of the planet with the living biosphere that forms the intangible Earth System, a single global system incapable of any legal abstraction of division. A key process of the Earth System is self-regulation, which consists of feedback loops formed by component parts of the system (both inside and outside of all sovereignties) that work synergistically to keep the system within well-defined states.

Humans and human activities are an integral part of the Earth System.

ARTICLE 3

The Planet and the Earth System

Throughout the history of planet Earth, on a geological timescale, the Earth System has always existed in a process of permanent transformation.

Recent scientific developments defined and described the *Earth System* as a whole, and provided a well-defined biogeophysical structure of the Holocene epoch, the only state of the Earth System that we know for certain can support advanced human civilizations.

The recognition that the planet Earth and the Earth System's state are two distinct concepts is a structural prerequisite to enable a global legal approach.

ARTICLE 4

The Qualitative State of the Earth System

The Earth System is a *single* and *complex system* that exists within the boundaries of well-defined states. It is now possible to understand the chemical, biological and physical processes of the Earth System that are conducive to maintaining a favourable state for humanity (i.e., the Holocene) and those that act to push the Earth System out of a stable, desirable state.

ARTICLE 5

Planetary Boundaries

The planetary boundaries (PB) framework provides a scientific basis upon which it is possible to define the features of the *Safe Operating Zone for Humanity* strongly oriented towards maintaining a relatively stable state of the Earth System, one that is very similar to that of the past 12,000 years (Holocene). From a human perspective, PBs are biogeophysical limits that define the state of the Earth System, exist through the identification of control variables, and the tipping points over which irreversible abrupt global changes may occur.

ARTICLE 6

A Limited Resource

The *favourable state of the Earth System* arose in an evolutionary process involving the interactions between the living biosphere as well as the geophysical part. Given that there are human activities that cause chemical, biological and physical alterations conducive to pushing the Earth System out of this desirable state, we can consider this "favourable state" as a vital good, exhaustible through its use. In this sense it is "an intangible natural limited resource" on Earth.

ARTICLE 7

The Source/Resource Relation

From a historical perspective, the *favourable state of the Earth System* is the result of interactions between the living biosphere and the geophysical properties, that is, in this sense the ecological infrastructures of biosphere are *sources* that contributed, and still contribute, to maintaining this resource.

ARTICLE 8

Remaining Ecological Space on Earth

From the moment we are aware that this favourable biogeophysical structure of the Earth System is exhaustible, internal relations are equally reconfigured among all users of that *resource*. We need rules to organize the relations established around the use of the remaining ecological space for human development, which, by being exhaustible, cannot be used in a free-access regime.

ARTICLE 9

Legal Indivisibility

The Earth System as a single and integrated system cannot be included within any already existing legal convention because it is impossible to divide it conceptually, materially or through any legal abstraction. Therefore it must be considered a common resource.

ARTICLE 10

A Common Intangible Space

Once the use of this limited vital good is not exclusive to any "user", and no "user" can deny access to any other, in global terms we are facing a situation where all people are exposed to the acts of others, creating an interdependence of benefits and harms shared on a global scale.

In this sense its use requires organization amongst users that defines privileges and responsibilities.

ARTICLE 11

A Primordial Resource

The exceptional stable conditions of the Holocene period, unique in the history of the Earth, are a gift that nature has produced for the use of all humanity, today and tomorrow. It's something that due to its indispensable value to life belongs to all members of the whole human race and represents more than the sum of individual interests of states. It is of supreme value and a primordial resource.

ARTICLE 12

The Patrimonial Dimension

The supreme vital value for humanity, the principle of intergenerational equity and the existence of the 'right' of future generations to receive and enjoy an ecological space that supports their survival confers a patrimonial dimension to the Earth System state within the limits of a Safe Operation Space since the transmission of a value is the main purpose of the concept of heritage.

ARTICLE 13

Common Home of Humanity

A planet in an undesirable state, which is not able to provide for human ecological needs, will not serve as our common home. In this sense, the common home of humanity, rather than the tangible geographic area of 510 million km^2 of the planet, is an intangible specific state of the Earth System, the "Safe Operating Space" (i.e., a Holocene-like state of the Earth System).

ARTICLE 14

Intangible Space of Interconnection and Innovation

The evolution of the international community added to recent scientific developments in Earth Sciences and the need to address a growing interconnection on global governance justify the expansion of the restricted legal contours of the common heritage of humankind or the world heritage to new situations where the survival of the human species and life on the planet are at stake.

a) The doctrine considered the common heritage of mankind regime flexible enough to adapt to the emerging challenges the discovery of new resources and values, such as scientific research;

b) It is of notable interest to understand that all the substitutes and derived concepts gravitating around the common heritage of mankind seek to plant a seed for the development of a normative framework as to offer alternatives to govern the global common goods, and not only the areas and resources beyond jurisdictions;

c) World heritage has already done the course from material cultural heritage to intangible cultural heritage. It seems that this same course can now be reproduced in relation to natural heritage;

d) The protection of the Earth System as a world heritage complies with the functions of UNESCO as a "laboratory of ideas, standard-setter, clearing house, capacity-builder in Member States in UNESCO's fields of competence, and catalyst for international cooperation".

ARTICLE 15

Common Heritage of Humankind and World Heritage Evolution

The Earth System within the limits of a Holocene-like state is a vital primordial resource that belongs to all humanity, present and future. By this fact it exists simultaneously inside and outside all sovereignties, and demands one theoretical evolution on the common heritage of humankind and world heritage concepts, which finds its expression in the provisions of this treaty.

Part 3 - Principles Governing the Intangible Natural Space

ARTICLE 16

Safe Operating Space for Humankind

The human way to represent this primordial resource is through a set of indicators within the larger system that regulates the stability of the Earth System. These quantitative interconnected boundary levels create the *safe operating space for humanity*, which allows for the delimitation and measurement of a non-territorial common heritage of all humankind. These indicators should also function as a standard reference to guide the future management of our use of the Earth System .

ARTICLE 17

Just and Fair Operating Space for Humankind

Planetary boundaries are not only a safe space in biophysical terms but could also be used to achieve equity, fairness and a just distribution of the remaining ecological space on Earth.

ARTICLE 18

Systemic Governance

The planetary boundaries are a truly integrated analysis where all boundaries are interconnected, where a critical transition of one boundary could have feedback consequences on the entire system. Therefore, this safe space represents more than the sum of the different indicators and demands governance based on a systemic approach.

ARTICLE 19

Equity

State parties have the right to use the Earth System without discrimination of any kind on the basis of equality, equity and in accordance with international law and the terms of this treaty.

ARTICLE 20

Accountancy

The common heritage will be this intangible space where accountability should be carried out by an international institution (the UN) with coordinating functions, that is, if we have a system of compensation between the different performances of each state on the Earth System state, each state will try to have the best balance (difference between positive and negative inputs), mainly through self-regulation.

ARTICLE 21

Common Standard Pattern

For collective action to become possible, some structural conditions are required. One of them is the ability to measure and compare each action in regard to the maintenance of the favourable state of the Earth System. If equality consists of treating equally what is equal and inequality what is unequal, knowing what is equal and what is unequal presupposes a fixed point, a standard pattern that only the law can offer.

ARTICLE 22

International Institutionalization

Taking into account the characteristic of non-exclusion of access to this common vital resource on a global scale, the application of fundamental principles of the common heritage of humankind to a specific state of the Earth System implies that its use should be managed in an international and institutionalized form.

ARTICLE 23

International Regime

State parties adhering to this Agreement hereby undertake to establish an international regime, including appropriate procedures, to govern the use of our primordial natural resource composed by a relatively stable state of the Earth System, one that is very similar to that of the past 12,000 years.

This provision shall be implemented in accordance with Article 22 of this Agreement.

ARTICLE 24

Main Purposes of the International Regime
The main purposes of the international regime to be established shall include:

(a) Earth System Services of Global Interest
The Earth System services of global common interest are all the biogeophysical processes performed by the ecosystems that contribute to regulating the stability of the Earth System within the safe operating space. These services, although originated in ecosystems located in territories under the jurisdiction of sovereign states, are spread diffusely in the Earth System, providing benefits to all humankind, thus they are inevitably global and a common interest.

(b) Credits over the Common Intangible Heritage
Earth System services of global interest are considered all the benefits of the Earth System provided by the geosphere and biosphere. Because they contribute to the maintenance of the state of the Earth System within the Safe Operating Space for Humanity, they generate a credit on behalf of the state that exercises sovereignty or sovereign rights over the ecosystem infrastructure that provided those ecosystems services.

(c) Debits over the Common Intangible Heritage
The chemical, biological and physical processes resulting from human activity that are conducive to pushing the Earth System out of the safe operating space generate a debit on behalf of the state that exercises sovereignty or sovereign rights over the place where this activity develops. Because they undermine the stability of the Earth System, they constitute a depreciation of the common heritage.

(d) Common Metric
It is necessary to build a common standard pattern that represents the impacts (positive and negative) of each country on the structure and functioning of the Earth System. Conceptually, this new metric should be an aggregation of indicators that represent the core processes regulating the stability and resilience of the Earth System. This new metric should be based on the best available scientific knowledge.

(e) **Life-Support Unit**
The common standard pattern could be named "LSU – Life-Support Unit" and should be composed of an aggregation of PB indicators ("control variables"): stratosphere ozone depletion, aerosol loading, climate change, ocean acidification, biogeochemical flows (e.g., nitrogen, phosphorus), novel entities, biosphere integrity, land-system change, and freshwater use.

(f) **Ecobalance**
Ecobalance is the difference between the positive and negative contributions of each state party to the maintenance of the *Safe Operating Space for Humanity*, that is, it is the difference between the production and consumption of LSUs. It allows us to realize the status of the relationship of each state with the common heritage, and should be the base criteria for the building of a system of contributions and compensations for its maintenance.

(g) **System of Contributions**
The basic criteria to establish the contributions of each state for the common heritage are the different balances of each country for the maintenance of the Earth System within the limits of a Holocene-like state of the planet. All parties, depending on internal policies, might improve their balance relative to the common heritage, either through the encouragement of environmental efficiency and preservation or the restoration of ecosystems.

(h) **An Intermediate Space**
The new legal fiction of the Earth System should function as an intermediate space between state parties, where each state could understand the contributions from all the others and define its own performance strategy in relation to the common heritage, taking into account the prediction of the behaviour of other state parties.

(j) **Agreed Value for Each LSU**
Using all the best available economic information about the cost of environmental damage and the benefits of Earth System services, we must construct one monetary value for the production and consumption of each LSU. This value will be defined through a Convention.

(l) **Coordination Functions**
With the definition of a new object of law and governance, a new or a reconverted international organization should emerge. It should have the

capacity to address the Earth System as a whole, tackle the sort of challenges we are facing and assure the coordination tasks. It consists of receiving and redistributing the contributions of each state party and gathering the different interests in play, negotiating and adopting the necessary resolutions.

(m) **Resilience Priority**
The funds resulting from the accounting system payments should be used for setting compensation and restoration agreements with countries that exercise sovereignty on priority ecosystems for the maintenance of the stable regulation of the Earth System.

(n) **Historical Responsibility in the Use of Common Heritage**
The different historical responsibilities are well recognized in the use of this vital heritage for humanity. The different negative and positive contributions, the previous lack of knowledge about the global and cumulative consequences of the human activities, and the recent knowledge of the role of well-determined ecosystems, whose destruction could result in abrupt consequences in the regulation of the Earth System, should be appropriately weighted in the formulation of correction factors in the redistribution system. The common purpose of restoring this heritage within the levels necessary to ensure the sustainability of future generations of all the people of the world is a common objective to all members of the human species. The past cannot preclude the construction of the future.

References

Rockström, J., Steffen, W., Noone, K., et al. (2009). Planetary Boundaries: Exploring the Safe Operating Space for Humanity. *Ecology and Society* **14** (2): 32. [online] URL: http://www.ecologyandsociety.org/vol14/iss2/art32/
Steffen, W., Richardson, C., Rockström, J., et al. (2015) Planetary Boundaries: Guiding Human Development on a Changing Planet. *Science* 15 January, 2015 / Page 1 / 10.1126/science.1259855. http://www.sciencemag.org/content/early/2015/01/14/science.1259855. abstract
Kiss, A. (1982). La notion de Patrimonie Commun de L'Humanité. *Acedémie de Droit International, Recuil de Cours, Vol.175* (TomoII).

CONTRIBUTORS

NATHALIE MEUSY

Nathalie Meusy is, since November 2008, the Head of the Coordination Office on Sustainable Development at the European Space Agency (ESA) in the Strategy Department attached to the Director General. Prior to the creation of this office, she launched the sustainable development initiative at ESA in 2007.

She has, since then, developed the first framework policy on sustainable development for ESA, to be applied in its environment and energy activities, its programme activities and in the governance and ethics of the whole organisation as well as the first report on sustainable development for a space agency in Europe. Nathalie Meusy obtained Law degrees from the Paris XI and Besançon Universities and studied thereafter Social Sciences at La Sorbonne University (Paris). She started her career in journalism and intellectual property related to photographic work (Magnum Photos Agency). Thereafter, Ms. Meusy joined ESA in 1987 as a lawyer-administrator in the Human Resources Department. She supported, as Head of Social Policies, all ESA establishments and directorates from a legal and social point of view for15 years.

About ESA: This is a Research and Development inter-governmental organisation in charge of space projects and programmes at European level, which now counts 22 Member-States (20 member-States in the EU plus Norway and Switzerland), 9 other EU Member States have Cooperation Agreements with ESA. Canada also takes part in some programmes under a Cooperation Agreement.

PAULO MAGALHÃES

Paulo Magalhães is a researcher at the Interdisciplinary Centre of Social Sciences CICS.NOVA (CICS.NOVA.FCSH/UNL). He has a degree in Law from the Catholic University of Porto and a post-graduation in Environmental Law at Coimbra University. Today is in PhD Programme "Human Ecology" at Universidade Nova de Lisboa where he works in the concept of "*Common Intangible Natural Heritage of Humankind*". He is the author and coordinator of the Earth Condominium Project that propose a new concept to managing our use of the Earth System.

PS: Chapters one, seven, nine and fourteen are an integral part of the author's doctoral thesis, to be presented at Faculdade Ciências Sociais e Humanas (FCSH), Universidade Nova de Lisboa, with scholarship of the Fondation Luso-Française Elise Senyarich.

FRANCISCO FERREIRA

Francisco Ferreira is a Professor with the Department of Sciences and Environmental Engineering of the Faculty of Sciences and Technology of the New University of Lisbon, Portugal, and a member of CENSE – Center for Environmental and Sustainability Research. His main research interests are within the areas of air quality and climate change. He has published numerous peer-reviewed articles in scientific journals and coordinated several national and international research projects. He was President of *Quercus*, an environmental non-governmental organization from 1996 to 2001 and a member of the national board until 2011. He was a member of the National Council on Environment and Sustainable Development and of the National Water Council. Until the end of 2015, and for almost ten years, he was the author and presenter of a daily show on national public TV entitled "The Green Minute". He is currently the President of ZERO – Association for the Sustainability of the Earth System.

WILL STEFFEN

Will Steffen is a Councillor on the publicly-funded Climate Council of Australia that delivers independent expert information about climate change, and is an Earth System scientist at the Australian National University (ANU), Canberra. He is also an Adjunct Professor at the University of Canberra, working with the Canberra Urban and Regional Futures (CURF) program, and is a member of the ACT Climate Change Council.

From 1998 to mid-2004, Steffen served as Executive Director of the International Geosphere-Biosphere Programme, based in Stockholm, Sweden, and is currently a Senior Fellow at the Stockholm Resilience Centre. His research interests span a broad range within the fields of climate and Earth System science, with an emphasis on incorporation of human processes in Earth System modelling and analysis; and on sustainability and climate change, particular in the context of urban areas.

CLOVIS JACINTO DE MATOS

Clovis Jacinto de Matos started to work at the European Space Agency (ESA) in 1999 in the Education Office. In 2014 he became the Executive

Secretary of the ESA Programme Board on Satellite Navigation, which coordinates the Galileo and the European Geostationary Navigation Overlay (EGNOS) programmes. From 2005 until 2016 he initiated and participated in the coordination of the interaction between the Galileo Programme and the scientific community in the domains of Earth sciences, time metrology and fundamental physics. Since 2012 he also became part of the team liaising with the EGNOS users in the domains of Aviation and Maritime transports. From 2008 until 2012 Mr. de Matos exerted is professional activity in ESA DG services as the ESA Long Term Plan Administrator. Between 2003 until 2007 he was the Officer of the General Studies Programme of ESA, where the future space missions of the Agency are first assessed. Mr. de Matos graduated in 1995 from Coimbra University, in Portugal, with a Master degree in theoretical physics and he also obtained, in 1996, a Master of Space Studies (MSS) from the International Space University (ISU), in Strasbourg France.

KLAUS BOSSELMANN
Klaus Bosselmann, PhD, is Professor of Law at the University of Auckland. He is the founding director of the New Zealand Centre for Environmental Law and teaches in the areas of international environmental law, global governance, environmental constitutionalism and legal theory. He has served as a consultant to the OECD, the EU and the governments of Germany and New Zealand, was a legal advisor to the Earth Charter Drafting Committee and has been a visiting professor at leading universities in Europe, North America, Brazil and Australia. Prof Bosselmann is Chair of the IUCN World Commission on Environmental Law Ethics Specialist Group, Co-Chair of the Global Ecological Integrity Group and executive member of other international professional bodies. He has authored over a dozen books including the award-winning *Im Namen der Natur* (1992), *When Two Worlds Collide* (1995), *Ökologische Grundrechte* (1998), *Umwelt und Gerechtigkeit* (2001) *The Principle of Sustainability* (2008), *National Strategies for Sustainability* (2014) and *Earth Governance* (2015).

ALEXANDRA ARAGÃO
Maria Alexandra de Sousa Aragão is Professor of European Law at the Faculty of Law of the University of Coimbra, Portugal since 1996. She has a Master's degree in European Integration and a PhD in Public Environmental Law. She is holder of Jean Monnet modules on European Governance and European Environmental Law. She represents Portugal at the *European Observatories* on *Natura 2000 Network* and *Water*

Framework Directive. She is member of the 'Avosetta' group of experts in European Environmental Law and of the Advisory Board of the European Environmental Law Forum. She has authored numerous works on environmental law and governance, and her research interests are mainly focused European environmental law and the core environmental principles: polluter pays, precaution, integration and high level of protection. A list of publications and research activities can be found in: https://apps.uc.pt/mypage/faculty/aaragao/pt .

PRUE TAYLOR

Prue Taylor teaches environmental and planning law to graduate and undergraduate students at the School of Architecture and Planning, University of Auckland, NZ. She is the Deputy Director of the New Zealand Centre for Environmental Law and a long standing member of the IUCN Commission of Environmental Law and its Ethics Specialist Group. Prue's specialist research interests are in the areas of climate change, human rights, environmental and commons governance, ocean law and policy, property rights and environmental ethics. She has authored numerous books and articles in these areas. Her book, *An Ecological Approach to International Law: Responding to the Challenges of Climate Change* (Routledge), won a NZ Legal Research Foundation Prize. In 2007 she received an outstanding achievement award from the IUCN in recognition of her contribution, as a world pioneer on law, ethics and climate change.

FEDERICO MARIA PULSELLI

Federico Maria Pulselli (1970) is researcher in environmental and cultural heritage chemistry at the University of Siena, Italy. MS degree in Economics, PhD in Chemical Sciences (environmental curriculum), his research activity is performed within the Ecodynamics Group, established by Prof. Enzo Tiezzi, and is focused on the study of multidimensional aspects of sustainability and application of environmental sustainability assessment methods and indicators such as emergy and energetics of systems and processes, LCA, GHG emission inventory and responsibility, welfare indicators, ecosystem services. He co-authored three books and more than 100 publications in international scientific journals and books.

ALESSANDRO GALLI

With 10 years' experience on sustainability issues and indicator related projects, Alessandro's research focuses on analyzing the historical changes in human dependence on natural resources and ecological services through the use of sustainability indicators and environmental accounting methods. Currently, Alessandro is a Senior Scientist and the Mediterranean-MENA Program Director at Global Footprint Network. Previously, he has been working as technical advisor with the Emirates Wildlife Society (EWS-WWF) on the Al Basama Al Beeiya (Ecological Footprint) Initiative in the United Arab Emirates. Alessandro holds his PhD degree in Chemical Sciences from Siena University.

Alessandro is co-author of several publications including 30 articles in peer-reviewed journals such as Science, Global Environmental Change, Ecological Economics, Ecological Indicators and Biological Conservation, as well as WWF's Living Planet Report 2008, 2010 and 2012. He is also member of the Editorial Board of the Journal Resources: Natural Resources and Management and acts as reviewer for several academic journals. Alessandro was a MARSICO Visiting Scholar at University of Denver, Colorado, USA, in April 2011.

Key Research Interest: ecological footprint, human dependence on natural resources and ecosystem services, global environmental changes (including their socio-economic drivers), land use, resource management, sustainability, sustainability indicators, environmental accounting.

SARA MORENO PIRES

Sara Moreno Pires is a researcher at the Research Unit on *Governance, Competitiveness and Public Policies (GOVCOPP) of the University of Aveiro* in Portugal, where she is currently doing a postdoctoral study on the assessment of the quality of local governance for sustainable development. She was an assistant professor and researcher at the Faculty of Law of the University of Coimbra from 2002 to January 2016, where she taught courses such as Urban and Regional Planning, Environmental Management, Administration Science or Research Methodologies at Public Administration degrees. She holds a *PhD in Applied Environmental Sciences* (University of Aveiro), a *MSc in Development and Planning: Environment and Sustainable Development* (University College London) and a *BSc in Economics* (University of Coimbra). Her research interests are mainly centered on the development and use of sustainable development indicators and their role on urban governance contexts. She particularly focuses her research on urban sustainability planning, environmental policies and monitoring in Europe and Portugal and is involved in several international research projects. Her research has been published at scientific journals such as *Journal of Environmental Planning and Management, Ecological Indicators, Cities, Journal of Cleaner Production* or *Regional Studies Regional Science*.

IVA MIRANDA PIRES
Iva Miranda Pires is associate professor at the Faculdade Ciências Sociais
e Humanas (FCSH), Universidade Nova de Lisboa; she has a degree in
Geography, from Universidade de Coimbra and a PhD in Human
Geography, from Universidade de Lisboa. She teaches at the Sociology
Department where she also coordinates the master and the PhD programs
in Human Ecology. She is a senior researcher at the Interdisciplinary
Centre of Social Sciences CICS.NOVA (CICS.NOVA.FCSH/UNL). Her
main scientific areas of research are social and economic geography and
regional planning, human ecology and sustainable development.

KUL CHANDRA GAUTAM
Mr. Kul Chandra Gautam, born on 1 December 1949 is citizen of Nepal.
Former Deputy Executive Director of UNICEF and Assistant Secretary-
General of the United Nations. He is a distinguished international civil
servant, development professional, public policy expert, and human rights
advocate with extensive professional experience in international
diplomacy, development cooperation and humanitarian assistance.

As a senior UNICEF official, he helped craft ambitious goals for child
survival, protection and development at the historic 1990 World Summit
for Children, many of which later evolved into the Millennium
Development Goals.

He received a Masters of Public Affairs (MPA) degree in development
economics at the Woodrow Wilson School of Public and International
Affairs at Princeton University, and Bachelor of Arts (BA) majoring in
international relations at Dartmouth College in the United States of
America.

As part of his UN assignments, Gautam has written extensively on
international development issues, including on child rights, basic
education, public health, nutrition, and on issues of democracy, human
rights, the peace process and good governance in Nepal. Gautam currently
serves in the boards of several national and international organizations and
public-private partnerships. A list of his writings, public speeches and his
professional affiliations are found in his website: www.kulgautam.org.

VIRIATO SOROMENHO-MARQUES
Viriato Soromenho-Marques (1957) teaches Political Philosophy, Philosophy
of Nature, and European Ideas in the Departments of Philosophy an
European Studies of the University of Lisbon, where he is Full Professo
Since 1978 he has been engaged in the civic environmental movement
Portugal and Europe. He was Chairman of *Quercus* (1992-1995). He